ALL THE KING'S FALCONS

All the King's Falcons

Rumi on Prophets and Revelation

JOHN RENARD

Foreword by Annemarie Schimmel

STATE UNIVERSITY OF NEW YORK PRESS

Published by
State University of New York Press, Albany

Printed in the United States of America

For information, address State University of New York Press,
State University Plaza, Albany, N.Y., 12246

Production by Cathleen Collins
Marketing by Nancy Farrell

Library of Congress Cataloging in Publication Data

Renard, John, 1944-
    All the king's falcons : Rumi on prophets and revelation / John
Renard : foreword by Annemarie Schimmel.
        p.   cm.
    Includes bibliographical references and index.
    ISBN 0–7914–2221–6. — ISBN 0–7914–2222–4.
    1. Jalāl al-Dīn Rūmī, Maulana, 1207–1273—Religion.   2. Prophecy—
Islam.   I. Title.
BP166.38.R46   1994
297'.24—dc20   94–2307
                                                                           CIP

10 9 8 7 6 5 4 3 2 1

to
Annemarie Schimmel
in gratitude for the inspiration of
her life of exemplary scholarship

Contents

Foreword

How should the falcon not fly
back to his king from the hunt,
when from the falconer's drum
he hears the call: "Oh come back!"?

Thus sings Mawlana Rumi in one of his great poems in which he speaks of the longing of the soul for the eternal home, the craving of the soul-bird for the primordial garden.

Soul-birds were a common symbol in the Ancient Near East, and in the Islamic world too this symbol was extremely prominent, in particular in Iran and the countries under her cultural influence, such as India and Ottoman Turkey.

In the work of Sana'i (d. 1131), to whom Rumi was deeply indebted for a considerable number of symbolic expressions and stories, the falcon appears, along with the other birds in the great *qasida, Tasbih at-tuyur*, "The Rosary of the Birds":

The falcon prays: "O Lord, protect the Prophet's community in their faith and keep them secure!"

Here, one can find a first connection with John Renard's definition of the prophets as the "Lord's royal falcons."

Fariduddin 'Attar (d. 1220) in his *Mantiq at-tayr*, "The Language of the Birds," sees the falcon as the bird that shows its unquestionable faith in his king; bonded to his master he does not even want to participate in the quest for the Simurgh.

Such a faithful adherence to the king is the traditional role of the noble bird of prey whose story Suhrawardi the Master of Illumination (d. 1191) had told shortly before 'Attar, describing dramatically how the bird suffers in the prison of this world before he finds his way home.

In Mawlana's work, all kinds of noble soul-birds appear as do the mean, black birds of the hibernal world of matter. With him as with many later poets the nightingale is the favorite because he is enamored with the rose—the two represent the eternal interplay of longing Love and unchanging Beauty, the story of the mystic who pines for the rose garden of Beauty whose fragrance reaches him in this world. The falcon, however (*baz, shahin*), is a more powerful bird, a bird of prey whose pride is, as Rumi mentions in passing, not to hunt mice but rather "to hunt angels."

But the proud and strong bird is often captured, as in Suhrawardi's story, by an old, miserable crone. That is Mrs. World, who keeps him imprisoned and hooded so that he well-nigh forgets his heavenly master whom he left due to a mistake and, as Rumi states, Adam's fall was certainly a faux pas of a divine bird, a dangerous mistake. Rumi describes the unlucky bird's fate in a poetically delightful story, telling how the royal white falcon refuses to eat the delicious pasta which the old woman offers him after she has cut his claws—and angrily she pours the boiling hot broth over his head. Then, the falcon remembers his former glorious state, his master and his kindness, and therefore tries to return home.

But when he returns, so Rumi says in some other place, he will return "on the wings of *karramna*, 'We have honored the Children of Adam.'" For he received his name *baz* because he comes back, *baz*, to his master. Mawlana's remark about the "wing of *karramna*" brings the reader closer to the relation between the strong falcon and the prophets. God addressed mankind in the Qur'an (Sura 17:70) with the word: "We have honored the children of Adam" and thus points to the high rank of human beings whose ancestor, Adam, was indeed the first prophet, as the Qur'an teaches.

According to a tradition related from the Prophet, "the prophets are the people who are most afflicted" because each and every one of them had to undergo trials and tribulations while living among the unbelievers who, like the old hag in Rumi's story, want to deprive them of their most important implements (as are the falcon's claws). In the midst of the infidels the prophets try to preach their message, but, as little as a crow or a raven listens to the story, the lonely, homesick falcon tells them about the beauty of the king and his palaces, of his power and glory, so little do the worldlings believe in the prophets' words.

There has been an increasing tendency among Western scholars and, even more, lovers and admirers of Mawlana to forget the deeply Islamic background of his poetry. Did not Jami call his *Mathnawi* "the Qur'an in the Persian tongue"!? Modern people tried to select from often very vague secondhand translations only those verses that speak of love and ecstasy, of intoxication and whirling dance. The role that the Prophet of Islam plays in Mawlana's poetry is hardly mentioned in secondary literature. But whosoever has listened with understanding to the *na't-i sharif*, that introductory musical piece at the very beginning of the Mevlevi ceremonies, feels, nay rather knows, how deep the poet's love for the Prophet Muhammad was, which is expressed in his words—the Prophet, "cypress of the garden of prophethood, springtime of gnosis, rosebud of the meadow of the divine Law and lofty nightingale." He is the one whose secrets are communicated through Shams-i Tabrizi, the inspiring mystical friend. And as Muhammad was the last in the long line of God-inspired prophets from Adam to Jesus, it is the believers' duty to acknowledge and honor those who brought in divine message in times past. Thus, their stories as related or alluded to in the Qur'an form part and parcel of Muslim faith.

Mawlana Rumi was a mystic and poet who belonged to both the "prophetic" and the "mystical" type of religion, and it is the first part of the two aspects of his teachings that is often overlooked. The great singer of heavenly love, who often reminds himself to be silent and who sings out his yearning for union with the Beloved was also well aware of the importance of the outward form, of the divinely inspired Law which constitutes, as it were, the outer rind in which the sap of life flows, or the pith without which the kernel of the apricot will not grow into a healthy tree. The prophets, who taught the different aspects of the divine will and brought prescriptions for the community, acting so to speak as physicians of souls, are important in Rumi's teaching and therefore appear in different roles in his work, be it in his lyrical poetry, be it in the *Mathnawi*.

The reader will be grateful to John Renard that he has chosen this topic as the basis for his investigations into Rumi's theological approach. Trained as a theologian and orientalist he is in a position to put Mawlana's prophetology into the central place where it belongs, and many of Mawlana's numerous allusions to the prophets offer a fascinating picture of the various aspects of a prophet's role. Thus, the book will be an eye-opener for many of Mawlana's admirers.

It is certainly no accident that Mawlana Rumi's most ardent modern admirer and interpreter, the Indo-Muslim philosopher poet Muhammad Iqbal, who emphasized the truly "prophetic" form of active religious life and warned his listeners not to lose themselves in an ocean of mystical dreams in which their activity would melt away, chose as his favorite symbol the falcon. The royal falcon, soaring high into the seemingly endless blue sky was, to him, the best symbol for the true "man of God" who out-soars the earthbound creatures on his way to the beloved Lord who yet can never be reached, as many new horizons the falcon crosses, but whose voice is heard everywhere when He proclaims: "We have honored the children of Adam."

Annemarie Schimmel

Preface

Jalal ad-Din Rumi (1207–73) has enjoyed a justifiably broad popularity among Muslims and non-Muslims alike for centuries. Three perspectives have characterized studies on Rumi in recent times. Perhaps the largest segment of his admiring public has thought of him chiefly as a mystic, a Sufi, and a source of spiritual inspiration. Various studies have investigated Rumi's mystical psychology or his teaching on a wide range of issues of major concern to shaykhs and seekers. In addition to academic works from this perspective, a number of books of a more frankly inspirational or devotional nature have appeared. Rumi's importance in the history of Sufism and in the fabric of Islam's devotional tapestry is thus well established and acknowledged.

Rumi has also won praise for his poetic achievement. It is true that some critics have only grudgingly acknowledged his skill as a bard. Perhaps taking too seriously Rumi's own characterization of his verses as no more enduring than the bread of Egypt, some have regarded his poetry almost as an afterthought and not integral to his creative process. Extensive literary studies have catalogued the poet's vast repertory of imagery and situated his various works in the context of his life history. Scholars and the general reading public alike will find Mawlana duly enshrined in the Poets' Corner of the cosmic mosque.

A third group of studies have looked at various theoretical aspects of Mawlana's thought, his metaphysics, and so forth. Among the more insistent themes are the tracing of Neoplatonic influences and the allegedly central role of the doctrine of the Perfect Person (*al-insan al-kamil*) in his thought. Rumi was surely well versed in the large themes of philosophical and theological writing as well as in the more traditional Islamic religious sciences. But he clearly did not think of himself as either a philosopher or a theologian. He seems not in the least temperamentally inclined toward scholastic, systematic analysis. Still, studies of this kind, the least numerous of the three types, can be helpful in sorting out the intellectual currents influential in shaping Rumi's view of the world.

What then is missing from material now available on the life and work of Jalal ad-Din? Although it may seem all too obvious to need saying, Rumi was a Muslim. Yet what one sometimes hears about his attitude to formal religious affiliation is that he cared not a fig to what community one belonged—and perhaps even went so far as to deny the importance of his own adherence to Islam. For reasons such as that, or perhaps because of the oddly persistent notion that Sufis have always drifted off toward the fringes of Islamic society, relatively little attention has been given to what one of the world's most prominent and popular Muslims thought and felt about Islam's most fundamental notions and principles. These eight chapters look at Rumi's insights into the meaning of the second half of the basic Muslim creed, namely, the nature and function of revelation through prophets.

Rumi is a Muslim miner, sifting the rare earth of Islam's prophetic lore. He searches for treasures embedded in the Qur'anic mother lode, and in the various veins that intersect it. From that mine he brings forth the rough gems of the tradition cutting and polishing them as only he can, so that they reflect his own insight into, and interiorization of, the central themes of Islamic life. *All the King's Falcons* explores Mawlana's views on ritual prayer, jihad, pilgrimage, fasting, his understanding of the significance of revelation, and his interpretation of the crucial events of early Islamic history as enshrined in the life of Muhammad.

All the King's Falcons seeks to bring together some elements of the various approaches to Rumi already in print, with specific attention to several of his mystical concerns, to the poet's craft in utilizing prophet imagery, and to crucial components of Rumi's theology of revelation. And it does so while focusing on the most distinctively Islamic of religious teachings. Chapter 1 offers a look at Rumi's place in the history of Islamic prophetology, a panorama of thought on the rhyme and reason of divine revelation through prophet-messengers. The chapter compares and contrasts Rumi's contribution to the development of Islamic mystical prophetology with main themes in historical, philosophical, theological, and theosophical prophetologies. Chapter 2 then explores Rumi's "theo-poetics" of revelation, under the aegis of his distinctive use of the already ancient image of the royal hunting bird. Like the majestic falcon itself (*baz*), its metaphor kept coming back (*baz mi-amad*) to Rumi. As we shall see, the image is multivalent: the falcon is the prophet, the prophet is the shaykh, the shaykh is the trainer of the falcon (the seeker, *murid*), and so forth in appropriately falconesque swoops and spirals.

Chapters 3 through 6 detail Jalal ad-Din's treatment of the major pre-Islamic prophets—Abraham and his two sons; Joseph and his father Jacob; Moses and his brother Aaron, and Moses' enigmatic guide, Khizr; and Jesus along with three other Gospel figures. Each section relates Mawlana's material briefly to that of classic "Tales of the Prophets" and to one of the Islamic world's premier prophetological works, the *Fusus al-Hikam* of Rumi's older contemporary Ibn 'Arabi. Treatment of each of the Royal Falcons highlights major theological and religious themes, and their relation to the mystical tradition. Rumi develops the prophets in part as metaphors for key facets of the mystical quest, unique paradigmatic embodiments of central aspects of Islamic spiritual life, although he does not do so in the complex and systematic way displayed in Ibn 'Arabi's *Fusus*.

In Chapters 7 and 8 we turn to the Seal of the Prophets. Both as the Muhammad of History and as the Ahmad of Faith, the Prophet of Islam exercised a fascination on our mystical-theological poet. An inventory of Rumi's use of prophet-imagery provides not only an overview of the main outlines of Muhammad's life story as Rumi knew it, but also a survey of the more subtle ways in which the Prophet has represented for Mawlana the highest in spiritual aspiration and attainment.

Rumi's literally thousands of direct references and oblique allusions to the full gamut of prophetic figures situates him very much in the midst of mainstream Islamic tradition. One can in that sense use this book as an introduction to a central theme in Islamic religious thought. Mawlana's use of prophetological imagery as a metaphorical vehicle for his views on the relationship of the individual to God similarly make this book suitable as a primer in the mystical tradition of Sufism. Rumi's own unique twist and variation on the classical theological and mystical themes, finally, can introduce the reader to one of the more colorful, imaginative, prolific, and influential figures in Islamic religious thought.

Acknowledgments

All the King's Falcons represents a revision and abridgement of a doctoral dissertation written originally under the solicitous direction of Professor Annemarie Schimmel, and presented in 1978 through Harvard University's Department of Near Eastern Languages and Civilizations.

My thanks to Professor Schimmel for her unstinting help then, and for her more recent suggestion to Mr. William Eastman that SUNY Press might like to look at this manuscript. I wish to thank also Professors William Graham and Wheeler Thackston of Harvard University for the helpful suggestions they offered upon reading the dissertation.

In lieu of the original sections on Adam, Seth, Idris, Noah, Hud, Salih, Jonah, Lot, Job, Shu'ayb, David, Solomon, Ezra, and Luqman, an Appendix provides a fairly complete index of references to those figures in Rumi's writings.

To the College of Arts and Sciences of Saint Louis University, and to its Department of Theological Studies, I owe thanks for providing release time and a place in which to devote special attention to completing the project.

For generously agreeing to read and offer helpful comments on a draft of the book I am grateful to Professor Fatemeh Keshavarz of Washington University in St. Louis. And thanks to Ms. Laura Hobgood and Mr. David Vila for their careful editorial assistance in preparing a final manuscript.

I wish to thank the editors of several journals for permission to publish revised versions of several chapters previously published as articles. Chapter 1 appeared in *Thought* 57:226 (September 1982): 285–99; chapter 3 appeared in *Journal of the American Oriental Society* 106:4 (1986): 633–40; and chapters 4 and 6 originally appeared in *Hamdard Islamicus* IX:1 (Spring 1986): 11–22, and X:2 (Summer 1987): 47–64.

For permission to quote moderately revised segments of translations of Rumi's works by R. A. Nicholson and A. J. Arberry, I thank the following: Samuel Weiser, Inc., York Beach, ME 03910, for selections from Arberry's *Discourses of Rumi*. My thanks to Mr. Robin Bligh of the Gibb Memorial Trust, Cambridge, England, and to Aris & Phillips Ltd., Warminster, England, publishers of works for the Trust, for permission to quote from R. A. Nicholson's translation of

Rumi's *Mathnawi*. I have taken the liberty of revising occasionally the classic translations of Nicholson and Arberry, in consultation with Rumi's text in Furuzanfar's editions, where the replacement of archaisms and noninclusive language appeared to make for a smoother reading, or where another choice of words translating certain technical terms seemed appropriate (e.g. homogeneity or affinity in place of congenerity).

Citation of Rumi's Works

References to Rumi's works in all citations are as follows.

Mathnawi: Roman Numerals I–VI (Book) plus verse number (e.g., IV:2710), as in Nicholson's Persian edition and translation (London: Luzac and Co., 1925–40). H. indicates heading above line number given.

Fihi Ma Fihi: F followed by page number in Arberry's translation, followed by page number in Furuzanfar's Edition (e.g., F 35/27); translation as *Discourses of Rumi* (New York: Samuel Weiser, 1972)/Furuzanfar's Persian edition (Tehran, 1338/1959).

Diwan-i Shams: D followed by poem number and verse (e.g., D 2714:12) in Furuzanfar's one-volume Persian edition (Tehran, 1351/1970). Two poem citations separated by a slash (/) indicates a doublet or nearly verbatim parallels. *Ruba'iyat* in same edition referred to as, e.g., R 643. References to Arberry's translations from the *Diwan* will be by volume and selection number; e.g., MPR1 104 and MPR2 376 refer to poem number in *Mystical Poems of Rumi* (Chicago: University of Chicago Press, 1968) and same, *Second Selection* (Boulder: Westview Press, 1979). Translation from the *Diwan* cited, e.g., ND 32 indicates poem selection number in R. A. Nicholson's *Selected Poems from the Divani Shamsi Tabriz* (Cambridge: Cambridge University Press, 1977). When the original research was conducted, the ten-volume edition was not readily available to me; the time and risk of error that would have been involved in converting the thousands of numbers to accord with the ten-volume edition led to my decision to leave those references unchanged.

Maktubat: M followed by letter number and page number (e.g., M 67/148) in the Persian edition of Yusuf Jamshidpur and Ghulam-husayn Amin (Tehran, 1335/1956).

In citations of multiple texts from F, D, M, or R, the prefixed capital
   letter will not be repeated. Citations of one or two items appear
   in parentheses in the text; those of three or more items appear in
   endnotes.
Citations from the Qur'an will be indicated by a Q followed by sura
   and verse number, as in Q 7:14.

CHAPTER 1

Rumi in the History of Islamic Prophetology

Some of Muhammad's earliest critics dismissed his Qur'anic preaching as a mere repetition of "fables of the ancients," warmed-over tales of the prophets of old. That criticism and others like it only served to convince Muhammad of the need to recount still more insistently the history of God's revelation through His messengers. For the Prophet of Islam and countless Muslims ever since, the very thing that so many detractors have singled out as nullifying the force of the Qur'an has become one of the strongest of all arguments for the authenticity of its revelations.

> We believe in God and that which is revealed to us and that which is revealed to Abraham, and Ishmael, and Isaac, and Jacob, and the tribes, and that which Moses and Jesus received, and that which the Prophets received from their Lord. We make no distinction between any of them, and unto Him we have surrendered. (Q 2:136)

Since Muhammad's death in 632, Muslim thinkers and writers have lavished considerable attention on the doctrine of divine revelation through a succession of prophets, an unbroken line that began with Adam and culminated in Muhammad. The history of Islamic thought evidences a fascinating variety of approaches to the subject. Our purpose here is to provide a brief introduction to five important contributions to Islamic religious thought as a context in which to explore Rumi's views on revelation through prophets.

After a summary of the Qur'an's development of the concept of prophetic revelation and its use of stories of the prophets, we will investigate five further interpretations of the theme: the historical, philosophical, theological, theosophical, and mystical approaches. Each section will include three elements. First, it will take a brief look at the way in which the individual approach in question interprets the Qur'an. Discussion of the method peculiar to each approach as it elaborates the theme of prophetic revelation will follow. Finally, each of the first four sections will compare one approach with that of Rumi, whose chief work, the *Mathnawi*, has earned the exalted honorific title, "The Persian Qur'an." Rumi is the foremost representative of the mystical approach to prophetic revelation. He complains that his critics belittle his work as being "merely the story of the Prophet" (III:4233ff.). The poet is in good company.

Qur'anic Prophetology

Though the Qur'an was "sent down" piecemeal over a period of some twenty-three years, between 610 and 632, Muslims regard it as a single revelation that must be read as a whole. One of its unifying features is its teaching on the nature of revelation and the role of prophets as messengers. God alone initiates the message and communicates it through prophets, without whom humanity would have very little chance of attaining to the ultimate truth.

The Qur'an teaches Muslims to make no distinction among the messengers, but it nevertheless states that some prophets have been exalted above others (e.g., Q 2:253, 17:55). Muhammad is unambiguously the Seal of the prophets. God sends His prophets to teach people the Oneness of God, to bring the good tidings of belief and to warn against the consequences of unbelief. Some, such as Moses and Jesus, have been "given a Book." As opposition to Muhammad's message increased, stories of earlier prophets who had likewise met with unbelief and persecution multiplied.

Since the Qur'an is not a systematic document, it does not develop a coherent theory or system of prophetology; nor, except in the case of Joseph, does it ordinarily recount the story of any one prophet all in one passage as a unified and continuous narrative. Segments on the various prophets occur sporadically as part of Muhammad's homiletical material. Episodes and minor details from the stories of more important figures, such as Abraham, Moses, and Jesus, appear several times, each text retelling the tale either by adopting a slightly different point of emphasis or by adding variant details. Some of the features of specific stories will emerge in the context of the five approaches.[1]

Historical Prophetology

The historical approach reads the Qur'an with an eye for the continuity and sequence of events that constitute a given prophet's personal history or "biography." Concerned with presenting a chronological narrative, this approach is largely interested in the story line and in gathering the myriad anecdotal details that render a story credible, engaging, and true-to-life, with a generous enough sprinkling of the fantastic to make it marvelous. Names, place descriptions, personal relationships and encounters, genealogies, ages of the characters, times and durations of events, all form a concrete mundane context in which the supramundane becomes at once more plausible and more arresting. The prophet appears as a specific individual, a historical personage. Because of its interest in the concrete actions of a prophet, the historical approach implies a folkloristic or "midrashic" exegesis that freely fills in details that it takes to be in any way suggested by the Qur'anic text.

Some works of this type gathered their information directly from earlier Qur'anic commentaries and rearranged it to fit a new framework. An example of folkloristic embellishment might be the inclusion of a conversation between a prophet and another character, not actually supplied in the Qur'an but which, given other details mentioned in the scripture, one can readily imagine. This last feature sometimes occurs in the mystical approach; but there the prophet's story generally unfolds in snatches and allusions rather than in a single narrative.

Early Muslim "universal histories," such as those of Ya'qubi (d. 897), Tabari (d. 923), and Mas'udi (d. 956), include the histories of the prophets prior to Muhammad within their surveys of the pre-Islamic world. Several writers of the fifteenth and sixteenth centuries agreed that "the historical information of the prophets is one of the branches of history. Scholars occupied themselves with this worthwhile subject. . . ."[2] According to Sakhawi (1427–97), there were also some historians who "took pride in restricting themselves to the prophets, in particular, Muhammad. Occasionally, they combined with the history of the prophets the history of the beginning of the Creation, or they restricted themselves to one of these two subjects."[3] The same author notes that one of the chief benefits of history is that the material it contains about the prophets and their way of behaving can prepare people for the next life and improve their religious convictions and "approach to religious matters. . . ."[4]

Two of the most important writers who restricted themselves to the lives of the prophets after giving an account of the Creation were Tha'labi (d. 1036) and Kisa'i (fl.c. 1200). In the preface to his *Tales of Prophets*, Tha'labi enumerates five aspects of God's wisdom in revealing to Muhammad the prophetic stories. Four hundred years later the historian's historian Sakhawi would reiterate those same five features as an epitome of the meaning and function of prophetic histories. These stories, he argues, prove that the "unlettered" Muhammad was the recipient of an authentic revelation; they both encourage imitation of the heroic prophets and caution against the behavior of the unbelievers; they demonstrate how specially favored Muhammad's people were by contrast with earlier peoples who had suffered far more severely; they educate; and they bring to mind noble prophetic deeds, hold out the hope of reward for the righteous, and show that good deeds live on for the edification of posterity.[5]

Finally, the tone and attitude of both Tha'labi and Kisa'i contrast markedly with that of Miskawayh (d. 1030), who assiduously avoided any mention either of the pre-Islamic prophets or of the specifically religious history of Muhammad. Describing his methods and motives, Miskawayh wrote:

I am beginning with reporting the historical information about the time after the Deluge, because the information about events before it can be little trusted, and also because that information is in no way useful for accomplishing the professed purpose of the work (namely, to mention experiences that could serve as examples). For the very same reason, we did not undertake to report the miracles and their political achievements, because the people of our time can gain experience for the tasks they will face in the future only from human behavior that is unconnected with anything miraculous.[6]

Jalal ad-Din Rumi rarely concerns himself with listing the prophets in anything like a chronological or progressive order, but he does make a point of describing a kind of prophetic heritage. Both Tha'labi and Kisa'i indicate a symbolic succession from prophet to prophet as well as a theological thread interwoven with the thread of chronology. However, one can understand the differences between Rumi's treatment of prophetic continuity and that of the two authors of the *Tales* as typical of differences in their respective overall approaches to the subject. Tha'labi and Kisa'i demonstrate the continuity by the use of various typological symbols, items handed down from one prophet to another as emblems of prophetic legitimacy: Adam's sarcophagus, Joseph's vesture, Moses's staff, and the stones with which David slew the Philistine Goliath, for example. The authors reveal their underlying preoccupation with historicity and verisimilitude in their use of such concrete signs.

Rumi, on the other hand, describes the prophetic heritage in a more spiritualized manner: the light of God is the heirloom of the authentic prophet.

One of the few texts in which the poet does line up the prophets more or less chronologically, tells of the light's passage from Adam to Seth, and thence to Noah, Abraham, Ishmael, David, Solomon, Jacob, Joseph, Moses, Jesus, and Muhammad. But then the light continues into the safe-keeping of the first four successors of Muhammad (the "Rightly Guided Caliphs") and of the prominent Islamic mystics Junayd, Bayazid, Karkhi, Ibrahim ibn Adham, and Shaqiq. This last feature is Rumi's way of dealing with the problem of how divine truth remains in the world after the passing of the last prophet. Aside from that one text, chronology is of little interest to the mystical poet, though he is ever careful to point out the solidarity and unified heritage of the prophets.[7]

Philosophical Prophetology

One of the most original results of Muslim culture's encounters with Greek thought was the evolution of a philosophical approach to prophetic revelation. Prophetic epistemology and the role of the prophet as lawgiver were the philosophers' paramount concerns. Their noetic-political perspective led them to regard the prophet as an elite subtype of humanity endowed with special powers: prophet is as prophet knows, and, on the basis of that higher knowledge, as prophet governs. Although the philosophers never used the Qur'an as a prophetological sourcebook in the same way that, for example, the mystics and historians did, still the philosophers were in general careful to try to reconcile their conclusions with the sacred text—or at least to demonstrate that their conclusions did not constitute an unacceptable departure from revealed truth.

Fazlur Rahman describes the background of the philosophical theory of prophetic revelation as follows. Islamic metaphysics managed to address itself point by point to all the major tenets of religious doctrine, but never quite made a perfect match of the two. A serious question therefore arose.

> Either there was a double truth, one apprehended by philosophy, the other by religion, or the truth was unitary but appeared now in rational, and again in a metaphorical, imaginative form. The first alternative, that of two truths, did not seem possible rationally and so the philosophers decided to pursue the latter line of thought. Religious truth is but rational truth, but instead of being expressed in nakedly rational formulas, manifested itself in imaginative symbols—a fact which was responsible for its widespread acceptance by, and effectiveness among, the masses.[8]

Further emphasizing the importance of prophetic revelation in Islamic philosophy, E. J. Rosenthal notes that the two sides of the "central problem in Islamic philosophy" are "the political character of prophecy and the affinity between *Shari'a* and *nomos* (Divinely revealed and humanly ordained law, respectively) which manifests itself in the concept of the prophetic lawgiver."[9]

Al-Farabi, Ibn Sina (Avicenna), and Ibn Rushd (Averroes) are the key figures. All three begin with at least a minimal acknowledgment that Muhammad had come proclaiming a divinely revealed universal law. Of the three, however, only Ibn Rushd preserved intact the notion of God's "sending down" the revelation; the two earlier thinkers reduced the revealing angel to the agent intellect. As the originator of the "psychological" explanation of prophecy, al-Farabi (870–950) identified the imagination as the seat of prophecy. According to Richard Walzer, the imagination is "characterized as preserving the impressions made upon it as a result of the activity of sense perception and either connecting those images which it preserves with each other or separating them from each other so as to produce either true or false representations of past sense experiences within the soul."[10] Imagination thus functions as a bridge between perception and reason. During sleep every individual's imagination can engage by "imitation" in activity that is independent of sense perception; but, for a select few, the gift of prophecy makes the fullness of imaginative activity possible even in the waking state. In the latter case the imagination becomes "connected" with the higher faculty of reason, allowing the prophet to acquire the highest type of knowledge. Nevertheless the prophet is not quite the equal of the philosopher in the attainment of knowledge's upper reaches. Speaking of the type of revelation al-Farabi attributes to political rulers, E. J. Rosenthal says that "God mediates to his (the ruler's) theoretical and practical reason a revelation which makes him a philosopher, and then to his imaginative faculty, making him a prophet, a warner, capable of directing men to their happiness."[11] Al-Farabi does claim, however, that both philosophy and prophecy can lead to ultimate truth.

Ibn Sina (980–1037) reversed al-Farabi's priorities by giving divinely revealed law preeminence, equating the ideal person with the prophet rather than with the philosopher, and only then placing the loftiest type of philosophy on a par with prophecy. He elevated the prophetic intellect to a level of its own, from which knowledge flows into the imagination, where symbols are formed. Of the exalted status of the prophet Ibn Sina says that

"If one combines with justice speculative wisdom, he is indeed the happy man. And whoever, in addition to this, wins the prophetic qualities, becomes almost a human god. Worship of him, after worship of God, becomes almost allowed. He is indeed the world's earthly master and God's deputy in it."[12] The ability to receive true knowledge exists accidentally in the non-prophetic soul and essentially in the soul of the prophet. In addition, since truly just laws can never be of human devising alone, and since God would never leave his creatures to founder in a quagmire of injustice, God is obligated to supply that one office through which just law can be known and promulgated—the office of prophet.

Of the three philosophers under consideration here, Ibn Rushd (1126–98) defended most successfully the necessity of the divinely revealed law as the only law capable of securing happiness for all humankind. He insisted that the divine will can be known only through prophecy, but he denied Farabi's claim that every ideal ruler must also possess the gift of prophecy. Every prophet may be called a philosopher; but not every philosopher may be called a prophet, for Muhammad was the Seal of the prophets. Even though professed adherence to mainstream Islamic teaching prevented Ibn Rushd from holding that a prophet might arise after Muhammad, his political realism led him to concede that a post-prophetic lawgiver might indeed appear. Still he insisted that it was the reception of a divine Law, not the performance of miracles, that constituted proof of prophethood. That divine Law is a gift given to all people through their prophets, while philosophy remains the province of a select few.[13]

Rumi mentions neither al-Farabi nor Ibn Rushd by name. On those rare occasions when the poet speaks approvingly of Ibn Sina, it is to acknowledge the greatness of the physician rather than to praise the philosopher. Rumi's fundamental attitude toward philosophers is that "no person of intellect will ever know the head's ecstasy of the drunkard; no person of reason will ever know the heart's rapture of reason-lost" (D 532:2, MPR1 64). Reason is a highway robber, and the "how and wherefore" are "sheer loss." In *Fihi Ma Fihi* Rumi says:

> For instance, you have an uncut cloth which you want to have cut into a tunic or cloak. Reason has brought you a tailor. Until that moment reason was fine, for it brought the cloth to the tailor. Now in this very moment reason must be divorced and you must abandon yourself wholly to the control of the tailor. In the same way, reason is fine for

the sick person until it brings that person to the physician . . . after
that, reason is no use. . . . (F 123/113)

Jalal ad-Din does not hesitate to use the technical terminology of the
philosophers, but he always uses it with a twist that allows him to shift his
fundamental point of view from an emphasis on human powers of cogni-
tion to a focus on knowledge as a divine gift. Rumi therefore locates true
knowledge in the heart rather than in either the imagination or the intellect.
Even with all its vulnerabilities and weaknesses the heart cannot lie; for all
of its alleged powers, the intellect cannot but lie. Union of the human intellect with the "active intellect" is simply unthinkable for the philosophers,
except perhaps for the more mystically inclined Ibn Sina. In Rumi's view,
the prophet stands above all considerations of reason, is in contact with the
divine mind itself, and actually becomes the "universal intellect."

Rumi never describes the prophet in terms of personal power, only in
terms of openness and receptivity. In that respect the mystic is closer to the
view of the theologians than to that of the philosophers. But the theologians are far more concerned with arguing the fine points of miracle working as a proof of prophecy than Rumi is. It is a question of emphasis. Rumi
would agree with the philosophers that the prophet's credibility must not
rest solely on miracles. As for the question of the prophet's function as
lawgiver, on the other hand, the mystic does not endow the political role
with nearly the prominence the philosophers give it. Rumi does not deny
that the prophets were humanity's teachers (Adam especially), judges and
kings (such as David and Solomon), or lawgivers (particularly Moses).
The mystic does give considerable attention to Muhammad's embroilment
in martial and other communitarian affairs. Such matters were a necessary
and integral part of Muhammad's mission. But to treat the prophet's gov-
ernmental function as the central issue and to regard it almost as an end in
itself is, for Rumi, like asking for a messenger after one has already come
into the presence of the Sultan himself, like looking for a ladder after one
has already climbed to heaven's roof. Except for the purpose of teaching
and assisting others, the way to happiness is worthless for one who has
found happiness (III:1400–5).

Theological Prophetology

In an attempt to counter the views of the philosophers and to guard against
any species of immanentism that might threaten the concept of divine revelation, traditionalist Islam developed a theological prophetology. The

theologians were interested most of all in preserving the mysterious and inexplicable character of God's communication to His people. They preferred to regard the prophet primarily as instrumental in the plan of God, the pen with which the divine calligrapher writes. Because their apologetic approach evolved as a way of dialoguing with the philosophers, the theologians employed much of the technical jargon of the philosophers. They gave their attention most of all to two issues: prophetic epistemology, which they believed the philosophers had overintellectualized and overhumanized; and evidentiary miracles as necessary proof of prophetic authenticity, which they felt the philosophers had devalued and underemphasized. Whereas many proponents of rationalism held that the Qur'an, God's speech, could not be regarded as an attribute of God and must therefore be created in time, the theologians staunchly defended a doctrine of the Qur'an as God's eternal, uncreated speech.

The first Muslim thinker to forge a convincing synthesis of the logical methods of the philosophers with the doctrinal concerns of the theologians was al-Ash'ari (c. 873–935), himself a former adherent of the rationalist Mu'tazilite school. One of Ash'ari's most prominent followers, al-Baqillani (d. 1013), authored a treatise on miracles and magic, emphasizing the vast difference between the two phenomena. His work is in many ways characteristic of an important aspect of theological prophetology. Baqillani discusses prophetic evidentiary miracles from every conceivable angle, distinguishing them from all manner of "unusual" happenings and focusing on the necessity of miracles as a legitimation of the lawgiving mission of the prophets. In connection with their interest in miracles and their desire to defend God's primary causality, Baqillani and his fellow Ash'arites espoused a doctrine of atomism.

Abu Hamid al-Ghazali (1058–1111) exerted an extraordinary influence on Islamic thought, and was known to the Scholastics as Algazel. Coming out of the Ash'arite tradition, Ghazali also held that apologetic miracles were important, but he insisted that miracles were only one of the many proofs of prophethood. If one is to be fully convinced that, for example, Muhammad received the highest type of prophetic call, one must rely on the personal experience afforded by prayerful study of the Qur'an and the Sayings of the Prophet. Ghazali employed the vocabulary of his philosophical adversaries to raise the prophet to suprahuman stature and to demonstrate the necessity of prophetic revelation. He parted company with the philosophers in several ways: by situating the entire process of revelation under the absolute control of God, and by denying that prophethood is in any way the right or prerogative of any human being of whatever predisposition or that prophets are of necessity implicated in any sort of politico-legal administration. Ghazali's emphasis on the element of personal religious experience was one of his great contributions to Islamic theology and was the key to his lifelong effort to reconcile mysticism with more traditionalist Islamic thinking.

Another major figure who also stood between philosophy and mysticism, but in a way that tended to drive them apart, was Ibn Taymiya (d. 1328). His fundamental conviction was that God is Lord and Creator and that people are meant only to serve and obey. Maintaining the clearest possible distinction between God and the world, he dismissed the immanentism of the philosophers' approach to prophetic revelation. Then, focusing on the prophet's moral role in helping human beings to obey God, Ibn Taymiya fended off the threat of antinomianism that he regarded as inherent in mysticism. He shared Ghazali's reticence concerning the philosophers' emphasis on the prophetic lawgiving function. Ibn Taymiya therefore refused to identify as a "state" the community Muhammad had formed, lest the Prophet be relegated to the status of ordinary worldly rulers. Muhammad's goal was "not to build an empire but a social order based on the special ideology that he had brought. The state, though a necessary function of this social order, is yet subservient to it and not dominant over it." Miracles remain essential to prophethood.[14]

Jalal ad-Din Rumi largely agreed with the theologians with respect to Muhammad's political involvements. As the poet makes clear in all of his references to the meaning of jihad, Muhammad's reconquest of Makka, and similar matters, his underlying theological principle is that people usually do not know what is in their own best interests and must be maneuvered into a position in which they can more readily receive the gifts God wishes to bestow on them. Muhammad had no purely political ambitions. On the question of miracles, Rumi stands midway between the philosophers and the theologians. Whether he is speaking of specifically prophetic evidentiary miracles, or of the sorts of marvels Friends of God also can effect, the mystic redirects attention from the individual who performs the miracle, or through whom it is performed, to those toward whom the miracle is directed. He sides unhesitatingly with the theologians in insisting that not a trace of human initiative is in any way causative of miracles. On the other hand, Rumi remains sympathetic to the philosophers' suggestion that it is a mistake to look for the substance of prophethood in thaumaturgy.

As for his understanding of the nature of prophetic inspiration, Rumi represents a development that is manifestly at odds with the theological traditionalists. According to the theologians, prophetic inspiration ceased with the last prophet. For Rumi and his fellow mystics, the saints are the successors to the prophets through a variety of inspiration. Jalal ad-Din agrees with Ghazali in this respect, although Ghazali's concern for the traditionalist approach prevented him from stating explicitly the conclusions at which Rumi arrives. The mystic holds, along with Ibn Sina, that prophetic consciousness is related to a more highly developed perceptive faculty. Inspiration is therefore at least theoretically available to individuals at all times, even after Muhammad. Rumi then proceeds to the logical but technically untenable conclusion that anyone can become a Friend of God or a prophet.[15]

Theosophical Prophetology

"Theosophy" here refers to a variety of Islamic thought that began in the latter part of the twelfth century, a highly personal, subjectivist religious philosophy amalgamated with mysticism. It stands somewhere between pure rationalism and pure intuitionism. Let us look at three significant representatives of this unusual development.[16] Ibn 'Arabi (1165–1240) and his much later follower Shah Wali Allah of Delhi (1702–62) consider the prophet a manifestation of some divine attribute, or as typifying some historical situation, or perhaps as a prototype of one of the stages in the mystic journey. In other words, they do not regard the prophet primarily as a distinct personality in his own right, not even to the extent that a character in an allegory is a distinct personality. In Ibn 'Arabi's view, the prophet's personal story is purely secondary, providing a framework within which to speak of the Divine Nature. Occasionally Ibn 'Arabi may single out one or two details from the traditional story of a prophet and then weave around them a theory that is often highly esoteric.

For example, in his *Bezels of Wisdom*, with each of its twenty-seven chapters devoted to a single prophet, Ibn 'Arabi often focuses on some aspect of a particular prophet that would have been only a small part of the narrative in Tha'labi or Kisa'i, and proceeds to transform it into a metaphysical centerpiece. The story of Joseph is the only prophetic tale that appears in the Qur'an as a unified continuous narrative (Sura 12). Ibn 'Arabi concentrates exclusively on Joseph's initial dream of the celestial bodies bowing before him, and its eventual interpretation when at last

Joseph receives his family in Egypt. The theosophist uses the dream to praise the wisdom of Muhammad's saying, "The people sleep and when they die they awaken," and to discuss the epistemological qualities and deficiencies of this world of shadows as contrasted with authentic prophetic revelation and inspiration. Ibn 'Arabi then virtually ignores every other facet of the Joseph story even though it is the most complete story in scripture.

In a similar vein, his chapter on Jesus begins with the animating power of God's spirit as manifested in Jesus through Mary and Gabriel. He then discusses the metaphysics of the life-giving breath by which Jesus can revive the dead, as evidence of the mingling of the human and divine—a most remarkable discussion to discover in the work of a Muslim. The entire chapter turns around the question of the relationship of the divine to the creaturely in Jesus.

Ibn 'Arabi's approach stands at the opposite end of the prophetological spectrum from the historical approach. Whereas the latter tends to highlight some of the prophet's more charming or engaging characteristics, the former frequently builds a monumental theory upon some small or even bizarre detail, weaving involved interpretations of recondite word associations. For example, Abraham was traditionally known by the honorific title Khalil ar-Rahman (Friend of the Merciful). Ibn 'Arabi explains that the word khalil really means "intimate and interpenetrating," and constructs his entire chapter so as to show how Abraham is the prototype of the person lost in love.

The Indian mystic Shah Wali Allah betrays the influence of Ibn 'Arabi, even to the point that the Indian besought God to make him the Seal of the Sages (those who stand intermediate between prophets and Friends of God) as Ibn 'Arabi had been the Seal of the Saints and Muhammad the Seal of the Prophets. As Ibn 'Arabi had associated each prophet with a particular facet of divine wisdom, Shah Wali Allah links key figures with specific types of knowledge needed by the human race at certain critical junctures in its history. He emphasizes the function of the procession of prophets in a vast cosmic journey of separation from God and eventual return to God.

Sadr ad-Din Shirazi, also known as Mulla Sadra (1572–1641), was also indebted to the thought of Ibn 'Arabi, "but whereas Ibn 'Arabi's method of writing is not philosophical—he works by analogies and images rather than rational proofs, Sadra's method is out-and-out rational and philosophical. Indeed, just as Sadra condemns philosophy without intuitive experience, so he denounces pure Sufism (mysticism) without philosophic training and pursuit."[17] He thus stands as an important link for us between the pure theosophy of Ibn 'Arabi and Shah Wali Allah and the pure mysticism of Rumi.

Mulla Sadra's position concerning prophetic epistemology shares some features found in the thought of Ibn Sina and the other philosophers. The ordinary human mind unaided cannot attain to certain transcendental truths. Prophets are therefore absolutely necessary. But where the philosophers hesitated, Sadra and the mystics did not fear to tread: the prophet is that exceptional individual empowered to achieve a total union with the realm of the intelligible. Fazlur Rahman explains further:

> Whereas in al-Farabi and Ibn Sina, the Prophet receives the Intellectual Truth as a totality which is then transformed by his power of imagination into a symbolic form and a verbal mode; according to Sadra, the Prophet's mind becomes totally identified with the Active Intelligence both at the intellectual level and the imaginative level— that is to say, it is not the Prophet's mind which creates . . . the symbolic or imaginative truth but his mind "perceives" or rather "becomes" that truth as well as the intellectual truth. This is because Sadra believes (after Ibn 'Arabi) in an objective, ontological World of Symbols or Images or the "lower Angels."[18]

Though Rumi and his fellow mystics would agree with many of Mulla Sadra's conclusions, they would never dream of arriving at them by the same method. And though the mystics might approve of Ibn 'Arabi's method of analogies and images, they would make every effort to disavow any need for the cognitive content for which the theosophist strove.

Mystical Prophetology

Jalal ad-Din Rumi represents the finest and most original achievements in a tradition of mystical poetry that began with Hallaj (d. 922), developed through Sana'i (d. 1131), 'Attar (d. 1220), Ibn al-Farid (d. 1235), and continued down to Muhammad Iqbal (d. 1938). The mystical poets generally read the Qur'an looking neither precisely for story line, nor for more traditionalist modes of expression (though they frequently quote the Qur'an), nor for very esoteric and abstract etymological associations. The mystics fill their poetry with original and richly evocative imagery. They are, like Ibn 'Arabi, addicted to playing on words as they strive to enhance the

Qur'an's already vivid word pictures; but the puns of the mystics are in general slightly less arcane than those of the theosophist. Seldom do the mystics attempt to analyze the metaphysical complexities behind the words they use. They do not, in short, intellectualize their imagery.

Poetic imagination is in fact, if not in theory, the principal means by which the mystical poets transport the reader to an understanding of prophetic revelation, an understanding that transcends even intellectual perplexity. Bewilderment is not an impasse. It is the beginning of true mystical knowledge.

The mystics consider the prophet the paradigm of the relationship between creature and Creator. A prophet is neither merely a historical figure, nor merely a personification of some divine attribute or of some other abstract quality, though these features do occasionally emerge from the poetry. A prophet is an exemplar, a person whose life story can exert a living influence on the life of the observant believer. To that extent the story line is more significant for the mystics than for the theosophists. But the mystics are more interested in the patterns of value and behavior beneath the specifics of the prophet's biography. The poets therefore fashion allegories and fables. They tell stories of human and animal characters who embody prophetic virtues and who are clearly types of the prophet. Occasionally they also use stories in which the prophets themselves symbolize someone or something else, that is, in which the prophets themselves are "types" of humanity or, very often, of the ideal mystic or spiritual guide. Here are some samples of how Rumi uses the allegorical fable and related allusions. We shall return briefly to these matters in the Afterword.

If one may speak of a thematic image in Jalal ad-Din Rumi's prophetology, it is that of the royal falcon. It is by no means the only image he employs, but it is so fully developed in several passages and recurs so frequently in fleeting allusions that scarcely any other image can compete with the royal falcon for the prophetological limelight. Rumi makes it clear that the falcon does not refer either to a single specific prophet or only to actual prophets. His rationale in using the image is to present a standard of life that is truly that of all the prophets, but which is also a touchstone for all believers.

Rumi relates in two segments how the king's favorite falcon flew from the palace into the custody of an old hag, a symbol of the world with all its false promises.[19] She clipped the bird's wings and talons and tried to feed it a stew to which the falcon was not accustomed. When the bird refused to eat, the angry woman poured the boiling broth on the bird's crown. Meanwhile, the king's anxious search brought him at length to the old woman's tent. His Majesty's tears sharpened the falcon's own anguish at separation from the king. Immediately after this first segment of the story Rumi tells of the adversity which Moses, Noah, and Muhammad had suffered at the hands of their enemies. In the second segment the poet makes an association between the eye of the falcon, weeping both from the pain of the boiling broth and from longing for the king, and the eye of Muhammad, which "turned not aside" on the night when Muhammad journeyed through the heavens in his Ascension: the prophet is not distracted from the vision of God. Then the falcon speaks and likens himself to the pre-Islamic Arabian prophet Salih, who had endured such pain among the unbelieving people of Thamud.[20]

Before proceeding to develop a variation on this first falcon story, Rumi spins a related allegory. A certain king had two slaves, one true and the other false. As the king grew to esteem the true slave more highly, the royal courtiers became more and more envious, even as unbelievers have always envied their prophets. Within that context the poet sets his story of the falcon who, momentarily blinded by destiny, fell among owls. Fearful that the falcon had come to take over their homeland, the owls attacked. Said the falcon:

> I have no desire to remain here; I am leaving and will return to the
>   Kings of Kings.
> Do not be undone in your concern, Owls, for I will not settle down
>   here. I will return to my home.
> You consider this ruin a viable dwelling place; but for me it is to the
>   forearm of the king that I must return.

The owls persisted in their suspicion that the falcon was a crafty deceiver, and they mocked his talk of returning to the king. In reply the falcon explained that even though he was indeed not the king's equal, he would gladly experience loss of self (mystical annihilation) for His Majesty's sake.[21]

Later in book two of the *Mathnawi*, Rumi recapitulates his theme in a story entitled "The cause of a bird's flying and feeding with a bird that is not of its own kind." How is it that a royal falcon should descend from the vault of heaven to the level of the low-born owl? the poet asks. Part of the prophet's mission is to sow unity where there is chronic discord, even as Muhammad had defused the tensions among the rival factions in Madina.

Rumi then recounts a story of the prophet Solomon, who understood the speech of the birds and who had often served as arbitrator among them. Addressing his readers on behalf of all the prophets the poet writes:

> Listen all you wrangling birds, be attentive like the falcon to the King's falcon-drum . . . (And the birds reply:)
> We birds are blind and oblivious, for we have never recognized that Solomon.
> We, like the owls, have been hostile to the falcons and now find ourselves left behind in this ruin . . .
> Their crow was a crow only in appearance; within he was a falcon [whose eye] did not wander.[22]

Rumi then explains the behavior of the birds. When the falcon descends among the owls they often mistake the royal bird for a crow (*zagh* in Persian), the owl's natural enemy, because the falcon brings a message that upsets the birds. In reality the falcon is one who lives ever in the presence of the king and whose gaze, like that of Muhammad on his mystical journey to the throne of God, "turned not aside." Finally, Jalal ad-Din often alludes to the royal falcon in the lyric poems of his *Diwan*. His entire prophetology is summed up in this one verse: "Nothing can deter the falcon from forgetting its prey to return to the King, once it hears from drum and drumstick the call, 'Come back.'"[23]

CHAPTER 2

Flight of the Royal Falcons

THE DYNAMICS OF PROPHETIC REVELATION

When someone lays a trap and by cunning catches little birds in
that trap so as to eat them and sell them, that is called cunning.
But if a king lays a trap so as to capture an untutored and
worthless falcon that has no knowledge of its own true nature,
and to train it to his own forearm so that it may become
ennobled and taught and tutored, that is not called cunning.
Though to outwardseeming it is cunning, yet it is known to be
the very acme of rectitude and bounty and generosity, restoring
the dead to life, converting the base stone into a ruby, making
the dead sperm into a human being and far more than that. If
the falcon knew for what reason people seek to capture it, it
would not require any bait; it would search for the trap with
soul and heart and would fly on the king's hand. (F 38/26)

Following through Rumi's metaphor of prophet as royal falcon, the present chapter describes Jalal ad-Din's "theo-poetics" of revelation in
three sections. The first explores the overall relationship between prophets
and the world into which they are sent. The second focuses specifically on
the nature of revelation and the key technical terms in which Rumi
expresses his view of it. Finally, we look at the prophets as mystics in their
relationships with God, and as servants in their relationships with the people to whom God sends them.

17

The Falcon on the Minaret: Prophets in the World

The Office of Prophet

Whenever a prophet is conceived, his star rises in the heavens (III:901). By God's favor, and not through any personal effort, a human being may be exalted to the rank of prophethood.[1] God bestows the office, not because of His own need of prophets, but because of His majesty which can turn dust into "princely riders" (II:906–7) and wanderers into prophets (V:784). God gives everlasting fame to whom He chooses, and casts the names of self-made kings into oblivion (I:1102–6). In His mercy God sent so many prophets because so few people sought His grace (IV:3318). Prophets are sent to show forth both God's wrath and His mercy, but mercy was God's primary motive in sending them (V:514–16; F 227/220). Thus the prophets became the visible caliphs of the unseen Lord, separate from God only in form; for every king's messenger is of the king's kind (I:673–76; III:2743ff.).

Before a prophet can be commissioned he must endure a period of trial: every prophet began as a shepherd and only later ascended to the care of God's people (VI:3287–95). The Merciful caused the world to seem narrow to the prophets (III:3538) in order to purify them of lust and greed (II:908; V:H.4025–26), of their own desires (F 174/165), of concern for their bodies and for fame (F 238/230, 192/184). Thus pronouncing death's sentence upon the egocentric self (*nafs*) (I:787), the prophets were shown the way out of the "prison of this world" and the narrowness of arrogance toward the freedom that is the essence of prophethood.[2] As Rumi describes it, "some individuals have so faithfully followed their intelligence that they have become entirely angels of pure light. They are the prophets and the saints. They have been delivered out of hope and fear" (F 90/78).

Once hatched from the silent egg of the world, the chicks become birds and fly to a world suffused with the glorification of God: "the work and business of the prophets and messengers is beyond the skies and the stars" (VI:3447–49). The prophet-to-be is born in time, but the prophet is made a prophet out of time. He witnesses the creation of the world and is infinitely more ancient than the world (F 149-50/140–41). Within such a man are hell, paradise, and a hundred resurrections (II:3105–6). Mawlana further details the making of the prophet:

> First they journeyed to the other world, coming out of their human attributes, the flesh and the skin. They surveyed the depths of that

world and this and traversed all the stages, so that it became known to them how one must proceed on that way. Then they came back and summoned humankind, saying, "Come to that original world! For this world is a ruin and a perishing abode, and we have discovered a delightful place, of which we will tell you." (F 177/168)

Upon their return from the "world of spirit" (D 200:22), the prophets were like people who had been snatched away from their homeland to become slaves in a foreign country. All persons share the experience of slavery in an alien land, but the prophets were like those taken captive at a later age. Their memory of home was that much more vivid and their desire to return that much more urgent. As a result, they needed only the faintest reminder to be transported back home. For them, the speech of God removed the veils of forgetfulness and they became immediately reunited with God. Most people are younger when they are taken into bondage and need more insistent reminders of home. To such as these the prophets were sent (F 81/69).

All the prophets were educated in the school of the "hidden mind" and the "inmost consciousness" of God. Their message was therefore not one to be taken for granted. On the contrary, they would have had every right to withhold their *risala* from those who had no desire to hear it; ". . . for they have come from the Sublime Palace./ They are not beggars, that they should be grateful to you, O impostor, for every service." Even so, the prophets did not disdain to deliver their message (III:3604–12). Though their office did not include the ability to make people receptive, as only God can do, they discharged their commission to "manifest the power of God, and by preaching to waken" humankind (F 227/220).

"Integration by discrimination" seems a fair, if paradoxical, characterization of the prophetic task. Part is connected to whole only in appearance, and the connections that most mortals discern are spurious. Prophets were therefore sent to demonstrate the true interrelationships of things precisely by pointing out the false relationships, the genuine incompatibilities in creation (I:2811–13). Each prophet was a shaker of the buttermilk churn whose shaking reveals that the true self is hidden, like the butter that goes otherwise undetected in buttermilk (IV:H.3030–35). A prophet could disclose falsehood by being always true himself, thus serving as the touchstone by which a counterfeit coin could be found out,[3] the light by which one distinguishes friend from foe, sibling from stranger (F 92/80).

Because the world was home to prophets and infidels alike (IV:818), prophetic discrimination necessarily took the form chiefly of spiritual correction as directed by divine command. Of themselves the prophets were supremely tolerant, overlooking the myriad faults of their people. When they appeared intolerant, it was strictly by order of God (IV:776–77; II:2890). All seekers were homogeneous with the prophets and were attracted ever closer to the truth through them (I:751; IV:2669–71). By the example of the prophets, who were seen by all to have "reason and a tongue, hands and feet," other people were inspired to examine themselves as to why they themselves had not arrived at the perfection embodied in the prophets. Through such self-scrutiny against the measuring rod of the prophet, a person could advance toward perfection (F 179/171). "Those who acknowledge the truth see themselves in the prophets and hear their own voice proceeding from them and smell their own scent proceeding from them. No one denies his own self. Therefore the prophets say to the community, 'We are you, and you are we; there is no strangeness between us' " (F 227/220).

The Unity of the Prophets: Affinities and Contrarieties

Shared humanity precluded strangeness between the prophets and those to whom they were sent, but it did not rule out envy. Not all of the people who have heard the words of a prophet have especially appreciated the image of themselves that they saw reflected in the man of God, the heart/mirror of the world. Some hated the prophets for what they hated in themselves (I:787–93), and became envious of the prophets because of their obvious affinity with the source of life. A simple visual image may help to illustrate the relationship that Mawlana depicts among the prophets, their sympathizers, and their enemies. At the center of the image stand the prophets clustered around the throne of God, all engaged alternately in mission and return, moving away from their source temporarily and then coming back. Standing around the prophets in two concentric circles are their likes and their opposites: those like the prophets gathered in the inner circle and moving centripetally, their contraries in the outer circle in centrifugal motion. We shall look at these three concentric circles, first at the prophets as examples of utter unanimity and homogeneity among themselves; then at those believers who are homogeneous with the messengers; and finally at those whose jealousy make them inimical to the revealed message.

"We make no distinction" among the prophets, says Q 2:136; to which Rumi adds, that to disbelieve in a single prophet is to display imperfect faith (IV:H.407). Conversely, whoever travels in the ship of Muhammad is a fellow traveler with all the prophets (D 3495:11). Following as one behind the banner of the Seal,[4] the prophets were the tightest of all confraternities. In their complete accord they were like many jugs poured into one basin (III:2122-23), like ten or even a hundred lamps whose lights were never in competition.[5] They were "of one breath" and constantly acknowledged one another in such a way that, for example, one must regard the religious communities associated with Jesus and Moses as compatible and in no way hostile to each other (M 67/148; I:326). Rumi even paints a picture of all the prophets raising their hands in prayer and singing together the Qur'anic song, "Let me see (you)" (VI:2445–47, Q 7:139). To the Jew who was relating his dream of the assembled prophets, all of them looked like Moses,[6] and since Mawlana describes the prophets as bathed in one light (II:906–22), one can understand how the Jew saw them as "of one face."

Nothing in creation can grow and reproduce without a second of its own kind. The prophets therefore "sought fellow travelers" on the straight road (VI:518), people who would recognize prophetic signs (II:1703–4). "Every bird flies to its own kind" (I:639). To hear words from a "familiar friend" gives a feeling of security (F 177/167). For the sake of such homogeneity God called the prophets from among the people, and Rumi further defines homogeneity as "a species of insight whereby people gain admission to one another" (VI:2992). Recognition of affinity is the prime requisite of faith; for without that recognition and the security that it fosters, there can be only unbelief, suspicion, and enmity (F 45/34).

According to Q 6:113, God said, "We appointed unto every prophet an adversary." As we shall see in later chapters, Jalal ad-Din portrays vividly the struggles of nearly every prophet with his contrary. In every instance, faulty perception was the cause of the adversary's unbelief. As Iblis saw only the clay in Adam (I:3961), as Joseph's brothers deemed Joseph of little value (II:1405–7), as Pharaoh and Nimrod were archetypical in their faulty estimate of God's power in Moses and Abraham (D 27:14), to mention only a few examples—so all unbelievers "saw the minaret, but not the bird upon it, (though) upon the minaret (was) a fully accomplished royal falcon" (VI:1140). Some unbelievers claimed to be followers of the prophets, but they were like bats claiming to have sight or like snakes insisting they were swimming fish (M 67/149). No infidel could ever "distinguish between a prophet (*nabi*) and a dolt" for the Magician (the Devil) made the prophets seem ugly (VI:4277, 997). Infidels are of the substance of Sijjin (Hell). Prophets are of one substance with 'Illiyin.[7] Mawlana says that unbelievers do in fact know the prophets as well as they recognize their own children, but deny their perceptions out of jealousy (III:3663–65).

The prophets' jealousy of any heart that contained "other than God" was always beneficial (D 123:11); but the jealousy of the unbelievers for the prophets was always evil (D 114:7). Envy blindfolded them to the inner truth of the messengers (II:3101–6, 3109–13), so that their fantasy made them dismiss the stories of the prophets as mere fantasy (D 1299:5). Mawlana speaks of the advent of the prophet under such adverse conditions:

> Every prophet came alone into this world: he was alone, and yet he had a hundred unseen worlds within him. By his power he enchanted the macrocosm, he enfolded himself in a very small frame (body of man the microcosm). The foolish deemed him to be lonely and weak: how is he weak who had become the King's companion? The foolish said, "He is a man, nothing more": woe to him that recks not of the end! (I:2505–8)

Envy then turned to spite, and to "blows on the nape," and even to death for the prophets, at the hands of those who used every conceivable means to fight them.[8] Calling the prophets "magicians and self-advertisers" and thinking the worst of them,[9] the infidels criticized the prophets' every move. If a prophet accepted a gift he was beggar, but if he declined he was a hypocrite. If he was sociable it was because he was actually covetous; and if he kept to himself he was proud (II:3065–66). It was the constant lot of the messengers to be afflicted by vile types (VI:2150), and as Rumi explains, the underlying reason for the opposition was that the infidels were excessively attached to material things. Their possessions were like rags used to bandage the sores of greed on a donkey's hide. The prophetic message was like the action of one who tries to pull the rags off of the sores (V:H.1149–53).

Under the pressure of unrelenting vituperation, even the prophets began to doubt that the message would be accepted. Their preaching to the envious was like beating cold iron. Twice Rumi quotes Q 12:110, "Until when the messengers (*rusul*) despaired . . . they thought they had been deceived." In one instance he explains that he has chosen the reading *kudhibu*, "they were deceived, or let down by God," rather than *kudhdhibu*, "they were taken for liars" by the infidels. God had not, however, forsaken the prophets, and did not leave them to wallow in despair for long (III:H.3077ff.; III:2033–40). Though the infidels appeared to have gotten the upper hand in the struggle, the angels interceded for the messengers (IV:27–28) and they overcame their adversaries. Prophets are a product of God's mercy while enviers result from the divine wrath; and God's mercy is stronger than His wrath (V:514–16).

"Enmity (proceeding) from wisdom is better than the love that comes from a fool," said the Prophet (II:1877; AM 156). In the case of the prophets and their adversaries, the positive effects of enmity were twofold. First, the infidels prompted the messengers to retaliate with evidentiary miracles.[10] Second, since things can be known only in light of their opposites, the unbelievers were revealing God in the very act of denying Him (F 92/80, 185/177). Rumi nevertheless believes that everyone who is not happy at the call of God and the sight of His prophets should forever remain a Gabr (Zoroastrian, R 1083). In the end, of course, unbelievers have always paid dearly for their false accusations; for "whenever anyone throws a stone at heaven, the stone comes down on his own head" (M 131/252). Conversely, for followers of the prophets in this world, the threats of evil people are empty (D 1658:6).

Prophets, Friends of God, and the "Complete Person"

From Rumi's vocabulary one may conclude that there are two grades of prophet, or at least that Mawlana would not disagree with Muslim tradition. Every prophet is a *nabi*, but not every *nabi* is a *rasul* (messenger). Mawlana does not, however, elaborate specifically on the distinction that one could infer from his terminology. Indeed, his use of the terms itself does not exhibit ironclad consistency. Nowhere does he state explicitly how a *nabi* differs from a *rasul*, and the poet gives the general impression that the theoretical distinction is of little consequence to him. Rumi refers to the prophets as a group or in general allusions, as *anbiya', paygham-baran, rusul, rasulan, mursalun*—always without further qualification. Among the individual prophets only a few are specifically entitled *nabi* (e.g., Noah, Isaac, Moses, Job, David, Muhammad, to name those most frequently so titled). *Rasul*, except in contexts that are not specifically prophetological, is usually reserved for Muhammad, as is the term *mursal* in the singular. Roughly the same may be said of *pay(gh)ambar* as of *nabi*, though the Persian term appears more frequently. As for the related substantives, *nubuwwa, risala,* and *payghambari*: Mawlana uses them sparingly and nowhere sets up a clear distinction among them. In the final analysis, one must conclude that Rumi follows the Qur'anic example of "making no distinction" among the prophets; and that, except for formulaic expressions such as "the *nabi* said . . ." that appear mostly in his prose, the poet chose his prophetological terms largely for the sake of meter.

Between prophets and the "Friends of God" (*awliya' allah*), often referred to as saints, however, Jalal ad-Din does elucidate specific differences. Muhammad was the last of the prophets, but God has not left his people without guidance since the year 632. Saints have arisen in every age since the Prophet and "because of him" (I:813; F 233/226). A seeker cannot discover his true hidden self until a prophet is sent or until the words of a saint, which are part of the prophetic message, fall on the seeker's ear (IV:3032–36). Just as the prophets gave strength to people by translating revelation into letters and sounds, "So with regard to the great saint and his letters and sounds though the mass of people do not know him and do not attain to him, yet they derive strength from him and are nourished" (F 164/156). Mawlana often implies by context that every prophet is a Friend of God, whereas only certain of these are prophets. Moreover, some holy persons who were not prophets lived during the time of the prophets.[11] Here again Mawlana echoes classical Muslim teaching. Beyond that, he occasionally likens Friends of God to specific prophets, such as Jesus and Moses.[12] The model (spiritual guide) *pir* is called both Friend and *nabi* (II:3101).

Parallels between sainthood and prophethood formed an integral part of Rumi's theological heritage. As there are, at least in theory, ranks among the prophets, so there are gradations in holiness: from the many who have achieved union with God, to the *abdal*,[13] to those "veiled ones" so concealed that even the *abdal* do not hear their names (III:H.3104; F 100/88), to the *awtad* ("pegs," F 233/226), to the *Qutb*[14] and the Imam who is both the Guided One and the Guide (I:817–18). Speaking of the light of God passed from the prophets through the generations of saints, Rumi explains the necessity of stratification among the saints:

> . . . the light has gradations in degree, Because the Light of God has
>   seven hundred veils: regard the veil of the Light as so many
>   tiers.
> Behind each veil a certain class (of saints) has its place of abode:
>   these veils are theirs, rank by rank, up to the Imam. (I:820–22)

By extension, the rank and station of the individual seeker is related to his or her attachment to the saint as body depends on its attachment to heart and intellect. To sit in the presence of a Friend is to sit with God.

Rumi also recognizes the saintly "miracle" (*karama*) as parallel, though distinctly inferior, to the prophetic or evidentiary miracle (*mu'jiza*). "If a Friend of God drinks poison it becomes an antidote, but if the seeker drinks it, his mind is darkened" (I:2603). Some individuals may even be able to travel from Konya to the Ka'ba in a moment (F 129/118). Such wonders are spectacular and awesome, to be sure; but one must not take them as a proof of the performer's friendship with God. Even the monks can deduce people's thoughts and work wonders (F 198/189). Do not put undue credence in such works, Rumi warns, for, "what is a true wonder (*karama*) is this: that God should bring you from a lowly estate to a high estate, that you should travel from there to here, from ignorance to reason, from the inanimate to life. . . . These are the true marvels" (F 129/118). Finally, the prophets and saints together are God's shield, "And that shield stands firm till the resurrection, age after age; now in the form of the prophets, now in the form of the saints; to the end that the God-fearing may be distinguished from the ungodly, God's enemies from His friends" (F 85/73).

Mawlana's views on the *kamil*, the so-called "perfect person," in relation to prophethood, fall into place here. Jalal ad-Din sees all of creation as a definitely hierarchized, even pyramidal, structure in which all forms of existence are at least potentially capable of evolving into higher forms. The *kamil* represents the perfection of that process of increasing spiritualization. A look at Nicholson's index entry "Man, the Perfect" indicates how many of the highest possible attributes that notable interpreter of Rumi ascribes to this cosmic personage (MCN 441–42). It is important to note, however, that Rumi himself never talks specifically of the *insan-i kamil*, and only infrequently of the *kamil*. The poet then contrasts the "perfect one," *kamil*, with the "deficient one," *naqis*, and describes their respective qualities thus:

> If a *kamil* take earth, it becomes gold; if a *naqis* has carried away
>   gold, it becomes ashes.
> Since that righteous individual (the *kamil*) is accepted of God, his
>   hand in (all) things is the hand of God.
> The hand of the *naqis* is the hand of Devil and demon, because he is
>   the trap of imposition and guile.
> If ignorance come to him (*kamil*), it becomes knowledge, (but) the

knowledge that goes into the *naqis* becomes ignorance.
Whatever an ill person takes becomes illness, (but) if a *kamil* takes
     infidelity, it becomes religion. . . .
To the *kamil* (every) mouthful and saying is lawful. You are not
     kamil: do not eat, be mute.[16]

Even a minimalistic interpretation of Rumi's description must allow that
the word *kamil* could as well be "prophet" or "Friend of God," and the
word *naqis* "infidel." For the poet, therefore, the *kamil* is the prophet and
the Friend of God as seen in a particular perspective: namely, as the ultimate refinement in creation's evolutionary capability.[17]

The Call of the Falcon Drum: The Nature of Revelation

The Prophetic Subject as Receiver of Revelation

In the final weighing of divine initiative against human capacity, Rumi
tips the scales in favor of divine influence in human affairs. Such an
assessment is difficult to avoid despite Mawlana's various attempts to
steer a purely neutral course across the deserts of predestination and
freewill, between which the high road of the Sunna threads its way like a
ribbon of cool water. Along that road the prophets lead all believers
(V:H.2963). Rumi manages to maintain the precarious balance convincingly enough in the area of overt ethical conduct;[18] but his epistemology
leans decidedly toward a theory of predisposition.

God had warned a gloating Adam that He could have given Adam's
place to Iblis (I:3893). Pharaoh could have been a Moses (F 184/176).
Rumi's God makes "the distracted soul to be a guide" and "the wayless
wanderer to be a prophet" (V:784). The sort of predisposition to which
Rumi tends is not, of course, a condition inherent in the person, but a result
of God's prior creative action. From its very inception the prophetic intellect is superior to all others. However, God is in no way constrained to
bestow such preeminence on this person rather than that; nor can the individual advance by his own effort alone.[19] A prophet is like an infant who is
able to hear his mother's words and then speak. Lesser persons are like
children born deaf; they must remain mute because they are unable to imitate their mothers' speech (IV:3037–40).

Mawlana employs a variety of metaphors to tell of the receptive capaci-
ties of the prophets. God spoke to many of them, and in the instances of
Joseph and Shu'ayb the poet says specifically that God's address "came to
the ear."[20] Jacob had an especially acute sense of smell (e.g., I:1902) and,
in fact, none of the prophets came to full life until they detected the "scent

of the unseen teacher" (D 303:7). Most frequently Rumi uses the imagery of sight and vision. Jacob's sense of smell became the servant of his eyes, so that his restored vision was the same as that by which all the prophets were "far-seeing" (IV:3222). In ecstasy, they see with the "eye of the heart" and thus "behold the Garden."[21] Vision must precede speech. Rumi therefore argues that the very claim of the prophets to vision is itself proof of their vision and of the veracity of the message. Since vision is transitive and requires an object as well as a subject, any denial of the vision of the prophets only serves to establish the existence of both subject and object. By so remarkable a logic Mawlana defends the prophets against the claim that they were "victims of a false presumption" (F 168/160).

In Plato's *Meno*, Socrates demonstrates the theory of "innate knowledge" by helping Meno's slave boy "remember" the geometry that he has merely forgotten from a former time. Rumi's image of the slaves brought from their homeland into another country is analogous to the scene from Plato's dialogue. A kind of innate knowledge, totally independent of sense, is the primary reservoir from which the message of the prophets flows. Communing with God in the "world without letters and sounds," the prophets were later sent into the world of letter, of water and clay, to give sensible shape to the message and to help believers recall their homeland. For the sake of forgetful, sensate beings, the message is dressed in "the garb of *'ayn* and *lam*," so that memory may be nudged by the senses (F 164/156; IV:2970). Adam therefore came into the world fully prepared to teach "the names," and Jesus spoke virtually with his first breath.

Mawlana gives a description of what happens to the sensible faculties in an encounter with the revealing God:

> Our senses and finite speech are obliterated in the knowledge and
> wisdom of our Sultan.
> Their (the God-intoxicated mystics') senses and understandings
> within (them) are (tossed) wave on wave, in (the sea of) "they are
> assembled before Us." (Q 36:32, 53)
> When night comes, it is again the time of (bearing) the burden: the
> stars, which had become hidden, go (again) to work.
> God gives back to the senseless ones their (lost) senses: (they return
> to consciousness) troop after troop, with rings (of mystic
> knowledge) in their ears,
> Dancing, waving their hands in praise (of God), triumphing (and
> crying), "O Lord, you have brought us to life." (I:3671–75; see also
> F 174/166ff.)

Nicholson notes that the "daylight" implied in the text and juxtaposed to the night of consciousness is the "divine *tajalli*" or manifestation. Rumi uses a number of terms for "revelation, manifestation, inspiration," in addition to *tajalli*. In order to analyze further the process of revelation we shall investigate each of those terms briefly.

The Vocabulary of Revelation

Many are the names of God's communication to humanity, but the most important of them for Rumi are *wahy*, *kashf*, *ilham*, and *tajalli*. Rumi bases his usage on that of the Qur'an.

Wahy: Already in the Qur'an, *wahy* had become a technical term for divine revelation. Though the term is most often referred to Muhammad, earlier prophets are also said to have been the recipients of *wahy*. Both the objective message and the subjective process of imparting it may be connoted by the word. Taking his cue from the scripture, Mawlana says that by means of *wahy* Adam received knowledge of the names (VI:2648) and learned that his sons were treating one of their brothers unjustly (M 84/174); Khizr was given license to perform "formally" questionable actions (I:224–26); Moses received messages at the Bush and Sinai (D 1847:16; VI:2437, among many references); Solomon was told to build the al-Aqsa mosque (IV:389). Many of the circumstances under which God delivered a *wahy* to Muhammad will appear in a separate chapter.[22]

God once made a *wahy* to the mother of Moses according to Q 28:7. She is told there to suckle her child before casting him into the river. In the *Mathnawi*, too, 'Imran's wife receives a *wahy*, but Rumi has transformed it into an assurance that her child would not be hurt when she threw him into the stove (III:953). Rumi does mention the command to suckle the child as well, but the command is not given by *wahy*. Mawlana believes that *wahy* is sent down on people other than Muhammad and the other prophets. In most of those instances, however, it is not called *wahy*, but the light of God (F 139/128). 'Imran's wife seems to be the one specific exception for Rumi, possibly because she is a prophet's mother.

According to Rumi, the Qur'an provides further warrant for some flexibility in applying the term *wahy*. A man who claimed to be a prophet defended his claim by quoting Q 16:70, "God has inspired (*awha*) the bee." How could the *wahy* of a human being, of one honored by God, be inferior to that of the bee? Nicholson interprets the man's argument as meaning that the *wahy* of the claimant, who is the perfect person, need not be given through Gabriel in order to be genuine *wahy*. Rumi thus allows *wahy* to become roughly equivalent to *ilham*, the inspiration given a Friend of God.[23]

Wahy is the guarantee of the truth of a creed. Among the many sects, one alone is the custodian of *wahy* and only its members are true believers. A believer must therefore be discriminating in his choice of creed (F 127–28/116). From *wahy* comes knowledge of jurisprudence (F 156/147), of the trades (F 151–52/142–43), of medicine and astronomy (IV:1294–97; VI:3143). All of these aspects of knowledge are the "words and sounds" of *wahy*, about which Mawlana likes to use a variety of auditory images.[24] Words and sounds are needed because the *wahy* itself is hidden in the hearts of a chosen few (IV:2179). Descending upon the "spiritual Ka'ba" of the heart,[25] *wahy* preserves the heart from error (VI:1601).

Mawlana explains the safeguarding quality of *wahy* by means of an analogy with the Qur'an: *wahy* is equivalent to the actual text of revelation (*nass*) given through the Holy Spirit (Gabriel) and therefore not subject to error. The derivative sciences mentioned above as the "words and sounds" of *wahy* are like *qiyas*, or the process of analogical reasoning deducing from the original text. Closely linked to the text, the activity of *qiyas* is not entirely negligible; but it is far less dependable than the actual text. Spirit is to the original text what the partial or individual intellect (*'aql-i juz*) is to the results of *qiyas* (III:3582–85). To state it another way: the prophet as recipient of *wahy* and possessor of spirit stands in relation to the abridged certitude of the original text as the ordinary person, the recipient of derived knowledge and possessor of partial intellect, stands in relation to the abridged certitude of knowing indirectly by analogy. Mawlana states further that the "spirit of revelation" (*ruh-i wahyi*) "also has actions conformable to (reason), (but) the intellect does not apprehend (them), for that (spirit) is exalted (above intellectual apprehension)." Thus the intellectual person may well regard the actions of the spiritual person as sheer madness, until he, too, allows himself to become spiritualized (II:3260–61). Only *wahy* can subdue the *nafs* (III:2560), and the revelation consumes the prophet totally in its flame.[26]

Kashf: Though Rumi allows himself some latitude in using the term *wahy*, it remains a characteristically prophetic prerogative. *Kashf* is a term of much less restricted application. The poet uses it to speak of uniquely prophetic communication, or of the special knowledge of the saints,[27] or of the knowledge that all seekers desire (III:3646). God is the *kashif* (IV:1014) to whom all things are *makshuf* (F 112/100). Rumi's most arresting attribution of the "unveiling" of *kashf* occurs in the verse, "He (the *'arif*) is both the command to do right and the right (itself), he is both the *kashif-i asrar* (unveiler of mysteries) and the *makshuf* (that which is unveiled)."

Ilham: Nicholson generally translates *ilham* as "inspiration." Rumi occasionally uses *wahy* as an approximate synonym for *ilham*; but the converse does not seem to be true. In other words, *wahy* may apply to the saint or the *kamil* (I:2081, 223–25), but Rumi never calls the source of prophetic knowledge *ilham*. One possible exception occurs in the story of how Qabil learned the trade of gravedigging from the crow, who, in a reversal of Rumi's usual usage, appears here as a prophetic type. A few verses earlier, Rumi had said that *wahy* is the root of all trades; but a few verses later, he says that the crow learned the trade of gravedigging through *ilham* (IV:1307). Recipients of inspiration are called the *ahl-i ilham*. They are the fountain of life (III:3295).

Tajalli: Nicholson explains that *tajalli* is the "self-revelation by which the One may be said metaphorically to become the many" (MCN IV:1667). God had revealed himself thus to Moses at Sinai (VI:2434), manifesting Himself without a veil so that the mountain crumbled.[29] *Tajalli* is roughly synonymous with *payda kardan*.[30] It also evokes images of light as the chief attribute of God's manifestation: Rumi calls union with God "the *tajalli* of the moon" (I:1464), and the "cycle of Ahmad" the rising of the "dawn of *tajalli*."

Jalal ad-Din's language of revelation seems to warrant the following conclusions: *wahy* and *ilham* carry a connotation rather of content or consequence than of the divine action itself. *Kashf* serves as a bridge between the two above terms and *tajalli*, in that *kashf* occurs in contexts suggestive of both the action of the revealer and that which is revealed. *Tajalli*, on the other hand, connotes God's doing, the event of theophany rather than the content of the revelation. *Wahy* is given mostly to prophets, though it can be related to others on rare occasions. *Kashf* is applicable to prophets and nonprophets alike without significant distinction, whereas *ilham* seems to pertain only to nonprophets. Virtually any seeker of God may experience the divine *tajalli*. In terms of content, *wahy* and *ilham* may impart every sort of beneficial knowledge, whether of the strictly mysterious or not as with trades or other practical affairs, secrets of the universe, etc. *Kashf* is the uncovering of the mysterious as a mystery, that is, of that which should not, and will never be, the common property of all human beings. *Tajalli* imparts an overwhelming sense of the brilliance and power of the Deity without necessarily conveying any further information.

Between God and the Prophets: Gabriel and the Spirit

Since the Creation, the angel Gabriel has been God's emissary to earth. When God commissioned the angel to go and collect a handful of earth for Adam's body, the earth dissuaded Gabriel from his mission by telling him he was meant for greater things. He was, said the earth, the greatest of the four angelic Throne bearers because of his superior awareness. He would become the messengers' messenger for he was the "life of the spirit of revelation," possessed of knowledge from the tablet of divine decrees. Because he was a "mine of reverence and respect," Gabriel honored the earth's plea in God's name not to embroil her in human affairs. God then sent Michael in his place (V:299, H.317, 1556–80).

Gabriel's next task, that of ushering the fallen Adam from Paradise (V:962–6), was not a pleasant one; but thereafter Gabriel became for all the prophets a bringer of "apples from Paradise" (V:2540) in the form of revelation (III:3583). If a prophet felt, as Abraham did, that the angel's intermediacy was unnecessary (III:4215–18; IV:H.2173–77), or where there was simply no room for him between the prophet and God, as during Muhammad's Ascension, Gabriel withdrew (I:2953). The angel escorted Jesus and Idris on their heavenward journeys (VI:2964ff.), put power into the incantation of Jesus and Moses (D 738:4), and Jesus was "produced from the breath of Gabriel" (V:3982). Mawlana's most remarkable description of Gabriel occurs in two texts in which the angel visits Mary. So beautiful that Joseph himself would have cut his hand, Gabriel "blossomed from the earth like a rose before her—like a fantasy that lifts its head from the heart" (III:3705–6). The angel describes himself in a later text as the "trusted" of the Lord and a "king and standard-bearer in nonexistence." Rumi continues the heart image as Gabriel addresses Mary:

> O Mary, look (well), for I am a difficult form (to apprehend): I am
> both a new moon and fantasy in the heart.
> When a fantasy comes into your heart and settles, it is with you
> wheresoever you flee—
> Except an unsubstantial and vain fantasy which is one that sinks like
> the false dawn.
> I am the light of the Lord like the true dawn, for no night prowls
> around my day.[32]

To Muhammad, Gabriel was a comforter on Mt. Hira (V:H. 3535–41), deliverer of *wahy* and of the Qur'an (F 171/163; I:2539). He ministered not only to the Prophet, but to others on behalf of the Prophet, as in the story of the suckling infant who addressed the Messenger. When the child's mother scolded and asked whence came its verbal proficiency, the following dialogue ensued:

> ". . . God taught (me), then Gabriel: I am Gabriel's accompanist in
> (this) declaration."
> She said, "Where is (Gabriel)?" It replied, "(I see him) shining above
> you like a perfect full-moon.
> He is teaching me the qualities of the Messenger and delivering me
> by means of that sublimity from this degradation." (III:H.3220–23)

Gabriel's power, derived from his vision of the Creator, was such that the dust from his horses' hoof could make the golden calf low at Sinai. His wings are the prototype of saintly "reason."[33] Reason alone, however, is limited. There remains a truth that even Gabriel does not know, and that would singe his wings (I:1732). One who does know that truth, the *'arif*, is a thousand Gabriels in human form (VI:4584). Gabriel longs to carry off even the tears from such a knower's eye and rub them on his own wings and beak (IV:2645–46). Unfortunately for the angel, once the spirit of Ahmad has "bitten the lip" of a knower, Gabriel can come no nearer lest he be lost in the flames (IV:1888–90). Many more images of Gabriel in the *Diwan* fill out Rumi's picture of the angel in essence and in action.[34]

Images of the Revelation

With this background of Rumi's thought on the receptivity of the prophetic subject, and on various aspects of the process initiated by God and mediated by Gabriel, we may now address ourselves to the questions: "What did God communicate?" and "What were its effects in the recipient?" Each of the next two sections of the chapter will treat one of these questions.

Mawlana speaks of the content of revelation poetically rather than discursively. Three types of imagery carry his message: light and fire, the water of life, and revelation as speech.

Light and fire: As an explanation of how *wahy* can be said to come down on people other than the prophets, Rumi quotes a famous Hadith and then comments on it:

"The believer sees with the light of God." When someone sees with God's light he discerns all things, the first and the last, the absent and the present; for how can anything be hidden from God's light? If anything is hidden, then that is not God's light. So the true meaning is *wahy*, even though they do not call it *wahy*.[35]

Light is therefore synonymous with *wahy*, and the related imagery provides Rumi a way of demonstrating the ongoing nature of revelation. His development of this light that inhabits the heart (IV:3397; VI:2756) is founded on his exegesis of the "light verse" (Q 24:35):

God most High has likened His light to a lamp for the sake of comparison; the Friends of God (and, by extension, the prophets) are likened to the glass of that lamp, also for the sake of comparison. God's light is not contained in phenomenal being and space; how then should it be contained in a glass and a lamp? How could the orients of the lights of almighty God be contained in the heart? Yet when you seek after it, you find it in the heart; not as being the receptacle wherein that light resides, but that you find that light radiating from that place.[36]

Among "persons of heart," or possessors of the light, there are degrees. The brightest are like the light itself; next comes the lamp; then the lamp-niche; and so forth, ever moving away from the source, from those whose very life is brilliance, to those who can scarcely bear the light even through tightly squinted eyes. There occurs a progressive despiritualization. In the outer circle, furthest from the source, are the "partial hearts," the squinters; they relate to the light as body to heart (I:817ff.). Living on "borrowed light," the squinters are bemused into thinking their bodies and senses are light. In that respect they share Moses' initial misperception at the Burning Bush: what they think is light is in reality fire (II:1256; IV:3223–25). Only the light of the prophets can extinguish that fire:

When the water of his light trickles on the fire, "chak chak" rises
    from the fire, and it leaps up.
When it makes "chak chak," say to it, "Death and woe (to you)" in
    order that this hell, your *nafs*, may become cold. (II:1257–58; see
    also I:3700–2)

Compared with light, fire is sheer darkness (IV:597), created by God so that His light might be made manifest by its relative opposite—relative because Rumi insists that God and His light have no opposite as such (F 92/80; I:1133–35).

God's light is a dyeing vat in which all things become of one color by losing their colors. Once the colors (and scents) of contingent existence have been dispensed with, obsolescence overtakes the "lamp with six wicks," that is, the five senses plus "common sense" (II:1345; IV:427). What faint light is supplied by the fire of sense draws a person earthward and remains hidden in the black of the eye. Now if that light, gross as it is, is invisible to the person of sense, it is not surprising that the far more subtle light of God goes unnoticed. Sense-light is as useless as a riderless horse; it needs the light of God to take the reins. Finally, Mawlana sums up by saying, "The light of God is an ornament to the light of sense: this is the meaning of 'light upon light.'"[37]

Transforming all things on which it shines, the light can make of Samiri's calf a *qibla* of grace; or leave the *qibla* itself a mark of infidelity by its absence. By that light unbelief becomes faith and the Devil becomes a Muslim (VI:2073–75). "The night and darkness of this world passes away, and the light of these words every moment becomes clearer. Even so the night of life of the prophets departed . . . yet the light of their discourse departed and came not to an end, nor ever will" (F 193/184).

The Water of Life: Since water shares the fire-extinguishing properties of the light of God, the water of life is also, by association, synonymous with revelation. Rumi makes the connection quite explicit: "know, then that the blessed water from heaven is the *wahy* of hearts and the true explanation (of every mystery)" (III:4319). Because of its affinity with the light, the contrary by which the water is made manifest is not drought, but darkness. Darkness is therefore beneficial to one who is willing to risk entering into it, holding aloft the lantern of universal reason (I:3687–91). One finds the water of life only in the "land of darkness," which is the body of the prophets and Friends of God.[38]

The "people of *ilham*" are the fountain of life from which God sends forth prophets and saints, "like a great, limpid water such as delivers out of darkness and accidental coloration every mean and dark water that enters into it." Weeds of care are swept away by its flow.[39] A note of caution is in order, however. Let whoever accepts the water's invitation to drink, do so in full awareness that this draught will effect a change. Anyone who imagines that the water of life consists merely in this world's delights will find those "sweet things" turned to fire, the Water's natural enemy, and his "double-vision" cured most painfully.[40]

Revelation as speech: God's speech, the Qur'an, existed in the days of Moses and Jesus and the other prophets, but it was not then in Arabic (F 93/81). From cover to cover the Qur'an is the story of the "cutting off of (secondary) causes" and of the glory of the prophets in battle against their enemies (III:2520–25). The Qur'an is by no means accessible to everyone: it is like a bride who does not disclose her face (F 236/229). Upon intimates, however, the Book works wondrous changes. Mawlana explains how this revelation transforms anyone who encounters it:

> When you have fled to the Qur'an of God, you have mingled with
>   the spirit of the prophets.
> The Qur'an is (a description of) the states of the prophets, (who are)
>   the fishes of the sacred ocean of majesty.
> And if you read and do not accept the Qur'an, suppose you have
>   seen the prophets and the saints (what will that avail you)?
> But if you are accepting (the Qur'an), when you read the stories (of
>   the prophets), the bird, your soul, will be distressed in its cage.
> The bird that is a prisoner in a cage, (if it) is not seeking to escape, it
>   is because of ignorance. (I:1537–41)

Like the light and the water of life, the Qur'an is unsettling, challenging, demanding change in one's approach to life in the world-cage. In fact, whoever drinks the water or "feeds on the light of God becomes the Qur'an" (V:2478).

Paygham (and its shortened form *payam*) also appears as one of the names of revelation. It simply means "message," and often occurs in contexts that do not appear to refer directly to the prophetic message. One cannot help but suspect, however, that Rumi seldom used the word without thinking of "the revealed message," especially where the term is associated with the word *payghambar.* In explicitly prophetological contexts, the term appears as a synonym for Qur'an (III:3421; VI:4728); refers to the teaching of any prophet (I:574); refers to Solomon's invitation to Bilqis to become a believer (II:H.1601); and refers to part of the content of a *wahy* given to Moses (IV:3575), to mention only a few of its occurrences.

Rumi also calls revelation "The Book" when he quotes the Qur'an's own references to itself as *al-kitab.* Alluding to Q 35:29, for example— "Then we gave the Book as an inheritance to those of Our servants whom we elected"—Mawlana suggests that the revelation descends especially upon "those chosen in eternity for the intimate knowledge and love of God" (I:747, MCN). Again, quoting the initial verse of Suras 10, 12, 13, and others—"These are the signs of the Book"—Rumi makes a parallel between the Qur'an and the hearts of those elect, where the "signs" of intimate knowledge are to be seen (II:1703–4, MCN). *Nuba* is an infrequently used synonym for the Qur'an, obviously connotative of revelation given through a *nabi* (IV:2220; III:2643). Finally, three other Qur'anically inspired names appear as well: the "remembrance," the "warning," and the "criterion."[41]

The Effects of Revelation on the Recipient

Mawlana's language of knowing is nuanced and its vocabulary varied. We turn now to a more precise examination of the characteristics of uniquely prophetic knowing and its effects in the knower.

All human beings possess reason or intelligence (*'aql*), but even the most intelligent person (*'aqil*) is not necessarily an authentic knower (*'alim* or *dana*). Rumi emphasizes the point by quoting a recurrent Qur'anic formula. Speaking of the *'aqilan* who possess an abundance of earthly *'ilm*, the poet says: "*la ya'lamun*"—that is, "they have no real knowledge" (III:2643; Q 30:5–6). Human intellect is only partial or particular, and as a result, most peoples' knowledge is fated to remain incomplete. Unaided *'aql* knows only descriptively rather than essentially (VI:4138–39; III:3642ff.) Such secondhand knowledge is easy prey to imagination and fantasy. Only by seeking the company of the prophetic intellect can one escape being a blind imitator and become a true knower.[42]

Prophets are the universal intellect and have bridged the gap between the partial and the universal.[43] Using a term he seems to reserve for prophets and Friends of God, Mawlana declares the prophets "endowed with reason" and possessed of a special kind of intelligence.[44] They are thus liberated from the snares of imagination. Through their knowledge of the unseen, prophets understand that one must be guided by spiritual or primary causes rather than by external secondary causes (IV:H.2562; I:843-49). God gave Adam the *'ilm* of the names of all things so that he became a knower (*dana*, I:1012, 1238). To Joseph He gave the kingdom of *'ilm*, far superior to the kingdom of beauty (VI:3104–5). To Moses He gave knowledge and discernment (*danish, tamyiz*) by teaching him to harvest and thus separate the dark spirits from the pure (IV:3020–29). Jesus He "endowed with knowledge" (*agahi*) so that knowledge and intimate knowledge became his possession.[45] Partial intellects may share in these "sciences of the prophets" (*'ulum*) if they are willing to subdue the *nafs* through the discipline of polishing the mirror of the heart (I:3459–61; R 865).

Polishing the mirror of the heart is the foundation and goal of asceticism in Rumi's view. From the seed of asceticism grows intimate knowledge: the sowing of struggle, obedience, and strenuous effort is like the body; the growth and harvesting are like the soul (VI:2090–92; F 213/204). Passing through a sea of blood (VI:4364), mystics put on the "garment of *ma'rifa*" through whose warp and woof the light of the spirit shines (VI:3062–63). The eye of one who allows God to be his *mu'arrif* ("one who endows with intimate knowledge") becomes the salvation of the two worlds, for God never turns his face from the *'arif* (VI:2859–60; III:3236). Because he feeds on, and faces the *qibla* of, the light of union (VI:1897; IV:H.1641), the mystic is protected from the *sarsar* of death[46] and is the Khalil (Abraham) of hospitality and kindness toward strangers (V:H.3644). He is liberated from the sixes (the directions) and fives (senses) of the game of backgammon played by the world and the Devil, and from all imaginings, for he is a thousand Gabriels.[47]

In *Fihi Ma Fihi* Rumi clarifies eloquently the interrelationship of the *'alim*, the *'arif*, and *zuhd*, the asceticism from which intimate knowledge grows. His text is given here in full with the original of the key technical terms inserted:

> The *'alim*, from the linguistic standpoint, is a person of higher degree than the *'arif*. God is called the *'alim*, but must not be called the *'arif*.[48] *'Arif* means one who did not know [*nami danast*], and then came to know [*danast*]; and this does not apply to God. From the standpoint of common usage however the *'arif* is the greater; for *'arif* is used to denote one who knows [*danad*] the world, transcending proof, by direct vision and face to face. By usage such a person is called an *'arif*.
>
> It has been said, "The *'alim* is better than a hundred ascetics." How should the *'alim* be better than a hundred ascetics? After all, the ascetic practices asceticism on the basis of *'ilm*; asceticism without *'ilm* is impossible. For what is asceticism? [*zuhd*] To forsake the world, and to turn one's face to obedience and the world to come [an exact description of how one attains intimate knowledge]. Well, it is necessary to know [*bidanad*] this world, its foulness and imperma-nence, to know [*bidanad*] the charm and permanence of everlasting-ness of the world to come, and to strive to obey, saying, "How shall I obey, and what is obedience?" All these things are *'ilm*. Hence asceti-

cism is impossible without *'ilm*. Hence the ascetic is both *'alim* and ascetic.

This *'alim* who is better than a hundred ascetics is nevertheless real, only its meaning has not been understood. There is another *'ilm* which God gives a person after this asceticism and the *'ilm* which he possessed at first. This second *'ilm* is the fruit of that *'ilm* and asceticism. Assuredly such an *'alim* is better than a hundred thousand ascetics. (F 58–59/47; VI:3881–H.3884).

Ascetics fall short of genuine union with God by the distance of love. Though Mawlana does not make the connection explicitly, he strongly implies that the "second *'ilm*" is synonymous with love. The service and striving that form the core of asceticism are in reality only a branch; love is the root. One performs service only at the behest of the beloved. If the beloved desires no service, the lover may desist from service without in any way diminishing his love (F 227/220). Service can therefore become a screen that hinders perception of higher needs. In that respect, reason is kindred to service; for though reason claims to be love's confidant, in reality it denies love (I:1981). Several poems in the *Diwan* highlight dramatically the chasm between reason and love. One of those odes records their conflicting claims beautifully.

> Reason says, "The six directions are the boundary, and there is no
>   way out"; Love says, "There is a way, and I have many times trav-
>   elled it."
> Reason beheld a bazaar, and began trading; Love has beheld many
>   bazaars beyond Reason's Bazaar. . . .
> Dreg-sucking lovers possess ecstatic perceptions inwardly; people
>   of reason, dark of heart, entertain denials within them.
> Reason says, "Set not your foot down, for in the courtyard there is
>   naught but thorns"; Love says, "These thorns belong to the reason
>   within you."
> Beware, be silent; pluck the thorn of being out of the heart's foot,
>   that you may behold the rosebowers within you.[49]

Reason's discursive orderliness is deceptively safe from the chaos and vulnerability of love's torrent (VI:910). Partial reason and love simply cannot coexist. "(If) you become reason," Rumi writes, "you will know reason perfectly; if you become love, you will know love's flaming wick" (VI:758). Following the example of the women of Egypt, one must be

willing to gamble reason away in exchange for the love of Joseph
(V:3237).

Finally, Mawlana brings together all that we have discussed for the past
several pages and explains it all as integral to his prophetological synthesis. "After all, the prophet is not that visible form; that form is the steed of
the prophet. The prophet is that true love and affection ['ishq, mahabba],
and that is immortal; just as the she-camel of Salih, his form is the she-
camel. The prophet is that true love and affection, and that is eternal." (F
234/226–27) Revelation's ultimate consequence is the transformation of
the recipient into love itself. In turn, the prophet seeks to pass on to his
people the message that God had spoken by wahy to the heart of Moses:
"O chosen one, I love you."[50]

To the Forearm of the King:
Functions in Relation to God and Believer

The Prophet and God

Jalal ad-Din has called the prophets a touchstone by which one can distinguish true coin from counterfeit. He has said further that the prophet is true
love and affection. It would therefore be quite consistent with Rumi's
thinking to say the prophet is faith; for "faith is discrimination, distinguishing between truth and falsehood, true coin and imitation."[51] Since
freedom is the essence of prophethood, faith and all that flows from it
must be of all things that which is most free of compulsion. Of the
prophetic attitude toward faith and works, Rumi writes: "The prophets are
determinists in regard to the works of this world, (while) the infidels are
determinists in regard to the works of the next world. To the prophets the
works of the next world are (a matter of) freewill; to the foolish the works
of this world are (a matter of) freewill" (I:637–38). Prophets and infidels
differ in regard to faith and works because the prophets' quest is spiritual,
that of the infidels intellectual. The intellectual quest attempts to satisfy
the seeker with answers based on secondary causes. In the end, the seeker
is trapped by the compulsion of logic, tangled in premise and conclusion.
At the heart of the spiritual quest is "either wonder or the father of wonder," which leaves the seeker free from "necessary" conclusions and
untrammeled by the machinery of mental fabrications (I:1496–1508). The
intellectual quest is both frantic and futile, whereas the spiritual gives
peace in the knowledge that what is sought has already been found.
Mawlana gives a fascinating explanation of this paradox of faith.

The human quest consists in seeking a thing which one has not yet found; night and day a human being is engaged in searching for that. But the quest where the thing has been found and the object attained, and yet there is one who is seeking for that thing—that is a strange quest indeed, surpassing the human imagination, inconceivable to human beings. For human quest is for something new that one has not yet found; this quest is for something one has already found and then one seeks. This is God's quest; for God most High has found all things, and all things are found in His omnipotent power. . . . Yet for all that God most High is the Seeker: "He is the Seeker, the Prevailer." The meaning of the saying quoted above is therefore, "O humankind, so long as you are engaged in the quest that is created in time, you remain far from the goal. When your quest passes away in God's quest and God's quest overrides your quest, then you become a seeker by virtue of God's quest." (F 198/189)

Logic leaves the seeker locked in an egocentric orbit. Only wonder can liberate one from the narcissism of the intellectual quest and direct the seeker toward the self-transcendence of prayer. The problem is not that intellect's search is bankrupt in and of itself, but that, composed of both intelligence and lust, human beings often allow that quest to be degraded into a closed system. Lust persuades the seeker that intellect is self-suffi-cient and can find all the answers within itself, and the quest becomes a sham. Lust sees all good things as belonging to itself by right, rather than by privilege. It then cajoles the intellect into believing that all goods must therefore be within immediate reach. When the partial human intellect is relatively free of the centripetal force of lust, it becomes aware of its own partialness and owns the need to look beyond itself for fulfillment. Thus did the prophets follow their intelligence and break free of lust (F 89–90/77–78). It may now be clear how Rumi can juxtapose prayer and lust, saying that, "The prophets offer their devotions, the enemies (of God) offer lusts" (II:2685).

> (Spiritual) ardor belongs to the saints and the prophets; on the other
>   hand, impudence is the refuge of every imposter;
> For they draw the people's attention to themselves, saying, "We are
>   happy (with God)," though within they are exceedingly unhappy.
>   (In the Story of the Jackal who pretended to be a Peacock,
>   III:730–31.)

Formal prayer was invented by the prophets, and, though it is not the "soul" of prayer, it is still helpful (F 24/11–12). "Hundreds of thousands of prophets" worshiped God (III:90) facing the *qibla* of patience (VI:1899), because "every prophet has received (on behalf of his people) from Him the guarantee (implied in the words) 'seek help' of Him 'with patience or prayer.'"[52] All of the prophets came poor into the world (D 3241:4) and so realized the need to ask God for his bounty even if God already knows what each person needs (VI:337–38).

God is the prophets' only friend (III:2930) because in the soul of their own prayer they are totally absorbed in God (F 84–85/73, 24/11–12). In that state God causes the prophet to be in fear, not so that he is afraid, but so that he becomes aware that all things—fear as well as security—come from God. Absorption therefore means that the prophet knows he need never look elsewhere for anything (F 56/44). Mawlana uses the language of the "Path" as forged by the classical Sufi theoreticians, but he employs their terminology rather loosely. For example, he speaks of the "states" (*ahwal*) of the prophets (F 137/126, 164/156), but he includes obedience among the "states" and refers to *nubuwwa* as a *maqam* ("station") (F 213/204, 184/176). Neither obedience nor prophethood occur in the list-ings of stations and states given by Sarraj or Qushayri or any of the classi-cal Sufi systematicians.[53] What is most curious, however, is that Rumi seems to have reversed the order of the classical authorities regarding the sequence in which the various stations and states are attained along the Path. Sarraj and Qushayri both give the *maqamat* (stations) before the *ahwal* (states) and indicate that the former are acquired by personal effort while the latter are totally dependent on God. Rumi agrees that stations are lasting and states fleeting; but he goes on to say that "there is many a one of the Sufis who enjoys a *hal*, (but) he that has attained to a *maqam* is rare . . ." (I:1434–38). Rumi clearly has in mind a slightly different meaning for the terms than did the classical sources with regard to the nature of the condition, but not with regard to the duration of the condition. For Rumi any *maqam* is more advanced than any *hal*: the state is like the momentary unveiling of the bride, the station is the king's being alone with the bride. It is therefore clear why Mawlana calls *nubuwwa* a *maqam*; the equation speaks eloquently of the prophet's relationship to the Lord.

There are other examples of Jalal ad-Din's use of classical terminology. He speaks of contraction (*qabd*) and expansion (*bast*) as resulting from disobedience and obedience respectively; of trust; of "passing away" and "survival"; of hope and fear.[54] Above all, Mawlana emphasizes patience and security as exemplified by the prophets. Hope starts the traveler on the road toward security and away from fear (F 21/9). Security is a *maqam*, unmentioned by Sarraj and Qushayri either as *hal* or *maqam*, in which right and wrong are revealed and distinguished (F 141/129). It is the diametric opposite of fear, which was like the fire of Nimrod from which God kept Abraham secure (I:547). From security come the teachings that the prophets passed along to their people, that the people might achieve security through faith.[55]

Rumi quotes Q 43:31, "And we have raised some of them above others in rank," and explains that Muhammad was above the other prophets in security. Within the *maqam* of security there are further *maqamat*, and the same is true of fear. Whereas the stations of fear can be discerned, those of security "have no indication"; Rumi therefore infers them on the basis of the Qur'anic text just cited. Mawlana uses "fear" and "security" to characterize in a more general manner the condition of prophets and their people on the one hand, and of infidels on the other. Moreover, the fear of which Rumi speaks here is not the *khawf* that Qushayri calls a *maqam* and Sarraj a *hal* (AS 76–79). Mawlana refers rather to the overall mood or attitude resulting from a fundamental orientation to this world; security, on the contrary, results from an otherworldly orientation (F 60/48).

Rumi appears to be making two inferences: first, the stations of security are not indicated, but since security is the opposite number to fear, whose stations are indicated, security may be said to have stations within it as well. Second, since security is the hallmark of one whose values are otherworldly, and since Muhammad is the foremost of the prophets, it follows that "it was in regard to security that Muhammad . . . was superior to all the other prophets." Rumi eschews facile definitions and too-tidy distinctions, however, and says that, after all, fear and security must necessarily flow into each other and elude categorization. The poet advises, "Know that the *maqam* of fear is that in which you are secure; know that the *maqam* of security is that in which you are trembling" (D 1845:16).

Patience, like security, is related to faith. Security flows from faith; patience is propaedeutic to faith (II:600–1; AM 122). Patience is the rope that drew Joseph from the well of this world and delivered him from the wolf of separation (II:1276–79; III:403–5). Patience is as acceptable to God as prayer itself (IV:1181). As notable examples of the virtue Rumi singles out Jacob, Noah, Job, and Luqman.[56] By means of patience in the face of unbelief and open hostility, the hearts of the prophets were polished (VI:2041–43). Mawlana describes that process and its implications for all believers:

(Yet) the bad associate is good (for you) because of the patience
(which you must show in overcoming its desires), for the exercise
of patience expands the heart (with spiritual peace).
The patience shown by the moon to the (dark) night keeps it
illumined; the patience shown by the rose to the thorn keeps it
fragrant.
The patience shown by the milk amid the feces (in the intestine) and
the blood enables it to rear the camel-foal till he has entered his
third year.
The patience shown by all the prophets to the unbelievers made them
the elect of God and lords of the planetary conjunction.
(VI:1407–10)

Prophets and Their People

Whenever a prophet encountered impenetrable resistance from the people
to whom he was sent, God allowed the prophet to enlist the aid of the inanimate world, to give knowledge to rod and stone and perform a hundred
thousand "evidentiary miracles." For every prophet there was a new miracle (mu'jiz, D 1112:8). Rumi emphasizes that God, not the prophet, is the
primary agent, and the messenger's role is merely to deliver the message.[57]
Evidentiary miracles are meant to be a witness to the truthfulness of the
messengers (VI:4350). Because their message is nonintellectual (na
ma'qul), so also are the witnesses to the message. The prophets "fling their
miracles at Saturn," circumventing secondary causes and thus removing
their action from the grasp of intellect (I:2143–45; III:2517).

Miracles are not, however, the cause of faith. They are performed "for
the purpose of subjugating the foe." It is the homogeneity of the prophet
with believers that wins hearts to greater faith (VI:1176–77; F 19/7). At
this juncture Rumi makes a subtle distinction that serves to reconcile two
apparently contradictory statements, namely the statement just made and:
"This indeed is the soul of all mu'jizat, that it (miracle) should bestow
everlasting life on the (spiritually) dead" (III:2502). Mawlana resolves the
tension in his most complete single statement on evidentiary miracles:

The mu'jiza that produces an effect upon something inanimate (is)
either (like) the rod (of Moses) or (the passage of) the Sea (by the
Israelites) or the splitting of the moon (by Muhammad).
If it (the evidentiary miracle) produces an immediate effect upon the
soul, (the reason is that) it (soul) is brought into connection (with
the producer of the effect) by means of a hidden link (i.e., the
homogeneity spoken of above).

> The effects produced upon inanimate objects are (only) accessory:
>   they are (really) for the sake of the fair invisible spirit,
> In order that the inmost heart may be affected by means of that
>   inanimate object. (But) how (much more) excellent is bread
>   (produced) without the substance (of bread), (namely) dough! . . .
> Miracles (proceeding) from the spirit of the perfected individual
>   affect the soul of the seeker as life (bestowed on the dead).
> The *mu'jiza* is (like) the sea, and the deficient (heedless) person is
>   (like) the land-bird (which perished in the sea); but the water-bird
>   is safe from destruction there.
> It (the miracle) bestows infirmity on any one that is uninitiated, but it
>   bestows power on the spirit of an intimate.
> Since you do not feel this bliss in your inmost heart, then continually
>   seek the clue to it from outside,
> For effects are apparent to the senses, and these effects give
>   information concerning their producer. (VI:1303–6, 1308–12)

One can say, therefore, that miracles aim at vanquishing the enemy through their effects, while the soul of miracles affects the heart of the believer by reason of his or her homogeneity with the prophet.[58]

A variety of prophetic roles and functions nurture and manifest sympathy and unanimity between prophet and people. One does not attain prophethood by personal effort, "but it is the way (*sunna*) (of the prophets), that whoever attains that station (*dawla*) lives a life of personal effort and virtue; that moreover is for the sake of the common people, that they may put reliance on them and on their words" (F 184/176). So, for example, when Muhammad was called to be occupied no longer wholly with God, but to turn toward the people, God told him to counsel and reform the people (F 78/66–67). Each of the prophets taught a way of believing, but all lead people to God: prophets are sent to connect part to whole (I:3086, 2811–13). People who follow the *sunna* of the prophets become their family and heirs, and thus the prophets become the link between Creator and creatures.[59]

Prophetic mediation appears in many guises in Rumi's works. From a theological point of view the two most important prophetic functions are the reflection or passing-on of the light of God, and intercession. It matters little whether the believer beholds the light from the "lamp of the last (Friends of God)" or from the "candle of those who have gone before (prophets)" (I:1950). All prophets and Friends of God are "theaters" of the divine light (F 92/80). Their sole work is "light and heat" (I:320), and anyone who follows their way benefits from their lunar illumination.[60] Angels, ranked along with the prophets and Friends of God according to their radiance, may be needed on occasion to show forth God's light to the believer; for not everyone is capable of looking directly at the Sun (I:3657–58; IV:451).

In addition to what we have already noted concerning the intercessory roles of various individual prophets, Mawlana says that every time a person in prayer turns to the right in salutation at the conclusion of *salat*, he is in fact turning towards the spirits of the prophets. That closing salutation begs of the prophets, "O kings, vouchsafe intercession, for this vile one's feet and mantle are stuck fast in the mire." One must not wait till the Resurrection to ask help from the prophets. Earth is the place to begin good works (III:2165–68).

Prophets are God's brokers in the marketplace. God is the purchaser, and the broker asks for no wages but the sight of the Friend. All believers must therefore be willing to trade with the prophets.[61] God's agents also act as physicians who alone can cure the malady of forgetfulness of the freedom of a former world and overconcern with this world.[62] Prophets heal by calling believers from this world and guiding them to the other. Talking of religion, they say, "This, this is the way of escape for you. By this we escaped from this narrow cage: there is no means of escape from this cage but this way, (That) you should make yourself ill (!), exceedingly wretched, in order that you may be let out from (the cage of) reputation."[63] As witnesses on the road to God (D 1856:4), prophets "show the way to the King" both by their active presence as shepherds,[64] and by their absence: "the going of the prophets . . . to mountains and caves, is not for the purpose of hiding themselves and on account of their fear of being disturbed by the people, but for the purpose of guiding the people in the right way and inciting them to abandon this world as much as possible" (III:H.4250).

For the sake of their people, prophets willingly enter the world of "letters and sounds" to become the teachers of humankind (F 164/156). Partial intellect is subject to the teaching authority of the universal intellect, namely the prophets themselves.[65] These teachers impart no new knowledge as such; they teach by reminding of a former state (F 44–45/33–34). Rumi offers a comparison to illustrate what occurs when a prophet instructs his people. God teaches people by using the prophet in the same way one would use a mirror to train a parrot. The teacher stands behind the mirror and dictates to the learner/parrot. The learner thinks the image in the mirror is the one speaking whereas the real teacher is unseen (V:H.1430; F 80/68).

Finally, the prophets are mosque builders. Abraham was involved in the construction of the Ka'ba; Solomon built the Farther Mosque.[66] Rumi refers to the early days of Islam as "the beginning of the edifice" (III:173) and tells of how the hypocrites tried to lead the believers away from Islam by constructing a kind of "anti-mosque," the "mosque of opposition" (II:2825ff.). Beneath the building imagery, however, Mawlana is talking about the heart of the prophet as the locus of revelation.[67] In this connection the poet relates the charming and lengthy tale of the "lover-killing mosque" of tribulation, and of the reckless lover who insisted on spending the night in the mosque, even though he was fully aware of the pain he would undergo there (III:3922ff.). More important for present purposes are the texts in which Jalal ad-Din associates the image explicitly with the prophets. One sums them all up beautifully:

> That edifice of the prophets was (raised) without greed (self-interest); hence the splendors (of its renown) increased so uninterruptedly.
>
> Oh, many a mosque have the noble (prophets) erected, but "the Farther Mosque" is not its name.
>
> The grandeur which at every moment accrued to the Ka'ba—that (grandeur) was derived from the acts done in pure devotion by Abraham.
>
> The excellence of that mosque (which the prophets build) is not from earth and stone, but (because) there is no greed or enmity in its builder.
>
> Their books are not as the books of others, nor their mosques nor their means of livelihood nor their houses and homes.
>
> Nor their observance of respect nor their anger nor their chastisement nor their slumber nor their reasoning nor their discourse.
>
> To each one of them belongs a different glory: (in each of them) the bird, their spirit, flies with a different wing.
>
> The heart is trembling at the mention of their (high) estate: their actions are the qibla of our actions (IV:1136-43).

We turn now to Rumi's treatment of some major individual prophets, beginning with Abraham.

CHAPTER 3

Abraham and Sons

Three clusters of images aptly sum up Rumi's treatment of Abraham and his sons Isma'il and Ishaq (Ishmael and Isaac). We look first at Abraham as a man of faith who struggled to arrive at true belief while immersed in an idolatrous family environment and culture. In this context Rumi locates Abraham's willingness to sacrifice his son. As we shall see, it is not always clear which of the two sons, Isaac or Ishmael, the poet considers the intended victim.

Second, Abraham engaged, as prophet, in speaking the word of faith especially to the people of Nimrod, whom Rumi portrays as the epitome of the stiff-necked infidel. Signs from God repeatedly legitimate Abraham's mission, particularly in the imagery of his emerging unscathed from Nimrod's fire. Finally, as an exemplar for all subsequent prophets and believers, Abraham functions in Rumi especially as model for pilgrims and people of prayer. Several images are important in this context, such as sacrifice, fire, and hospitality, to name a few. Rumi allegorizes on the details of Abraham's story to give the prophet a timeless, paradigmatic quality.[1]

Abraham the Man of Faith

Abraham's father, Azar, made his living carving religious images. In his busy shop he fashioned idols of hope and fear (D 876:8); but God laughed at Azar's handiwork (D 2991:5) and chose to deliver Abraham from his idolatrous upbringing. Rumi sees the idol shop as an engaging metaphor for his own poetic art and his realization that he must undergo a conversion from idolizing his own words:

Before this I sought a purchaser for my discourse, and now I wish of
   you to buy me from my words.
I have carved idols enough to beguile every person; now I am drunk
   with Abraham, I am sated with Azar.

47

An idol without color and scent arrived; my hand was put out of
    action by him. Seek another master for the shop of idol-making.
I have cleared the shop of myself, I have thrown away the idols;
    having realized the worth of madness, I have become free of
    thoughts.
If an image enters my heart I say, "Depart, you who lead astray!" (D
    2449:1–5, MPR2 313)

According to Q 4:125, God made Abraham His Friend (Khalil), evidently
as a result of Abraham's being "true in faith" (literally, a *hanif*, seeker after
the one God). Rumi refers to the prophet far more frequently as Khalil
than as Ibrahim; and it is interesting to note that Ibn 'Arabi is so fascinated
with the prophet's status that he builds his entire treatment of Abraham
around a play on the meaning of *khalil* as "intimate, interpenetrating," so
that Abraham becomes the prototype of the person "lost in love" (FB
90–92).

Abraham began his journey of faith very early in life. It started when he
"came forth from the cave" (II:3077), a phrase to which Nicholson adds in
his translation "(of idolatry)." Rumi is actually referring to the legendary
detail of Abraham's being reared in a cave where he was born (on the 10th
of Muharram) in order to keep him hidden from the murderous Nimrod.
Kisa'i says it was the very same "cave of light" in which Idris and Noah
were born, whence Gabriel led Abraham at the age of four (QKT 137–38),
and where, as Rumi mentions in an ode, the child "sucked from the fingertips of a lion."[2]

One of the poet's favorite Qur'anic stories tells of how Abraham, fresh
out of the cave according to Kisa'i (QKT 138) and Tha'labi (QT 65),
beheld in succession a star, the moon, and the sun. He thought each in turn
was his Lord; but as each fell below the horizon, Abraham realized he had
been freed of false belief. He said, "I love not things that set" (*la uhibbu 'l-
afilin*), words that are for Rumi the quintessence of God-centeredness, so
that he often uses only that phrase or its first two Arabic words to recall the
entire story.[3] To the sun and moon the Prophet said, "No!" To his father's
people he said, "I am free from you." To God he said, "I have surrendered."[4] As is his wont, the poet alludes to the story without actually
retelling it, using only key terms from the text of the Qur'an to suggest
both the central meaning of Abraham and the stance required of every
authentic seeker of God.

Khalil's repudiation of all that is not God led him to take action against
the idolatry of his father's people for "How can Khalil agree with Azar?"

(VI:2125). Like the object of mystical vision, which is an idol in form but a breaker of idols in reality, Abraham knew that only by being shattered can an idol receive spirit and intellect (*jan* and *'aql*).[5] Abraham's willingness to fracture someone else's idols was, of course, but a prelude to more stringent demands yet to be made on his monotheism. His response to the further testing of his faith appears in the story of Nimrod's fire, to be discussed shortly, and in Abraham's preparing to sacrifice his son.

Addressing the seeker of God, Rumi asks: "It may be that, like Abraham, you have broken the idol; but will you entrust the idol of your body to the fire?" (V:2505). He explains elsewhere that the body is like Ishmael, the spirit like Abraham, who pronounces the funeral *takbir* (*Allahu akbar*) (III:2145). The poet uses the story as an occasion to exhort the believer to be patient in suffering. To the chickpea boiling in the pot and rising again and again to the surface with a hundred cries for mercy, the housewife offers the consolation that a higher destiny awaits it if it will allow itself to be consumed. Thus does Abraham offer solace to his sacrificial victim. Alluding here to the Qur'anic text in which Abraham dreamt he must sacrifice an unnamed son (Q 37:101), the poet inserts the name of Ishmael (III:4159–75). As we shall see, however, Rumi seems on the whole to be ambivalent as to whether the intended victim *(dhabih,* D 704:10) was to be Isaac or Ishmael.[6] One could perhaps argue for the ultimate preeminence of Ishmael in this role on the basis of his being mentioned in the *Mathnawi* while Isaac is not.

Ishmael, as other prophets, cared not whether his body would continue to exist (F 238/230). Rumi sees him as the epitome of indifference, the body who willingly dies for the spirit. Gladly he lays open his throat "to love and his dagger" (VI:2985), takes a "drink from the cup of Khalil's blade," and gains knowledge through obedience to the universal intellect. Willingness was Ishmael's greatest virtue. He knew that as a sacrificial victim for love (*qurban*) he would be protected and that the knife would not harm him.[8] He was free from "care for his head" and did not recoil from offering himself. For the chickpea and for all humanity as well, Ishmael is the model of the proper attitude toward death.[9]

Both Ishamel and his father trusted in God, who in turn provided a ram to be killed in place of the boy (VI:1347–48, 2476). Let that not detract, however, from Ishmael's free offering of himself. It was by means of his participation in the light that is the heritage of all the prophets that he was able to make his oblation. Falling into the stream of that light, Ishmael laid his head before Abraham's flashing blade (II:914).

Isaac's role in Rumi's works is in some ways nearly identical to that of Ishmael. The poet is not always entirely clear as to whether there is a serious distinction between the two sons of Abraham, for in one of the odes the two are even mentioned together as sacrificial victims (D 738:5). Isaac, too, was *qurban*, was protected from ultimate harm from the knife, and was happy to submit to his father's dagger.[10] For the sake of comparison, it is interesting to note that Ibn 'Arabi chose Isaac as the sacrificial victim. Kisa'i tells a lengthy story about Isaac in the role of *dhabih*, giving only a passing mention of a tradition that favors Ishmael (QKT 160–62). Tha'labi has collected a larger list of variant accounts about the victim's identity (QT 80ff.).

Rumi mentions Isaac only in the *Diwan*, and Isaac is the only prophet who is never mentioned explicitly in the *Mathnawi*. It may be that the poet had decided later in his life that, even if the sons of Abraham should be considered as two distinct personalities, Ishmael's importance so far outweighed that of Isaac as to render the mention of Isaac superfluous. In any case, Khalil's laying dagger to throat must be seen as the loving playfulness of the divine king (D 2058:8). Abraham's utter trust in God allowed him to emerge from the experience with both faith and progeny unscathed (VI:1347–48).

Abraham the Prophet

Several "signs" especially associated with Abraham's prophetic office came about as a result of his faith and trust. "Khalil's faith and entreaties brought about what would otherwise have been impossible" (II:1647). When Abraham was in need of food to substantiate his reputation for hospitality, God turned a bag of sand into flour. In the same way, the poet moralizes, God pays the debts of all who rely on Him completely[12] Jalal ad-Din makes only the scantiest allusions to this story, and he does so in such a way as to imply that the tale was well known to his audience. Kisa'i records this version of the story. As punishment upon Nimrod's people for refusing to accept Abraham as God's Messenger, God stopped the rain and thus endangered Nimrod's food supply. After Nimrod had impounded all food and grain,

> Abraham went outside the city to a sand dune and called his Lord to turn the sand into food for the faithful. God granted his prayer and made it food of Paradise, from which the believers took as much as they wanted; and the infidels took from Nimrod until his supply was

exhausted, whereupon the people began to incline to Abraham. One day, while Nimrod was standing at the gate of his palace, Abraham came near carrying a bag of wheat he had brought from the sand dune. "Abraham," called Nimrod, "what have you there?" "Food," answered Abraham. "My Lord has provided sustenance for me and for all who believe in Him and in me." Nimrod ordered him to open the bag; and, putting in his hand, he drew out red sand. Then Abraham put in his hand and drew out grains of wheat the size of pistachio nuts. On each grain was written, "A gift from the Magnificent to Abraham the Friend." (QKT 145)

Abraham's most celebrated gesture of hospitality is mentioned in Q 11:69–73 and 51:26. There we are told that anonymous messengers bring news that Abraham will have a son. Abraham then killed the "fatted calf." Evidently on the basis of the tradition that Abraham's guest must have been angelic, Rumi's four brief references to the story identify the guests all under the name of Gabriel.[13]

Abraham had his nemesis, as did all of the prophets. His prophetic role is delineated most sharply by contrast with Nimrod's delusions of grandeur. The ill-tempered monarch's attempts to exterminate the newborn Abraham, whose birth had been foretold by astrologers, finds parallels in the stories of Moses and even of Muhammad as Rumi knew them. Recalling the legendary details recorded in the *Qisas*, the poet describes at some length Nimrod's forgetfulness of God's loving care for him in his own orphanhood, and his ungrateful slaughter of a hundred thousand innocents in order to protect himself from his predicted adversary (VI:H.4831–54). Qur'an 21:68–70 describes Abraham's conflict with Nimrod, but without mentioning the evil king by name.

Failing in his first attempt to eradicate his enemy, Nimrod was to try again later by throwing Abraham into a fire. Rumi describes how in the interim Nimrod indulged his hybris further by trying to intimidate Abraham with his alleged power over life and death. *Fihi Ma Fihi* elaborates twice on Q 2:258. The scriptural text reads:

Have you not turned your attention to one who disputed with Abraham about his Lord, because God had granted him power? Abraham said, "My lord is He who gives life and death." He replied, "I give life and death." Abraham said in answer, "But it is God who causes the sun to rise in the East; you then, make it rise from the West." In that way was the one who disbelieved confounded.

Rumi gives two different interpretations of Abraham's last statement. In his first interpretation, Rumi says that Abraham seemed at first to have been silenced by Nimrod's assertion that, "I, too, when I banish a man, as good as cause him to die, and when I appoint a man to a post it is as though I bring him to life"; but in reality the prophet's challenge to Nimrod concealed a more profound meaning, "namely that God Most High brings the fetus out of the east of the womb and sends it down in the west of the tomb" (F 200/190–91).

In his second allegorical exegesis, Jalal ad-Din explains that the sun represents the state of the disciple, rising in the orient of obedience and striving, and setting in the occident of self-will and sloth.

> Inasmuch as through obedience and strenuous effort and noble actions the *'arif* [i.e., one who possesses intimate knowledge, a mystic] attains illumination and spiritual intoxication, refreshment and ease, and in the state of abandoning such obedience and effort that happiness goes down like the sinking sun, these two states of obedience and abandoning obedience have been for him his east and west. [He then goes on to paraphrase Abraham's challenge to Nimrod as follows:] "so if you are able, by bringing to life in this state of apparent setting, which is godlessness and corruption and disobedience, now in this state of setting make manifest that illumination and ease which rose up out of obedience." (F 213/203)

The following verse in this Qur'anic context, 2:259, continues the imagery of God's power over life and death. That verse tells the story of the resuscitation of a certain unnamed individual's long-deceased donkey. Tha'labi comments on the same verse just before he recounts the story of 'Uzayr (Ezra), noting the considerable controversy as to the identity of the man in the story: some say Ezra, some Jeremiah, some Khizr (QT 307–10). Rumi chooses to associate the story with Ezra, and also recounts another story evidently based on the *Qisas* literature, in which Ezra serves to highlight God's ultimate power.[14]

Then, in various texts, Rumi resumes with his commentary on Q 2:260, where direct reference to Abraham returns in the scriptural account. There Abraham asks God, "Show me how you bring the dead to life." The poet offers a psychological interpretation of the text. God told the Prophet to dismember four birds and place their parts all separated at some distance. Rumi then describes at surprising length the inner meaning of each bird, allegorizing each into a "heart-oppressing" quality that must be purged from every seeker of God. The duck, cock, peacock, and crow symbolize the qualities of greed, lust, arrogance, and desire respectively. Together they amount to what the poet calls the "gallows of reason," which renders human beings incapable of receiving the prophetic message. All four act like crows (another fleeting reminder of the falcon metaphor, by contrast), in that each robs intelligent people of their intellect.[15] While the several texts in the *Mathnawi* focus on the psychospiritual symbolism of the birds, the handful of one-line allusions in the *Diwan* to the "birds of Khalil" emphasize more clearly their resuscitation as a metaphor of spiritual renewal.[16]

The story of Nimrod's attempts to kill Abraham by hurling him into a fire provides the occasion for what are undoubtedly Rumi's favorite Abrahamic images. Nimrod's frustration mounted as his final means for destroying Abraham proved instead to be a "fortress" for the Prophet (I:1842). The fire became as submissive as an anklet (III:3102) and refused to set its teeth on the chosen one (I:861). Khalil was like a gold coin, tested and proven; like a horseman he held the reins of the fire; like a moth he rested content in the flames.[17] For Abraham the fire became coolness and safety, his nurse, his wine.[18] It was a delightful garden full of every kind of blossom and tree.[19] However, what one person sees as roses, another regards as thorns: for the likes of Nimrod the fire is only death and anguish (VI:4291). The flames did not harm Abraham because God had given the fire an eye that distinguishes the authentic from the inauthentic (IV:2412), thus using the fire for the opposite of its normal purpose as a proof that He is able to turn fear into security.[20]

Fire is the antithesis of light. Abraham was able to enter Nimrod's blaze fearlessly only because he already possessed the terrible brilliance that is the heirloom of the prophets (II:913; I:3700–3702). In one of the odes Abraham tells the fire it will live forever, but the fire knew the truth. Abraham would long outlive its flames, and heaven and hell both would become Abraham's servants because he was protected from all that is not God (D 1186:5–6). Rumi seems to be alluding here to a hadith in which hell says to the believer, "Your light has extinguished my fire."[21] Abraham possessed light because he was *'aql* and *jan* whereas Nimrod was *nafs*. In other words, the poet likens light to intellect and spirit, and fire to the "lower self" or the ego (II:3310-11). Mawlana elaborates on the symbolism:

Now this "fire" is the fire of sensuality, within which lies the root of sin and error.

> External fire may be quenched with some water; the fire of
>   sensuality pulls to hell.
> What is the remedy for sensuality's fire? The light of religion: It will
>   extinguish the fire of the unbelievers.
> What kills this fire? The light of God: Make Abraham's light your
>   master,
> So that your woodlike body may be delivered from the fire of your
>   Nimrod-like ego. (I:3697–3701, SPL 88)

The wonder of the fire in Abraham's case is that it made him still more receptive to light, for the flames polished his mirror (heart) pure (VI:2042). Abraham transcended the "spirit and angel," passing beyond the fire to direct mystical vision. Twice Rumi alludes to Gabriel's coming to assist Abraham and Abraham's refusal of his help, since the angel's presence would prove only an inconvenience and a barrier (III:6–10, IV:H.2973ff.). Kisa'i tells how when Abraham was catapulted forty cubits into the air as he was being hurled into the fire, Gabriel met him in flight and asked, "Abraham, have you any requests?" "From you, no," Abraham said. "God is my keeper; how excellent is his guardianship!" (QKT 147) 'Attar, one of Rumi's greatest formative influences, also refers to this tale when he tells how Abraham refused to deal with the angel Azrael who had come to require his soul of him: if he refused help from Gabriel even then, how could Azrael expect Abraham to let an angel come between him and his God at a time like this?[22]

Since fire is utterly opaque when compared to the true light, fire is the land of darkness into which one must journey in order to find the water of life (R 1808/ 1816). One must, like Abraham, allow form to be consumed so that spirit may thaw. Alluding to the hadith mentioned above, Rumi sums up the implications for the seeker:

> Until you burn up the form, your spirit will be frozen, like idol
>   worshippers far from springtime and security.
> In firelike love, be happy like silver; since you are a child of
>   Abraham, fire is your dwelling.
> By God's command, fire becomes tulip and rose for the true, clusters
>   of basil, willow and lily.
> The believer knows the spell and recites it over the fire; the heat
>   remains in it no more, it remains shining as the moon.
> Blessed be the spell through which peace befalls in a fire which can
>   transform iron into a needle. (D 2043:4–8, MPR2 254)

When Nimrod's plan to destroy Abraham in the fire proved a fiasco, the king's blind hatred of Abraham (D 914:23, 923:12) turned on God. Nimrod's ultimate folly was his attempt to fly heavenward on vultures' wings to assassinate the Creator Himself. He naturally refused Abraham's offer to act as Nimrod's *pir* providing for him thereby a ladder to heaven—a far surer means of ascent than the discursive reason of carrion-eating vultures (VI:4125–42, 373)! In the end, irony of ironies, the headstrong Nimrod was destroyed by a gnat. Rumi refers only in passing (R 21) to the story of how one gnat, of the many God sent in a plague, entered Nimrod's brain and tortured him from within for forty days. Nimrod had an iron bar made and had his highest ranking aides strike his head now and then to still the gnat. Then a very strong officer hit too hard. Nimrod's skull split and, as Kisa'i records, "the gnat emerged like a chick from an egg, saying, 'There is no god but God; Abraham is the apostle of God and His Friend'" (QKT 149–50).

Abraham the Exemplar

In Q 16:124 God commanded Muhammad to "follow the religion of Abraham"; and in Q 60:4, the Prophet is told, "Truly you have a good example in Abraham." Rumi cites both texts together (V:H.1265). Elsewhere, too, the poet exhorts disciples to "make the light of Abraham your teacher," so that the body may be delivered from the fire of the *nafs* (I:3701–2, 1606). The victory can be won because there is an "Abraham-like" flame in the body that can subdue the fire (IV:3763). It is the spirit of Khalil that allows one to "see in the fire Paradise and its palaces by the light" (II:1557). Those who can become moths to the fire are "kin of Khalil" (V:435ff.). 'Imran's wife, the mother of Moses, had been assured by a revelation that her son was of "the stock of Khalil," so that she could confidently entrust her child to the fire of the stove. Pharaoh had ordered the destruction of the child, but as a descendant of Abraham, Moses experienced no harm in the oven (III:948ff.).

Rumi mentions two aspects of Abraham's being and meaning that remind the disciple of the prophet's humanity. First, as lofty a rank as Abraham enjoyed as God's prophet and friend, there remains a kind of word or knowledge that God did not communicate to him (or to the other prophets), but that is available to the mystic (*'arif*, I:1732). This is less a statement about Abraham's status than about the unsurpassable eminence of mystical union with God. Second, Abraham also had his moment of idolatry when he slipped into the world of imagination (*khayal*), which is so powerful it can overcome even a "mountain" like Khalil (V:2648–53). The poet is referring here to the scriptural text in which Abraham said of the heavenly luminary, "This is my Lord" (Q 6:76). Nevertheless, Abraham is also the model of the spiritual guide, the *pir*, who can help the seeker to bypass knowledge based only on opinion and arrive straightway at the knowledge of direct experience: the former knowledge is like searching for the *qibla* in the dark of night; the latter, like standing before the Ka'ba at midday (VI:4125–39).

Only through prayer can one imitate Abraham's example, only through seeking the "station of Abraham." Rumi discusses the literalist notion that the *maqam Ibrahim* refers to a specific place near the Ka'ba, traditionally said to have been built by Abraham. But he adds that there is another possible interpretation:

> . . . according to the spiritualists, Abraham's station means you cast yourself Abraham-like into the fire for God's sake, and bring yourself to this station by toiling and laboring in God's way, or nigh this station. One has then sacrificed oneself for the sake of God; that is to say, his self is no more of moment in his sight and he has ceased to tremble for himself. To perform two inclinations of prayer at Abraham's station is excellent; but let it be such a prayer that the standing is performed in this world, and the bowing in the other world. (F 173–74/165)

Rumi goes on to say that the physical Ka'ba (whether or not actually built by Abraham) is a "branch" of the Ka'ba of the heart, and that all of the Ka'ba's grandeur is a result of Abraham's acts of devotion.[23]

Prayer was the dominion of Khalil (D 1309:8). The poet portrays him as the model of prayer when he says, ". . . the foundation of prayer is the abandonment of the body and the abandonment of sons, like Abraham, who was offering his son as a sacrifice in order to perfect his prayer and giving up his body to Nimrod's fire" (V:H.1265). Rumi also likes the image of Abraham as the man who sighed, the clement, tender-hearted man of Q 9:114 and 11:75. Where there is no sighing, says the poet, there is no ecstasy; and Abraham was the epitome of the *awwah*, the sighful person (F 163/155). Sana'i, from whom Rumi may have inherited a fondness for this Abrahamic epithet, explains the inner meaning of the Qur'an's onomatopoeic description:

. . . the *waw* of *awwah* gave him the sincerity of his faith [the translator notes that *waw* is the first letter of *wafa'*, which he renders "sincerity"], the majesty and beauty of his belief,—then when the *waw*
goes out of *awwah* there remains but *ah*, a sigh,—how wonderful!
[The translator notes that another manuscript says *ah* is "the essence
of the affirmation of the light," since it is composed of *alif*, which
means "one," and *ha*, which stands for *huwa*, "He."] *Ah* remains, a
memorial of Him; His religion remains as a manifestation of Him.[24]

God gives a hundredfold in exchange for the most languorous sighs, says
Rumi in one context directly related to this quality of Abraham
(VI:883–86). Elsewhere in the *Mathnawi* he tells a marvelous story that
may well have been inspired by the implicit example of the "man of
sighs."

A certain pious man hurried to the mosque to take part in the Friday
noon community ritual prayer. As he arrived he saw people emerging from
the mosque, and he asked why everyone seemed to be departing early.
Another man explained that the Prophet Muhammad had just finished
leading the people in prayer, and had already given the final blessing. The
distraught latecomer

> Cried "Ah!" and the smoke from that sigh arose [again *ah*]; the
>   aroma of a bleeding heart wafted up on that *ah*.
> One of those from the congregation said, "If you will give me that
>   *ah*, I will give you my formal prayers."
> The man replied, "The sigh is yours in exchange for the formal
>   prayers." The other man carried off that sigh as though it were a
>   hundred petitions.
> While he slept that night, a voice said to him, "You have purchased
>   the water of life and healing.
> In honor of your choices and trade, I have accepted all the ritual
>   prayers of my people." (II:2771–79)

Rumi has left us with only a small sample of prayer from the lips of
Abraham, but it suggests one final significant way in which the poet
viewed the prophet as exemplary. Playing the intercessor in an exchange
vaguely reminiscent of the Genesis 19 story of his bargaining with God
over the fate of Sodom and Gomorrah, Abraham secures provisions for all
people even though he realizes God will not extend his unconditional
approval to all (F 172/164). His prayer seems characteristically generous

of the sighful man whom Rumi sees here as the prototype of the mystic ('*arif*), who in turn embodies the hospitality that is one of Abraham's hall-marks. Rumi likens the human body to a guesthouse to which a variety of spiritual states, thoughts, and feelings come every day seeking lodgings. "The mystic ('*arif*) who takes cognizance of those inner movements of sorrow or joy, is like a generous person who extends hospitality and kind-ness to strangers, as Khalil did. Khalil's door remained open to receive guests with a warm welcome. Whether infidel or believer, whether trust-worthy or suspicious, all his guests saw a smile on his face" (V:H.3644). On the whole, Rumi emphasizes the symbolic and often frankly allegori-cǎl meaning of Abraham far more than the narrative aspects of the prophet's saga. As we shall see, one can say much the same of the hun-dreds of allusions to the other prophetic figures in his works. Let us turn now to Mawlana's treatment of the prophet Joseph.

CHAPTER 4

Joseph and His Family

Joseph is unique among the prophets for several reasons. In the Qur'an only Joseph has his story told all at once, in unified fashion, in the twelfth Sura. Outside of the Surat Yusuf, the prophet appears only twice in all of the Qur'an: once in a list of eighteen prophets whom God has guided (Q 6:84), and once saying that Joseph had brought clear proofs and still people refused to believe (Q 40:34). It is remarkable that the only prophet to merit a featured role through an entire Sura should not be mentioned in other lists of prophets that occur often in the Qur'an. Similarly it is noteworthy that Joseph is nowhere said to have been sent to a specific people and rejected by them, as are most of the other prophets. Jalal ad-Din Rumi, too, regards this son of Jacob as a special case. In the stories of the other messengers of God, it is the people to whom they are sent who suffer calamity and distress most noticeably. In Joseph's story, it is the prophet himself who experiences multiple setbacks. Vindicated ultimately, his very survival and final exaltation are the unmistakable mark of God's protection.

Mawlana's treatment of Joseph includes all of the prominent elements of the Qur'anic account: Joseph's inaugural dream; the brothers' ruse to separate him from his father and their claim that the wolf had eaten Joseph; the prophet's being sold into slavery and being bought back by the Egyptian; Zulaykha's attempted seduction; Joseph's imprisonment and subsequent reprieve and rise to power in Egypt; the journey of the brothers to seek food in Egypt; Joseph's detaining of Benjamin; the return of the prophet's shirt to Jacob and the father's recovery of sight from the scent of the shirt. Four pairs of images offer a sense of how Rumi has placed his own stamp on the story of Joseph: they are the images of beauty and beast, pit and prison, shirt and scent, dream and light.[1]

Before discussing those images, however, it will be helpful to see briefly how Rumi's treatment of Joseph's father, Jacob, serves both as a summary of those same themes and as an important background against which to appreciate the poet's more detailed presentation of Joseph.

Jacob's affinity for Joseph contrasts markedly with the brothers' antipathy for Joseph.[2] The brothers were for Jacob (and Joseph) what Nimrod was for Abraham, types of the prophet envier who does not see beyond bare appearance. Joseph's siblings regarded him as a draft animal; in Jacob's eyes he was a houri.[3] Jacob anguished while the brothers lied and hated (III:H.3029ff.). Shepherding Joseph by his loving care, Jacob regarded the envy of the brothers as a wolf whose malevolence far surpassed that of the actual wolf.[4] Separation from Joseph left Jacob with the intense grief that marks a true lover.[5]

Jacob had as much patience as Job had tribulation (VI:875; D 2953:2), but his liberation from suffering also matched Job's ultimate recompense (M 117/228). For bearing the pain of loss, Jacob experienced all the greater ecstasy in reunion with his son.[6] The old man who had grieved himself into blindness regained his vision when he received the scent of Joseph's shirt. From Egypt came the breeze that was the "mercy of the Merciful," and the sense of smell gifted that of sight.[7] "Jacob hungered for Joseph, and the aroma of bread came to him from afar."[8] When at last Jacob actually saw Joseph, the father was like a blossoming tree (D 3368:11; R 734). He drank a hundred wines from the cup of Joseph's face while the brothers quaffed poison (V:3300–3301; III:H.2039).

Like all the other prophets, Jacob was a beneficiary of the "light of the highest heaven." His heart was truthful, illumined by the light that rewarded him for patiently enduring separation from his beloved in submission to the destiny of God (VI:2756; II:917). Let us turn now to the four pairs of images with which Rumi characterizes Joseph.

Beauty and Beast

Joseph's long and eventful odyssey toward union with God began with a most painful separation from his father Jacob.[9] His scheming brothers contrived the theft in their envy of Joseph's close relationship to Jacob (D 36:4; 1425:5). As Joseph's dream had shown, he was the "*Law Laka* of the Brothers," the one to whom all the brothers must defer (D 3130:5). Rumi views Joseph's astonishing beauty as the reason for his favored position (and perhaps the result as well); and the real beast in the story was the consuming envy of the brothers.

Seldom celebrated for its comeliness, the wolf might understandably be jealous of the storied elegance of Joseph. Envy of someone else's beauty results from blindness. Because the brothers so envied Joseph's gifts while they were all still in Canaan, they would be unable to recognize him later when they went to buy grain from him in Egypt.[10] They feigned concern for their "lost" brother, and grief over him; but the wolf can have no love for Joseph apart from its lust to devour him (II:2057; V:476). Ironically, even as the brothers behaved wolfishly towards Joseph, they began to regard him as the wolf. Recognition of Joseph's beauty for what it is is equivalent to faith; wolfish jealousy is the mark of the unbeliever. Mawlana goes to considerable lengths to emphasize the relationship of belief to the perception of inward reality, and of unbelief to "form-worshipping."

As archenvier, the Devil is a wolf (VI:499): the unbelief that he embodies also characterizes the brothers' attitude to Joseph so that he becomes their wolf.[11] Mawlana fashions numerous images of the wolf to highlight both the necessity of the accurate perception of faith and the devouring hunger of unbelief.[12] The wolf can be brought into submission, however. Only a Joseph can transform the wolf of *nafs* (D 1576:2) into a shepherd (D 2634:7).

Joseph's brothers failed to recognize his true worth and so were content to sell him to the Bedouins for a mere eighteen coins.[13] Rumi says, quoting Sana'i: "When the tongue of envy turns slave-dealer, you may get a Joseph for an ell of linen."[14] Human perception is fickle. God the painter portrays both Josephs and *'ifrits* (demons), the beautiful as well as the ugly; both reveal His artistic mastery (II:2538). Hidden grace allows one to see both in creation and to be aware that appearance alone is deceptive (I:3755). A lover sees beyond unchanging forms and thus remains in love even though the beloved may seem to change from Joseph to wolf. The lover knows that the wolf may also become a Joseph (F 49/37; II:1420). Unbelievers see only the outward significance of the saints and prophets; their eyes, ears, and hearts are sealed, so that they see the wolf but miss Joseph (F 38/26).

In spite of Joseph's hateful treatment at the hands of his own brothers, the prophet prayed that they be forgiven (D 929:5ff.; M 10/56). Joseph experienced his enslavement as a major trial, but it freed him from slavery to creatures so that he could be the slave of God alone (M 110/218). The Bedouins paid almost nothing for Joseph, but when they sold him at auction in Egypt, the lord of the land went into bankruptcy to purchase the striking young man.[15] Joseph's appearance in that Egyptian bazaar was so dazzling that every shop shut down because of the fire his beauty had set (D 1798:6; 2391:2). The bazaar thus becomes for Rumi the image of this utterly unexpected and intoxicating presence of the prophet among a far-away people.[16] Once Joseph had arrived in Egypt, it became the "Egypt of union," the desire of Jacob and all who yearn to be reunited with their source. Every shop in the bazaar was transformed into a sugar-seller.[17]

No sooner had Joseph been bought by the Egyptian than the vizier's wife fell madly in love with the prophet.[18] Zulaykha pursued Joseph but God's love caught him (D 27:26). She tried to imprison Joseph for his beauty (D 2019:7) by locking all doors and surrounding him with pictures of herself together with Joseph. Ironically, she was following the example of the Creator, who places signs of Himself everywhere so that one cannot but see them (D 3073:5). Joseph escaped because he trusted God (V:1105–7; VI:3637–40), but not before Zulaykha had torn Joseph's shirt as he was running away (D 581:19), and he had "torn her veil"—that is, had forced her secret into the open (D 136:2; 631:4). Because of his trust in God Joseph also escaped his first and third incarcerations (the pit and the prison, as we shall see shortly). In Zulaykha's prison Joseph's trust made him a lion, so that the fire of lust was quenched by God's water (V:3873).

Proof that Zulaykha had instigated the attempted seduction was that Joseph's shirt had been torn in back. The vizier's wife then contrived to gain the sympathy of the other women of Egypt by demonstrating that no mortal could resist Joseph's beauty. She threw a feast and brought Joseph into the hall just as all the diners were peeling their oranges. All those present drank one cup of the wine of Joseph and delivered themselves the kindest cut of all (IV:2099). Their power of choice "wounded its hand" and spread its wings (V:2975–76). They gambled away their intelligence ('aql); reason ran away from home (D 2484:9) leaving the lovers utterly beside themselves.[19] Those women were "foolish in respect of their hands," but became the models of such lovers as live by Rumi's advice: "Sacrifice your intellect in love for the Friend, for in any case intellect originates where He is."[20]

One of Rumi's most brilliant pieces tells of how love for Joseph took possession of Zulaykha:

Zulaykha had applied to Joseph the name of everything, from
    rue-seed to aloes-wood.
She concealed his name in (all other) names and made the inner

meaning thereof known to (none but her) confidants.

When she said, "The wax is softened by the fire," this meant, "My beloved is very fond of me."

And if she said, "Look, the moon is risen;" or if she said, "The willow-bough is green (with new leaves)";

Or if she said, "The leaves are quivering mightily"; Or if she said, "The rue-seed is burning merrily";

Or if she said, "The rose has told her secret to the nightingale"; or if she said, "The king has disclosed his passion for Shahnaz (= "the king's delight")";

Or if she said, "How auspicious is Fortune!" or if she said, "Give the furniture a good dusting";

Or if she said, "The water carrier has brought the water"; or if she said, "The sun is risen";

Or if she said, "Last night they cooked a potful of food" or "The vegetables are cooked to perfection";

Or if she said, "The loaves have no salt (savour)"; or if she said, "The heavenly sphere is going round in the contrary direction";

Or if she said, "My head aches," or if she said, "My headache is better";

If she praised, it was his (Joseph's) caresses (that she meant); and if she blamed, it was separation from him (that she meant).

If she piled up a hundred thousand names, her meaning and intention was always Joseph.

Were she hungry, as soon as she spoke his name she would be filled (with spiritual food) and intoxicated by his cup.

Her thirst would be quenched by his name: the name of Joseph was a sherbet to her soul;

And if she were in pain, her pain would immediately be turned into profit by that exalted name.

In cold weather it was a fur to her. This, this (is what) the Beloved's name can do (when one is) in love.

The vulgar are always pronouncing the Holy Name, (but) it does not do this work (for them) since they are not endowed with (true) love.

That (miracle) which Jesus had wrought by (pronouncing) the Name of *Hu* (He, God) was manifested to her through the name of him (Joseph). (VI: 4021-39; see also D 4:1/18:1)

Zulaykha's anguish at separation from Joseph made her old, but at Joseph's prayer her youth was restored.[21] Joseph's beauty was such that it became the very image of God's rejuvenating glory, and the sight of the prophet was like life-giving rain to the aging Zulaykha.[22]

Mawlana tells a story, in the *Mathnawi*, of a friend who, upon returning from travel, visited Joseph. The visitor gave the prophet a mirror as a present. Rumi explains the significance of the gift in *Fihi Ma Fihi*. Because Joseph's beauty is the image of God's, Rumi asks, "What is there that God most High does not possess and of which he is in need? It is necessary to bring before God most High a heart mirror-bright, so that He may see His own face in it."[23]

Before moving on to Rumi's second prominent image pair, let us mention one more facet of the gem of Joseph's beauty. After such trials as shall be described shortly, Joseph was to rise to a position of authority in Egypt.[24] He became overseer of the grain supply. When famine struck the land of Canaan, Joseph's brothers journeyed to Egypt to trade for grain. The prophet knew his kin but they did not recognize him. Joseph arranged to have his favorite brother, Benjamin, brought to Egypt.[25] Then as the brothers were about to return to Canaan a second time, Joseph hid the king's cup in Benjamin's saddlebag so that the young brother could be detained on the pretext of theft (F 75/64, 208/200). In the end, the prophet offered a prayer of gratitude for God's goodness in bringing his family to Egypt to seek wheat, and in making him overseer of the food (M 38/95). Through all that famine of desire and separation, Joseph's beauty was the food that sustained them.[26]

Pit and Prison

For the crime of beauty (VI:957) Joseph was thrice jailed: once by his brothers, once by Zulaykha, and once by the Egyptian vizier. To the visitor who brought the mirror, Joseph explained his experience of the pit and prison. "Like the moon in the interlunar period on the wane," he knew that he would soon wax again.[27] Joseph was like a secret whispered into a well by one who did not want it to come to ungrateful ears.[28] The pit was a kind of fasting for Joseph (D 2344:9) but it was not all misery; it became a garden (VI:3511; D 1769:9) in whose depths Joseph saw the seven heavens (D 1863:14), for "this moon" makes every place paradise (III:3811). The prophet was patient in his suffering (D 3186:8–9; 3217:6), and the breath of God came to him to reveal his destiny (V:4058) and to assure him that God was doing His work for him (D 1457:9ff.).

All the world's a well. Joseph must be drawn up on the rope of patience by the knower of God, who stands outside the hexagonal (six-directional) pit and lowers the bucket of his body into the world of space to help all "Josephs" who have been beguiled by their brothers and have failed to seek guidance.[29] The *Diwan* speaks often of the cord and bucket by which the prophet was liberated from the well.[30] Joseph's emergence is an image of the Resurrection, a deliverance from separation by the rope of remembrance (D 1838:6). When the prophet came up from the depths to greatness, the water boiled up after him out of affection. And "Who is that Joseph?" asks Rumi. "Your God-seeking heart, bound as a captive in your dwelling," to whom God recommends patience.[31]

When Joseph was incarcerated in Egypt, God turned his confines into a garden and a castle (D 2823:12; 1769:10). From that dungeon the prophet was later redeemed by a king who was in reality an image of the divine King (D 631:3). For a while Joseph lost his absolute trust in the sustaining power of the King and asked a fellow prisoner to intercede for him with his lord the Pharaoh. To convince Joseph that no prisoner can receive the gift of freedom from another prisoner, God let Joseph stay in jail for several years. Even God wondered "what ailed the falcon that had seen the Sultan." In his moment of weakness, Joseph preferred to fall like a bat into blackness rather than live in the sun; he preferred sand and mirage to sea and cloud. Even so, God did not leave Joseph entirely to his own devices. By giving Joseph the gift of absolute attention to his liberator, God restored the prophet to true freedom in spite of his chains.[32]

Shirt and Scent

Another of Mawlana's favorite images is that of Joseph's shirt and its sight-restoring properties. While Joseph was still in Egypt he sent a courier to Jacob in Canaan with instructions to place the shirt on Jacob's face. The old man had gone blind from weeping over the lost Joseph (D 2557:3). His eyes were brightened by the scent of his son. Most often the image denotes any power that allows a person to see clearly and accurately.[33]

The breath of Joseph, the "breeze from the Egypt of union," is a faint promise of the "breath of the Merciful from the Yemen" that, according to Muslim tradition, Muhammad later experienced.[34] Joseph's shirt received its most powerful associative value from the restored "eye of Jacob." In this context, since the scent made the eye receptive to the light, the shirt becomes a convenient bridge to Rumi's light and dream imagery (IV:3221–25).

Light and Dream

Joseph "fetched light from God" into his cheek and countenance and inmost self (VI:3058). His gift for interpreting dreams was the chief result, so that he could explain the dreams of others as well as his own (II:918; V:1995). The recollection of his own dream of the celestial bodies bowing to him sustained him during his years in prison (III:2333ff.). And whenever he walked through his town in Egypt he illumined whole neighborhoods (VI:3091ff.; D 2807:30). Joseph thus serves as the model for every enlightened holy person (IV:3397–3400). One who sees by the light of God is far more blessed than one who has the beauty of Joseph:

> God gave him in addition to the kingdom of beauty, the kingdom of interpretation (of dreams) without his having studied and taken lessons.
> The kingdom of beauty led him to prison; the kingdom of knowledge ('ilm) led him to Saturn.
> Because of his knowledge and skill the King became his solace: the kingdom of knowledge ('ilm) is more praiseworthy than the kingdom of beauty. (VI:3103–5)

As the notes to this chapter suggest, Rumi makes hundreds of passing allusions to Joseph, whereas this prophet takes center stage in relatively few extended narratives. In that regard, Rumi's Joseph is the literary mirror reverse of the Qur'an's Joseph. By contrast, Rumi features Moses in anecdotes and frame narratives perhaps more often than he does any other prophet. To that very important figure we now turn.

CHAPTER 5

Moses and Company

By piecing together Rumi's hundreds of references and allusions to Moses, we can assemble a remarkably complete and detailed panorama of the prophet's personal history. As we scan this picture, we can visualize scenes from Moses' infancy, his first encounter with God, the contest with Pharaoh, and his leading the Exodus. In overall outline, Mawlana's portrayal of Moses agrees with that of the Qur'an and of Tha'labi's *Qisas al-Anbiya'*. A section focusing on the distinctively prophetic qualities of Moses will follow a look at how Rumi interpreted the major events of the prophet's life story.[1] Finally, we discuss Moses' special relationship to the enigmatic Khizr.

Birth and Infancy

Pharaoh dreamed of the coming of an archenemy named Moses.[2] He consulted with his astrologers, ascertained the date destined for the child's conception, and proposed to thwart that destiny by contriving to separate all Israelite wives from their husbands on the appointed night. The king broke sacred tradition and invited all the men to the city square (maydan) for a public unveiling of the royal countenance. Pharaoh then bade the Israelite husbands spend the night in the plaza and ordered his treasurer 'Imran to sleep at the king's door. At midnight, however, 'Imran's wife came and woke her husband, and the two became God's way of foiling Pharaoh's scheme. 'Imran said to his wife:

> A steel struck upon the stone, and a fire was born—a fire that shall take vengeance on the king and his empire.
> I am as the cloud, you the earth, and Moses the plant. God is (as) the king on the chessboard, and we are checkmated, checkmated.
> (III:884–85)

As happens "whenever any prophet enters into the womb" (III:901), Moses' star ascended at his conception. All who had been sleeping in the maydan saw the star and raised a shout. The king awoke only to have his astrologers inform him that he had been hoodwinked. Nine months later the Egyptian tried a second ruse. He invited all the women who had given birth that month to a reception at which all the mothers would present their children and receive gifts. Pharaoh then murdered all the infants. Suspecting the worst, 'Imran's wife had stayed home. When Pharaoh's soldiers found her out, Moses' mother received a revelation that her son was a latter-day Abraham and that she should cast the baby into the stove. The soldiers moved on, convinced their work had been done for them. Tipped off by informers, they returned later with orders to make a more careful search. God then revealed a new course to 'Imran's wife: she should put Moses into the Nile in a cradle. "In the house Moses was in fear; in the water he was secure."[3]

Rumi's characterization of the pharaonic debacle occurs in two slightly different versions. In the long section just summarized, Mawlana suggests that 'Imran's wife hid with the child in her own house. Elsewhere, perhaps for the purpose of turning the story into a pedagogical tool, the poet says that while Pharaoh was outside committing infanticide, his enemy was safe inside the king's own house. In those contexts the story's point is that one ought first to search within for the enemy of the self, the *nafs* (II:768–75; IV:1916–17). Another explanation may be that Rumi takes Moses to have been rescued from the Nile by Pharaoh either before or during the infant slaughter; for he says that Pharaoh had not recognized Moses when he drew him from the water (D 3356:17) and the king may have had the baby safe in the royal house during the carnage.

A further Qur'anic detail appears also in other allusions related to God's order to consign Moses to the Nile. 'Imran's wife is told to suckle the child before casting him adrift, so that Moses will always be able to discriminate between a wet nurse and his actual mother. Rumi makes several references to the detail and Ibn 'Arabi makes much of the point in the *Fusus*.[4] In due time, however, Moses was taken from his mother's breast on a journey to Midian. Painful though the separation was, by means of that journey Moses would become the *mawla* (master, protector; D 214:8).

First Encounter with God

Rumi refers several times to Moses' killing of the Egyptian,[5] his flight to Midian, and the ten years he spent as a shepherd employed by Shu'ayb.[6]

He describes the shepherd's endless care and patience in bringing back a lost sheep (VI:3280–86). We read also of Shuʻayb's daughter Safura, who out of "love for that light of true guidance, sacrificed both her eyes" and married Moses (VI:3083–85; D 60:1). After Moses had completed the years of service agreed upon as the dowry for Safura, the son of ʻImran received his prophetic commission. Let us look at Rumi's three favorite images for describing Moses' early relationship with God.

The Burning Bush, the Staff, and the White Hand

Traveling with his family, "Moses went to fetch fire: he beheld such a fire that he escaped from (searching after) fire" (I:2788). He perceived fire from a certain tree, but what he thought was fire was in reality light.[7] What he saw was "a hundred dawns and sunrises" (D 598:5; M 8/54). The tree was not consumed. On the contrary, because it was a "theater" of God (D 525:7) and the very love of God itself (D 1684:10), the radiance of its light made the tree still greener.[8] That fire was not what it appeared to be, for it was meant as a test (D 142:3), meant to cook the raw.[9] "From the direction of the bush" Moses heard the voice of God addressing him as "My darling" (D 1414:1) and saying "I am God."[10] The prophet became curious and, like Khalil, he ran toward the fire,[11] for he thought he might find a gift there (D 123:6–7). What he found exceeded all imagining.

A conversation ensued in that valley (D 788:12) and Moses became the *Kalim*, the interlocutor, the man who spoke with God.[12] Rumi gives several charming versions of the bush's address to Moses. In each case the prophet is instructed to discard his sandals so as to become utterly free from all attachment to self and the two worlds.[13]

> When Moses proceeded towards the burning bush, the bush said, 'I am the water of Kawthar; take off your shoes, and come! Do not fear my fire, for I am water and sweet at that; you have come to prosperity; the seat of honor is yours, welcome! You are a pearl of pure lustre, a ruby of the mine, the soul of place and placelessness; you are the nonpareil of the age; where are other creatures beside you?' (D 45:8–10, MPR1 6)

Commenting on Qur'an 4:162, "And unto Moses God spoke directly," Mawlana explains that God spoke "not with letters and sounds, with throat and tongue," but in a manner accessible only to the prophets (F 164/156). Elsewhere Rumi discusses the question of whether Moses' "station of converse" rendered him superior to Muhammad, whose station was that of seeing (F 103/91-92). Both of these matters will be taken up more fully later in this chapter.

God's first sign to Moses that his mission would be assured of success arose out of His instructing the shepherd in the many unsuspected uses of his staff. Most of those wondrous applications will be related properly in the next section. Here we need advert only to God's initial command at the burning bush. He told Moses: " 'Let it fall from your hand,/That you may behold its good and evil; after that, take it up (again) by command of Him.'/Before his dropping it, it was only wood; whenever he took it up by His command, it became good" (IV:3576–78). Moses then began to see with the "eye of the invisible" and no longer regarded the staff as mere wood. God's command to drop the staff was meant, like the order to discard the sandals, to effect in Moses a total surrender to God and freedom from all that is not God.[14]

A second sign by which God persuaded Moses to accept his mission was the transformation of Moses' hand into a torch ablaze with harmless leprosy. God made the hand such a dazzling white that it "slapped the sun" in triumph (IV:3522; V:1539). Its light derived from Moses' own bosom, for Moses' body was no longer a "screen" blocking out the moon of God.[15] The mirror of the prophet's heart reflected for him the "formless infinite form of the unseen" (I:3486). That, Rumi teaches, is proof that human perceptive faculties provide the model for the heavens themselves (VI:1933–35).

Again, the "eye of the invisible" allowed Moses to see that his hand was no longer a hand, but light (V:3934). Nearly all of Rumi's many references to the white hand in the *Diwan* are rather general allusions to the hand's brightness or illumination, or to its function as an emblem identifying Moses.[16] Two images do stand out, however. One likens the breast to the Ka'ba—"Having circumambulated around our own breast, we bring out of the soul's pocket the white hand" (D 1531:4, MPR1 187). Another suggests the white hand's identity with the water of life: both are to be found only in darkness.[17]

Moses and Pharaoh

Moses' relationship with his nemesis, Pharaoh, is both the largest single portion of the prophet's personal history and the most fully developed portrait of any of the prophets in relation to their respective foils. The story will unfold here in terms of the general character of their duel of wits, the miraculous properties of the staff as Moses' principal weapon, the plagues, with special attention to Nile imagery, and finally Moses' relationship with his brother Aaron.

The Battle of the Contraries

Rumi suggests that the tongue of Moses was knotted lest Pharaoh discover his "proof" (D 1437:2, MPR1 137). The poet nevertheless employs several extended conversations between Moses and Pharaoh, as means of conveying a number of important prophetological themes. Their first discussion shows the Egyptian trying to intimidate the Israelite into calling off his mission. In the end, he argues, his superior might will surely annihilate the powerless prophet. God instructs Moses to give Pharaoh the time he says he needs to assemble his magicians for the contest. Pharaoh's arrogance would shortly be shamed by Moses' humility (D 405:6; 82:12). Round one ends with Moses telling the king he will not confront him again until he has gathered his tricksters (III:1067–99). Rumi notes that Moses could afford to laugh at Pharaoh's blindness (D 923:12), even though he would face much more of the king's mockery just as Muhammad would have to endure the taunts of Abu Jahl (D 1967:10). Round two, in which Moses and the magician match wonders, will be detailed separately. Meanwhile, Mawlana comments on the inner meaning of the Moses/Pharaoh enmity.

Moses possesses reason, Pharaoh imagination; the two qualities are eternally at loggerheads. The king is a world-burner; Moses inflames the spirit. Pharaoh inquires as to the prophet's pedigree and lineage. When the prophet replies that he and his are of water and clay with a God-given soul and heart, Pharaoh retorts that Moses is an ungrateful murderer who has forgotten that it was Pharaoh who nurtured him. Moses defends his involuntary manslaughter by contrasting its accidental nature with the premeditation of the king's infanticide. Again the king cites the ingratitude of Moses' public slander, only to have Moses assure him that the sting of his rebuke will be nothing compared to the sting of the Resurrection. Moses is in fact doing Pharaoh a favor by inviting him to repent. A garden must first be apparently destroyed before it can produce. Moses evokes a series of "you must die in order to live" images, and insists that it is because Pharaoh is a sensualist that he cannot see the increase behind apparent diminishment. Pharaoh is the type of the merciless king whose *qibla* is hatred, a leader of this world's army against the troops of the unseen. He is the rusty iron that has reason-the-polisher in chains.

Moses then makes himself a Joseph by telling Pharaoh that he (the king) has been troubled by horrid dreams of his true self destined for hell. Repentance is still not out of the question, however, and if Pharaoh would profess the faith in public he would forthwith receive four desirable gifts: health, long life, a twofold empire far greater than his present kingdom, and perpetual youth. Pharaoh is not uninterested. He tells his wife of the offer and she is astonished; she reminds the king of the import of Moses' words: "God is showing solicitude for Iblis" (IV:2604). Before he can decide, Pharaoh feels he must consult his vizier Haman, a type of the prophet-envier. Rumi exposes the true colors of their subsequent, ill-taken consultation:

> The Egyptian was a kindred soul of the reprobate Pharaoh; the
> Israelite was of like soul with Moses, the Kalim.
> Haman was more congenial (than anyone else) to Pharaoh: he
> (Pharaoh) chose him out and brought him to the high-seat in the
> palace.
> Inevitably he (Haman) dragged him (Pharaoh) from the high-seat to
> the lowest depth, for those two are homogeneous with hell.
> Both, like hell, are burning and contrary to light; both, like hell, are
> exceedingly averse to the light of the heart. . . .(IV:2705–08;
> cf. also IV:1637-38)

Moses was neither haughty like Pharaoh nor angry like Haman (D 1845:4).

Just when he was on the point of opening himself to belief, Pharaoh was duped by his vizier, the *nafs*. What Kalim had worked a hundred days to nurture in the king, Haman obliterated in an instant (IV:1240–41, 1245). "The morsel, felicity had reached his (Pharaoh's) mouth, when he (Haman) suddenly cut his throat" (IV:2772). It was enough to cause Moses to despair of ever converting the Egyptian monarch.[18]

In the dialogue between Moses and Pharaoh, Jalal ad-Din has created one of his most extensive dramatic settings for the staging of the fundamental principle, "Things are made clear by their opposites." Reminiscent of the cosmic syzygies of the ancient Gnostics, the inimical pair of king and prophet are a link in the chain of dyads that began with Adam and Iblis and will end, as we shall see, with Muhammad and Abu Jahl (F 92/80).

Rumi provides some remarkable analysis of the larger implications of the Moses/Pharaoh contest, in Book I of the *Mathnawi* and in Discourse 46 of *Fihi Ma Fihi*. Moses is to Pharaoh as antidote to poison, light to darkness, leader to lost, full moon to eclipse. However, since God has no opposite in reality, but only in form (F 92/80), Mawlana depicts Pharaoh praying in secret at night, asking God anguished questions about why God has shackled him rather than Moses, when he, no less than Moses, is also God's servant. Pharaoh almost broke free of the chains of differentiation as he prayed. Within him, below form's surface, "a Moses came into conflict with a Moses." God used the formality of antagonism between a Pharaoh and a Moses purely for pedagogical purposes, so that by spotlighting the formal opposite of the divine, God Himself might be shown forth (I:H.2447–68).

Not to leave the Egyptian king entirely ill thought-of, Rumi goes on to point out the importance, even necessity, of Pharaoh's role in the plan of God. In this case of "reversed shoes" (I:2481), the lot of Iblis could as easily have fallen to Adam, that of the wolf to Joseph, that of Pharaoh to Moses (D 2548:7). Everything depends on the favor of a God who is not merely capricious, but purposeful in His choices. Mawlana allows that Pharaoh "made a great personal effort in the way of bounty and charity and the dissemination of good." However, he was like the commandant of a garrison who treats his troops kindly in order to secure their support in his bid for a coup d'état; his beneficence was scarcely meritorious. Still, Pharaoh was not beyond redeeming. Profoundly influenced by al-Hallaj in his doctrine of opposites, Jalal ad-Din recounts the sympathetic epilogue in his own words:

Nevertheless one cannot entirely deny God's favor to Pharaoh. It may be that God most High favored him secretly, causing him to be rejected for a good purpose. For a king is both vengeful and gracious; he both bestows robes of honor and consigns to prison. The spiritualists do not deny God's favor to Pharaoh altogether. The literalists however consider him to be a man wholly rejected; and that is beneficial for the proper maintenance of external priorities. The king puts a man on the gallows, and he is hung in a high place in the presence of the assembled people. He could also suspend him indoors, hidden from the people, by a low nail; but it is necessary that the people should see and take warning, and the execution of the king's decree and the carrying out of his order should be visible. After all, not every gallows consists of wood. High rank and worldly fortune are also a gallows, and a mighty high one. When God most High desires to chastise a person, He bestows on him high rank in the world and a great kingdom, as in the cases of Pharaoh and Nimrod and the like. All those eminent positions are as a gallows on which God most High puts them, so that all the people may gaze upon it.[19]

Moses' Rod and Its Uses

Perhaps the single most fecund tree in Rumi's orchard of imagery is the staff of Kalim. Before describing the battle of faith-power versus sorcery in the arena of Pharaoh's court, a look at the rod itself and the array of associated imagery will be helpful.

Rod Imagery: Most often Rumi likens the rod to a dragon (*azhdaha*) called forth to subdue the fire-breathing Egyptian.[20] He paints his most colorful description of the dragon as he pictures Moses on his way home after agreeing to give Pharaoh time to call in his sorcerers:

> He was going (on his way), and at his heels (went) the dragon wise
>   and loving, like the hunter's dog.
> Like the hunter's dog, wagging its tail: it made the stones (crumble
>   as) sand beneath its hoof.
> With its breath it drew in stone and iron (to its jaws) and visibly
>   chewed the iron into small fragments.
> In the air it was making itself (rise) above the zodiac, so that Greeks
>   and Georgians would flee from it in panic.
> From its palate it cast out foam, like a camel: Whomsoever a drop hit
>   was smitten with tubercular leprosy.
> The gnashing of its teeth would break the heart; the souls of black
>   lions would be distraught (with terror).
> When that chosen one (Moses) reached his kinsfolk, he took hold of
>   the corner of its mouth, and it became again a staff.
> (III: 1100–1107)

Closely related to the dragon are the images of the serpent (*mar* and *af'a*) and of the rod as devouring maw. Mawlana's references to the *mar* are usually unembellished;[21] but he does elaborate once on the snake's impact on Pharaoh, who "humbly begged for a reprieve": "Whether the miracle was a dragon or a snake, what has become of the pride and wrath proper to his divinity?" (V:2442–44).

Vast as Pharaoh's empire was, the rod made one mouthful of it (II:919). In fact, its throat can accommodate all that is unauthentic or crooked

(III:37–40). As dawn devours night (IV:1663) the staff gobbled up Pharaoh's sorcery.[22] The staff can thus engulf all things because it is love itself (D 2919:12, 2274:3). But no loftier honor could be accorded the staff than that it be singled out as a type of the Qur'an, which "swallows up (all) infidelities, like a dragon" (III:1209). As that rod is superior to all others in all but appearance, so are the Book's mystic letters above all other letters (V:1314–18).

In addition to its more animated activities, the staff's role is at times more passive and instrumental, under Moses' control as hand and foot are under the heart's control (I:3568).

Staff as Weapon: Moses is occasionally fitted out as a soldier sallying forth ill-armed against innumerable Egyptian swords. Though the rod's appearance hardly inspires terror, it proves to be vastly superior weaponry.[23] Referring to the staff as a whip or cudgel, Moses tells the Pharaoh that he is an ass that must be disciplined and turned out of the stable whose inhabitants he is oppressing (IV:2802–5).

Staff as Caduceus or Healing-Wand: As a type of the instrument of healing, the staff/serpent is associated several times with the breath or incantation of Jesus. In all instances Rumi uses the combination to stress the underlying power of God vis-à-vis the deceptively easy accessibility of the forms of wood and word.[24]

Whatever its specific application, the staff always underwent a change from its essence (*mahiyya*) as staff (F 145/135). Only the hand of Moses could render the rod so versatile merely by letting go of it;[25] and only those with clear vision will be able to see the staff in the hand of Moses (D 931:9).

Miracle Against Magic

Moses' sincerity provided the key to the staff's enhanced versatility (V:2775), exposing the magic of the sorcerers as fraudulent. Mawlana speaks of the apparent similarity between the demonstrations of Moses and those of the king's minions, of the consequent need for the discriminating eye of faith, and of the final discrediting of the charlatans' ploys.

Ignorant people look at both magic and miracle and see only sleight of hand. They fail to see that magic issues in a curse from God, miracle in divine mercy (I:277–80). Moses expressed to God his concern that such ignorance might nullify his endeavors. God assured Kalim that He would supply discernment enough to make His case (IV:H.1670–77; F 155/147).

"In the hand of Moses the rod became a witness; in the hand of the magician the rod became motes in the air" (II:306). Pharaoh's magicians turned
cords into snakes, but the dragon-rod of Moses made a snack of their
magic; for magic is the world's insincerity which only love—both the rod
itself and the effect of the rod's power—can devour.[26]

Two stories illustrate the point that God did indeed grant some of the
Egyptians discernment, as he had promised Moses. Pharaoh's summons of
all the realm's tricksters reached two especially clever young sorcerer's
apprentices. They immediately conjured up the shade of their late father
and asked him how they might undo Moses. Steal the prophet's rod while
he sleeps, they were told; but know that if he is awake even while sleeping,
he is no mere magician. The two youths experienced a sudden change of
heart when the rod at the dormant Moses' side became a dragon and
afflicted them with a nearly fatal ague. The prophet, however, honored the
offenders' apologies and invited them to infiltrate the ranks of magicians
in Pharaoh's court (III:1157–1250).

Assembled later in the royal audience hall, those magicians upon whom
Moses had "poured wine" and who now shared the prophet's intoxication,
"deemed the gallows to be their beloved" (IV:2100; D 1135:14). Pharaoh
had threatened to cut off their hands and feet if they did not humiliate
Moses (III:H.1721–28). They scoffed at his threat by actually deferring to
the prophet; their respect for him "cut off the hands and feet of their con-
tention." They made glad reparation (I:H.1615–20), for "they perceived
themselves to be subsisting without this body and that the body had no
connection with them" (F 238/230). In the end, the sin of the magician was
redemptive and led to forgiveness, and "disobedience became obedience"
(I:3833–35).

Continuing Struggle: The Plagues

Rumi relates two other episodes in Moses' campaign against the king. The
prophet so charmed the water of the Nile that it turned to blood, not by
mixture, but essentially (IV:3524), whenever an Egyptian went to drink it.
For the Israelites the water remained potable, since the grace of God rendered the Nile intelligent (IV:2819). Even the Egyptian's request to have
an Israelite fill the jug for him did not solve the problem.[27] Pharaoh had
once before jeopardized Egypt's water supply when he claimed to be
divine and the Nile stopped flowing. When the king prayed for a reprieve,
God relented and gave Pharaoh command of the river, even as the *nafs* is
sometimes given the upper hand (III:1054, MCN). Pharaoh's repentance

had been short-lived, however, and the sanguinary plague was a result of his relapse. Mawlana adds an unexpected twist in the imagery of the deathlike Nile (IV:1660). An inexplicable transposition in two texts has the Nile, rather than the Red Sea, drowning the Egyptian army.[28]

In another plague, locusts destroyed all crops and brought a famine upon Egypt (IV:3581). Pharaoh-the-*nafs* could bear hunger no longer and went to beg a reversal of fortune from Moses. God instructed Kalim to restore produce from the earth. But after a moment's gratitude, Pharaoh and his people fell victim to renewed rebelliousness (IV:4598ff.).

At this point we must advert briefly to the role of Moses' brother Aaron in the prophetic battle against Pharaoh, one of Rumi's more extended metaphors for the greater jihad. Aaron (Harun)[29] does not appear as a distinct personality in Rumi. Every time the poet mentions him he is in the company of Moses. The phrase "like Moses and Aaron" (D 2090:4) is Rumi's equivalent to "like two peas in a pod." Together, the two prophets went to Egypt. God had warned Pharaoh that he was by nature a jackal and that it was sheer folly for him to play the peacock. Moses and Aaron were the genuine peacocks whose caudal brilliance would humiliate the drab Egyptian (III:875). As redoubtable a pair as the "two dervishes" (III:1167) were, however, Mawlana advises that if the untrammeled *nafs* had been Pharaoh, it could have compassed the ruin of a hundred like Moses and Aaron (III:1053–55). The unity of the brothers is perhaps best summarized by Rumi's statement that, even if Moses had not had the rod and the white hand, Aaron would have recognized him through his intimate knowledge.[30]

The Exodus: Moses as Guide

A chronicle of Israel's experience of freedom emerges from Rumi's poetry in several major moments or stages: the crossing of the Red Sea, trial in the desert, water from the rock, the revelation at Sinai, and the worship of the calf. Finally, under the heading of the conquest of the land, we shall group five stories that find no more suitable place in this reconstruction of Rumi's prophetology.

The Red Sea

Again thanks to Moses' sincerity and ingenuity (V:2775; D 567:14), the sea blocking the way of the Israelites was enabled to comprehend the prophet's words (III:1015), so that it bore Moses on its shoulders

(III:3102) and became his dance floor (D 2366:1). Moses could scarcely be sad in the water's midst, for he was a mountain peak (D 3434:8). As friend of the prophet and enemy of Pharaoh, the sea discriminated between Israelite and Egyptian (I:862; D 14:4). The rod split the water and became a bridge,[31] tying "veils of dust" raised from the sea's bed.[32] That dust was the body of the Friends of God (D 2199:7) and la ilaha illa 'llah (D 2407:2), and the water became a sea of temptation into which the Egyptians were drawn to drown.[33] "Pharaoh drowned like a reed in the waves; Moses sat on the parting of the waters like oil" (D 2043:11). As Muhammad was to split the moon, Moses split the sea (D 2840:2) and lives on as a cleaver of all such obstacles to freedom.[34]

Trial and Miracles in the Desert

One barrier surmounted, Moses faced the task of guiding his people through a trackless waste. Though Moses attended utterly to God, his Lord nevertheless saw fit to occupy him partially with human affairs (F 78/66). As the intellect is the commander of the body and requires the body's obedience, so stood Moses in the midst of the children of Israel to demand their allegiance. When they disobeyed, they experienced the contraction (qabd) of desert disorientation. When they obeyed, they felt the expansion (bast) of deliverance (F 65/53; 77/66). "This world is the desert," Rumi explains, and Moses is the type of the spiritual leader without whom the people remain lost.[35]

In the life-begrudging climate of the wilderness Moses provided water and food. At the touch of his staff twelve fountains flowed from the rock of the body (D 613:6), and the staff of love released a hundred thousand springs from a stony heart (D 2901:6). As a water giver that rod was like the sword Dhu'l-Faqar.[36] Had Moses so desired, the stone would have yielded milk (IV:1241). In that "sweet desert" of Moses, the wanderers received a forty-year supply of manna and quail,[37] succulent dishes, and bread from a cloud (I:3733). The son of 'Imran could only marvel at the continued skepticism of the Israelites in the face of such bounty: "During forty years the platter and tray came from heaven, and at my prayer the river ran from the rock./ These and a hundred times as many, and all these diverse (evidences) did not make that vain imagination fade away from you . . ." (II:2041–42).

Revelation and Rebellion at Sinai

Numerous one-line allusions and one rather extended story form Rumi's kaleidoscopic image of the romance of Moses and the mountain. Mawlana tells how Moses approached the mountain in desire of union with God[38] and called out "show me (Yourself)."[39] In the story of the Christian, Jewish, and Muslim travelers, we hear the Jew's tale of a dream in which he followed Moses to Sinai and was privileged to witness the theophany. A light, so brilliant that it obliterated the mountain as well as Moses and the Jew, gave birth to a second and still brighter light, whereupon Sinai disintegrated.[40] Exploding into three pieces, one of narcissus, one of pearl, one of ruby and amber (D 14:9–10), Sinai was scattered far and wide. One piece fell into the sea and sweetened its brine; one fell into the earth and sent forth a healing spring; and the third flew to the neighborhood of the Ka'ba at 'Arafat. When, still in his dream, the Jew recovered consciousness, he saw that Sinai remained intact, except that under the foot of Moses it was inwardly melting, overturned and leveled (VI:2428–42, 2484).

Moses' sincerity (V:2775) allowed him to receive the light of revelation so that at its encounter with the prophet and the divine *tajalli*, Sinai was intoxicated (I:26), lit up (V:3914), turned to rubies (II:1332) and blood (D 144:3), became a perfect Sufi, and began to dance.[41] Thus does Moses-the-spirit give life to Sinai-the-world/body/heart.[42] Moses himself was likewise ecstatic at God's *tajalli* at Sinai.[43] Notwithstanding the splendor and responsiveness of Mount Sinai, Rumi warns that one must not invest Sinai's stone with a value not proper to it. Those who give thought to the rock of Tur will die; they must rather go to God's Kalim who has come to serve (D 3234:7).

Israel's unbelief in the face of God's ongoing revelation through Moses is epitomized in the rebellion of Samiri and his followers.[44] Rumi alludes to the Qur'anic "lowing calf" (Q 20:96) and says that a mere handful of dust from the hoof of Gabriel's horse was enough to animate the idol (IV:3331–32; D 2714:18). In his conceit Samiri typifies the disciple who feels he has outgrown his need for guidance (II:1982). Moses was again amazed and angered that a people so skeptical of a hundred thousand clear miracles could be so easily seduced by a handmade calf (II:H.3026–42; M 68/150). The poet points out the implications for all seekers:

Like the people of Moses in the heat of the desert, you have
  remained forty years in (the same) place . . .

Daily you march rapidly till nightfall and find yourself in the first
   stage of your journey.
You will never traverse this three hundred years' distance as long as
   you have love for the calf.
Until the fancy of the calf went out of their hearts, the desert was to
   them like a blazing whirlpool.
Besides this calf which you have obtained from Him, you have
   experienced infinite graces and bounties.
You have the nature of a cow; hence in your love for this calf (those)
   benefits have vanished from your heart. (VI:1788–93)

Conquest of the Land

Five curious groups of references in Rumi appear to be associated with
events of the post-Exodus period, though it is impossible to pinpoint all of
them accurately. One text relates that Bal‘am son of Ba‘ur asked God not
to prosper Moses' siege of a certain city (possibly Jericho). Bal‘am had at
one time enjoyed divine favor—Rumi even calls him the Jesus of the
time—but his encounter with Kalim was his downfall (I:H.3298–3300,
MCN). At some point in the wanderings of Israel a man was killed and his
murderer went undiscovered. Moses was commanded to sacrifice a cow
and strike the dead man with its tail. The dead man revived and testified
against his killer.[45]

Another story says that Moses built the *bab-i saghir* (the small gate) in
Jerusalem, a gate designed to force the haughty literally to bow down upon
entering. No other mention of Moses in explicit connection with
Jerusalem occurs in Rumi (III:2996, H.2998). Mawlana makes one cryptic
reference to a miracle story in which a goat's hair became silk as Moses
and Safura pulled it off the animal's hide.[46] Finally we find numerous allusions to Qarun, the Korah of Numbers 16. He is said to have learned
alchemy from Moses and to have amassed for himself such great wealth
that the earth opened and swallowed him with all his gold and palace.[47]
Qarun became an example of the fate that awaits those who try to lord it
over the people of a prophet and who trust in their wealth rather than in the
Creator.

Moses the Prophet

We can now make a summary survey of Moses' specifically prophetic
qualities: his prayer, miracles, knowledge and inspiration, light, and the

"Moses of the spirit." Though Rumi seldom refers to Moses specifically as *nabi* (II:768; D 2159:3) or *pay(gh)ambar* (III:912; D 854:8) or *rasul* (III:1189), Mawlana clearly regards the son of 'Imran as the greatest and most important of the messenger-prophets prior to Muhammad.

Prayer

God once ordered Moses to call to Him with a sinless mouth. Moses replied that he had no such mouth, so God instructed him to call "by the mouth of another" (III:H.180–81), after which the Lord proceeded to teach Moses "by the mouth of another" a humbling lesson in prayer. As Moses was traveling he overheard a shepherd praying and took the poor man to task for addressing the Creator in an unduly familiar manner. God soon informed Moses that the shepherd's prayer was quite acceptable, unconventional as it was, because it arose from a burning spirit. Moses realized that he owed the shepherd an apology (II:H.1720ff.; VI:1091–92).

Rumi expands on God's instruction on prayer, and adds "or (else) make your own mouth pure" (III:185). That is apparently what Moses did, for we find him addressing God several times, sometimes praying for others, sometimes asking for information for himself. Moses was much vexed by the facts of pain and evil and the predominance of the unjust. He asked God to reveal the mystery to him as He had revealed all things to the angels through Adam, namely, the knowledge that the secret is in the end, not in the beginning, in the fruit not in the leaves (II:H.1816ff.). The prophet later asked the same question again in slightly different words, wondering why God creates and then destroys. God's answer gave Moses the vision he had asked for earlier (II:1821). God told him to sow seed corn, let it grow, and then harvest it (IV:H.3001–29).

Although Rumi does not say it in so many words, the second major aspect of Moses' prayer is intercessory. In the story of the man who wanted Moses to teach him the language of the animals, Kalim carried on a running conversation with his Lord, asking advice on the man's behalf. At length he secured for the man the gift of faith (III:3265–98). More spectacular results occurred at his behest as well. Throughout his struggle with Pharaoh the prophet was in constant contact with God.[48] Israel's survival in the desert was facilitated by their leader's intercession (II:2041; F 145/135).

Prayer is clearly the wellspring of Moses' prophetic charisma. From the two chief qualities of his prayer just discussed, personal and intercessory, there flowed his miraculous power and the gift of inspired knowledge, which in turn constituted the light by virtue of which he lives on as the Moses of the spirit.

Miracles, Knowledge, Inspiration, and Light

When Moses prayed, God worked miracles though him. Rumi refers explicitly to the *mu'jizat* of this prophet principally in two contexts. Miracles are usually the antithesis of magic, which Rumi uses as a backdrop against which to highlight prophetic wonders.[49] The miracles performed on the stage of desert sand were of quite the same magnitude as those wrought in Pharaoh's court; for some reason (perhaps only by chance) Rumi calls them explicitly *mu'jizat* only once (II:2038–42).

When Moses was perplexed he questioned God. He received knowledge (*'ilm*) in return. God explained to the prophet that the "'question is the half of *'ilm*, and this ability (to ask questions) does not belong to every outsider.' [To which Rumi adds that:] Both the question and answer arise from *'ilm* just as the thorn and the rose from earth and water" (IV:3007–08). Elsewhere, in context with Moses' staff, the poet writes that *taqlid* is like a staff on this journey: it must be transformed into the sword *Dhu'l-Faqar*. In other words, one must trade *taqlid*, unquestioning acceptance of authority, for incisive and penetrating knowledge (D 3496:3).

Mawlana often speaks of how God inspired Kalim. The Knower communicated with the prophet by inspiration or unveiling to advise a course of action, to correct, to exhort, even to reproach.[50] Moses did not cling selfishly to his knowledge, but was understandably cautious about passing it along to people who were not ready for it. As a type of the shaykh or spiritual teacher, Moses at first refused the request of the man who wanted to learn the language of the beasts and birds. When the seeker said he would be content to learn only the tongues of domestic fowls and dogs, Moses relented on God's advice (III:3265–98).

Moses' relationship with Khizr makes it clear that Kalim's knowledge had its limits. As we shall see at the end of this chapter, the law-giving, law-abiding Moses presented a marked contrast to the much freer Khizr.[51] Kalim made his journey to the Two Seas in search of love (VI:1127–29), about which Moses received his most sublime *wahy*. God spoke to the heart of the prophet and said, "O chosen one, I love you" (IV:H.2921–28).

"We sent Moses with our signs, commanding him: Bring forth your people from darkness into light" (Q 14:6). Rumi describes the illumination of Moses chiefly by means of four images, all of which have been treated in detail and need only to be grouped together here specifically with reference to light: the bush, the white hand, Moses as light/Pharaoh as darkness, and Mount Sinai. So manifest was the light of this prophet that even as the earth was gaping wide to engulf Qarun, it "saw the light of Moses and showed kindness" to him (II:2368).

The Moses of the Spirit

Through the gift of light Moses lives on. Mawlana thus capsulizes the inner meaning of the story of God's Kalim:

> The mention of Moses has become a chain (obstruction) to the thoughts (of my readers), (for they think) that these are stories (of that) which happened long ago.
> The mention of Moses serves for a mask, but the light of Moses is your actual concern, O good person.
> Moses and Pharaoh are in your being: you must seek these two adversaries in yourself.
> The (process of) generation from Moses is (continuing) till the Resurrection: the light is no different, (though) the lamp has become different.
> This earthenware lamp and this wick are different, but its light is not different: it is from Beyond.[52]

The individual can embody the spirit of Moses through faith, for that spirit is "the flaming torch of (true) religion" (IV:2363). To those who see by the light, a Moses exists in every dervish-cloak (II:2348) and in everyone whose breast becomes a Sinai (V:2524; I:3552).

One must not act toward one's Moses the way Pharaoh of old behaved (II:453). The Moses of the spirit arrives always in time to confront every Pharaoh (D 336:2; R 1926), plucking out the moustache of the Pharaoh of the body (D 1131:7) and giving to all pure, sugar-making kindred spirits of the prophet victory over the egotistical, hatred-mongering Egyptian (D 498:3–4). Since the coming of this Moses, none need be of the family of Pharaoh (D 2500:2; 3167:1) for the Kalim of love has attacked the Pharaoh of existence with the rod of annihilation (D 1970:2).

Khizr the Prophet and Guide

We come at last to a figure important both as an associate of Moses and as a character in his own right. The protean Khizr is the most inscrutable of all the prophets, particularly in scenes of his not always cordial relationship with Moses. On the basis of that relationship, Khizr evolves into the model of the *pir* of unassailable authority, which derives from Khizr's unique knowledge of the water of life.[53]

Khizr and Moses

Several of the episodes described in Surat al-Kahf appear in Rumi's works. We will treat them here in the order in which they occur in the Qur'an. As Moses was traveling in search of the confluence of the Two Seas (D 929:13), he mistakenly left his breakfast fish behind one morning. "At the touch of Khizr the roasted fish came to life and took its abode in the sea" (VI:2640; D 841:9). Moses then retraced his steps to find the one who had raised the fish to life, hoping that Khizr would consent to be his guide. Rumi comments on the mystery of Moses' need for a guide even though he already possessed the perfection of prophethood. Moses sought guidance because he no longer cared only for himself (III:1959–63). When his people chastised him for abandoning them, Kalim replied:

> Do not make this reproach, do not waylay the Sun (Khizr) and the Moon (Moses).
> I will fare as far as the "meeting place of the two seas," that I may be accompanied by the sovereign of the time (Khizr).
> I will make Khizr a means to (the achievement of) my purpose: (either) that, or "I will go onward" and journey by night "a long while."[54]

Khizr is explicitly called a means (*sabab*) for Moses. He agreed, reluctantly, to allow Moses to accompany him; so the two journeyed on.[55]

During the first segment of their travels, Khizr suddenly sabotaged the ship in which they were sailing. His bizarre action was, however, eminently defensible. Rumi echoes the reasoning of the Qur'an as he explains, "Khizr scuttled the boat for this purpose, that the boat might be delivered from him who could have seized it by force."[56] In his "staving" were a "hundred rightnesses," and that strange maneuver alone would have been enough to win for Khizr the title "lord of the lesser of two evils." The boat, Mawlana continues, is the body (D 2521:10); a Sufi must be broken and thus purified by the Khizr of love (D 408:1–2).

Khizr again applied his end-centered ethical principle when he killed a youth whom he and Moses encountered farther on. Rumi notes that Khizr cut the lad's throat (I:224). The Qur'an does not mention that detail, and it seems likely that Rumi has included it here because he wants to associate the slain youth with Isma'il, whose throat Abraham was prepared to cut at God's command (I:224-27). The poet does not include the Qur'anic justification of Khizr's act—"and as for the lad, his parents were believers and We feared lest he should oppress them by rebellion and disbelief" (Q 18:81)—possibly because it would not dovetail neatly with the Isma'il parallel.

Moses found Khizr's apparent license quite unreasonable (II:3262–64). His imagination was screened from comprehending the *'ilm min ladunn*, the esoteric divine knowledge to which Khizr had access (I:237; D 2010:3). "Shamefaced by disbelief" (II:436), Moses questioned Khizr once too often and the guide declared a parting of the ways (II:3515–16). At this point we come to Rumi's treatment of Khizr as a prophet significant apart from his relationship to Moses.

Khizr the Pir and Model of Dervishes

After the example of Moses, every disciple must eventually seek the guidance of Khizr.[57] Khizr could communicate with his spiritual progeny through dreams, by appearing to them as a messenger of God (III:192–97). Friends of God to whom Khizr has imparted special knowledge might also be delegated to appear in dreams (IV:678). In general, this prophet exerts an influence upon seekers through shaykhs who have become Khizrs. Thanks to Khizr, the *pir* exercises carte blanche authority over disciples. "If one who bestows (spiritual) life should slay, it is allowable; he is the caliph, and his hand is the hand of God" (I:226; I:2972-73). Any *murid* who does not wish the *pir* to declare a parting of the ways must surrender without question to his "Khizr" (I:2969–71; II:3527–30). If so exalted a figure as Moses sought Khizr, how much more should a lesser person submit to his tutelage. The great mystic Bayezid al-Bistami, too, searched for a Khizr (II:2231). Through the *pir*, Khizr remains present, "soul-increasing and help-giving and perpetual" (VI:187).

Khizr and the Water of Life

There is ample reason for Khizr's position as the standard of spiritual leadership. Unlike Moses and even Muhammad himself, Khizr was always wholly occupied with God (F 78/66). One aspect of his absorption with his Lord was his privileged access to the water of life, which enabled him to share in the immortality enjoyed also by Jesus and Ilyas.[58] Freedom from the fear of death is both the essence of the spirit of Khizr (III:717) and the prime requisite for anyone who would search for the water of life. "Life depends on dying (to self) and on suffering tribulation: The water of life is in (the land of) darkness."[59] Khizr transforms into Alexanders all who come begging with their pitchers.[60]

Khizr drinks from the wellspring of spirit (D 97:4; 2012:5), whose water not only reflects real things, but contains the real (VI:3242–43). Flowing through all of creation as the evolutionary sap that robes the world in green (D 482:7), the water elevates all beings to a new stratum of existence. "Every plant that turns its face towards the (animal) spirit drinks, like Khizr, from the fountain of life" (VI:127). The greening of humanity is effected through the "river of the speech of the Friends" who know what Khizr knows. A seeker fills his jar at the river. Carrying away wine from Khizr's cup (D 3285:9), the seeker's heart is filled with knowledge and his eye illumined. Rumi suggests that the water is equivalent to the *anwar-i 'aqli* (intellectual lights); and he states explicitly, "Know, then, that the blessed water from heaven is the *wahy* of hearts and the true explanation (of every mystery.)"[61] Suffice it to say here that it is to Khizr that the seeker owes gratitude for blazing the Fountain-finding trail. "(If) you are a follower of the prophet, tread the Way . . ." (III:4319).

One final aspect of Khizr is his relationship to the prophet Ilyas. Rumi clearly associates Ilyas' prophetic function with that of Khizr. Six of the poet's seven allusions to Ilyas place him side-by-side with Khizr in relation to the water of life. One reference in the *Mathnawi* says that Ilyas remains in the world like Khizr, transforming earth into heaven (VI:188). Five of the odes mention both Khizr and Ilyas in the same verse, three times in connection with the water;[62] once in such a way that they appear as two sides of the same coin (D 2709:3); and once as a pair who symbolize immortality (D 815:8). Rumi's final mention of Ilyas makes it nearly impossible to escape the conclusion that the poet thinks of the prophet as practically identical with Khizr. The sixth verses of odes 836 and 838, referring to a prophet who guides to the water of life, are exactly the same except that in the first ode the name of Khizr is substituted for the name of Ilyas.[63]

CHAPTER 6

Jesus and the Other Gospel Figures

In order to round off the image of Jesus that emerges from Rumi's works, it will be helpful to see the Messiah in the context of the other prominent figures from the Gospel (Injil). Those personages are Zakariya (Zacharia) and his son Yahya (John the Baptist), and Mary. Here then, is a collage of Rumi's thought and imagery around the Gospel figures, beginning with his picture of Zacharia and Yahya and then moving to Mary and Jesus.

Zacharia and John

On three occasions Rumi talks of Zacharia's prayer for a son and of the prophet's ensuing dialogue with God.[1] When Mary was presented in the Temple, the coveted charge of looking after the child fell to Zacharia. Each time he brought food to Mary he found that the equal of what he brought had already been supplied her. In response to Zacharia's curiosity about the matter, Mary informed him that all who rely solely on God will lack nothing. Zacharia was thereupon inspired to present his desire before the Lord: he wanted a son who would spontaneously devote himself to God.[2] God promptly answered that he would fulfill the old man's wish. At that point Zacharia apparently realized afresh the impossibility of his request, given both his and his wife's decrepitude. Reassurance came from God in the form of a reminder that the Creator has no need of secondary causes. He could easily produce from Zacharia a hundred thousand children "without wife and pregnancy" (F 80–81/69). As a sign that his word would materialize as promised, God told Zacharia that he would be mute for three days (II:1675–78).

Finally, two odes refer to Zacharia as Father of John (D 3060:7, 3375:1). In a very veiled allusion to Zacharia's martyrdom Rumi speaks of reason being sawn in half (IV:2306), and the *Qisas* report that the Father of John was sawn in two while miraculously concealed in a tree.

John, son of Zacharia,[3] was conceived by a woman sterile and aged, and married to a decrepit husband (F 182/173–74). While he was still in the womb, John described, and bowed to, Jesus who was also yet unborn (II:H.3602ff.; F 66/54). The infant prophet continued to learn rapidly, for Rumi calls him "old in wisdom" even in children's school (V:H.1271). Nicholson gives a note on this last verse about how in the *Qisas*, John reproached the children who wanted him to play with them, saying "I was not made for games." John's seriousness was a lifelong trait. Twice Mawlana alludes to a hadith which says that the prophet wept a great deal (F 60/48) and habitually frowned out of fear (D 1211:7). In God's presence however, John turned a somersault along with David and Joseph (D 738:3). Aside from three other cryptic allusions to John in the *Diwan*, Rumi tells how a mountain once spoke to and befriended the fleeing prophet and sheltered him, driving off with a rock slide the Jews who were in pursuit.[4]

Mary

Gabriel as "Holy Spirit" (*ruh al-qudus*) visited Mary in human form. The "life-increasing, heart-ravishing" presence terrified her (III:3701; D 3072:7). From her earliest youth Mary had learned to take refuge in God (F 182/173) and in her fright she cried again "*la hawl*," the beginning of the common Arabic expression "there is no help . . . and no power except in God." The Trusted One (Gabriel) explained to her that he was himself the very refuge she sought, one sent by God (III:H.3700–3710, 3767–83). Mary became pregnant when Gabriel breathed into the neck opening of her mantle.[5] She was like trees and Gabriel the breeze: from the two there came rose-faced Jesus.[6] Various texts in the *Diwan* speak of the impregnating breath of Gabriel and of the '*arif* (one who possesses mystical knowledge); but that breath is also the light and the call of God.[7] Since Mary had no husband, Jesus was conceived "without a father" "by a king unseen."[8] Mary had only to behold the fruit of Paradise for her fruit to be produced without orchard.[9] It is important for Rumi that Mary carried her secret treasure in silence.[10] Thought, like Mary, is pregnant with a hundred Jesuses (D 2297:12); Jesus would soon become the speech counterpart to Mary's silent thought when he emerged speaking from the womb.

A Rustam was concealed in Mary (VI:1884), but the true import of her burden was not hidden from everyone; the embryonic John the Baptist bowed in worship to Jesus. John's mother was thereby enabled to inform

Mary that she bore a king within her, a *rasul* (messenger), an *'ulu 'l-'azm* (possessor of greatness). There was a feeling of mutual respect between the two unborn prophets, and Jesus returned the bow to John. Rumi immediately follows the above story by responding in advance to any objections that such a meeting between the mothers of Jesus and John would have been a historical impossibility. The poet explains that there are many ways of being present to another.[11]

When Mary felt the onset of labor pains she went toward a withered palm tree, the way the heart in quest of the universal mirror at last arrives at its dwelling place.[12] In turn the blossoming of the sterile tree became the mirror image of Mary's giving birth without seed. The tree's seed was Mary's pain and anguish.[13] Since Mary was pregnant with the lights of the Messiah (D 796:5), her pain was a treasure like "light on light" (D 565:6, Q 24:35). And the Mary of endless love begot the Messiah of wonder.[14]

Jesus

Turning to the poet's explicit treatment of Jesus[15] we find that Mawlana likens the newborn prophet's cradle to a body into which Jesus-the-spirit has come.[16] Scarcely had Jesus emerged from the womb when he began to speak. His speech arose both from Mary's beauty and from her pain, and "part of her spoke on her behalf without her" (VI:3204–5, 4549). Jesus spoke on Mary's behalf in that his speech was meant to set aside suspicion as to the nature of his birth, to prove he had been born of the will of God and not of the flesh (IV:3044). With God as his teacher (IV:3403), Jesus could explain in the cradle at the age of two days (D 619:5), "Without having become a youth I am a shaykh and a *pir*."[17] In this connection Rumi quotes Q 19:27–28, in which Mary is said to have brought Jesus to her folk. When they raised an eyebrow, suspicious of Mary's integrity, the infant Jesus spoke up and removed Mary's disgrace (M 60/139). Jesus "struggled" and delivered the proof that he was God's servant and the recipient of the Book. In spite of his precocious eloquence, however, there remains a word of union that even Jesus cannot utter.[18]

Jesus' Public Ministry

Personality and Teachings: Jesus laughed much, because of his trust, whereas John wept much. Following his quoting of this hadith in *Fihi Ma Fihi*, Mawlana records a discussion between the two prophets as to which is the proper attitude, laughing or weeping. The poet then uses their discussion as a backdrop against which to bring out his own belief that any response to, or thought of, God can be God's dwelling place.[19]

Jesus had a sense of humor, but he had a more austere side as well. "The way of Jesus . . . was wrestling with solitude and not gratifying lust." [20] By a severe regime he sought release from a world in flames (D 1974:3; 2624:13). He was a homeless (D 1955:8) desert wanderer. One day he was about to take shelter from a rainstorm in a jackal's den but was prevented from doing so by a revelation that reminded him he must remain without a home. Jesus models the behavior of one who strives to be grateful for the loving favor of being driven to the road by constant reminders that he is a pilgrim (F 53–54/41–42). Rumi alludes twice in parallel texts to the story of how Jesus once failed to trust God completely when he carried a needle with him in his wanderings. Symbolizing lack of total dependence, that tiny needle was as much a veil as was the vast treasure of Qarun.[21]

One of Rumi's stories tells why Jesus once sought solitude. The rather lengthy passage depicts the prophet fleeing to the mountains to escape fools. He was apprehended on his way by a man who asked why this healer and master of the spells of the unseen should be in flight. The Messiah replied that folly was hopeless and would not yield even to the healing man. One must shun fools, for they steal religion away (III:H.2570–98).

Most frequently, however, Jesus is depicted much involved with people, teaching, responding to questions and needs. Jalal ad-Din refers in passing to the Messiah's asking his band of disciples, "Who are my helpers for God?" quoting Q 61:14 (M 74/161). A "sober-minded" apostle once asked Jesus about the most difficult thing in existence. The Messiah replied that the wrath of God was the hardest of all, and that the only safety from it was the abandonment of one's own wrath. We also find Jesus expressing his amazement at how one living being can eat another living being of its own kind. His puzzlement may seem at first to be some sort of argument for vegetarianism; but Rumi says Jesus was referring to the way a shaykh "eats" the disciple by imposing strict demands.[22]

Miracles: Above all Rumi talks of Jesus in relation to the miraculous, especially to healing and bringing the dead to life. Each day people would gather at Jesus' door hoping to be delivered from every imaginable malady. Jesus was a man of prayer and only by that means was he able to fulfill the hopes of those who sought him out. As a good monk, the son of

Mary would first attend to his litanies, and then go out to pray over the afflicted and send them skipping home.[23]

Breath of the Messiah: *dam-i masih* appears frequently in Rumi as an all-inclusive topos for Jesus' dominion over life and death, health and sickness. Q 3:45 and 5:110 appear to be the inspiration for the poet's extensive development of the image. Those verses tell the story of how the youthful Jesus fashioned a bird of clay and animated it by breathing on it. From the Qur'anic storehouse Mawlana delivers one detailed summary of the original story and dozens more of oblique allusions; "The water and clay, when it fed on the breath of Jesus, spread wings and pinions, became a bird and flew."[24]

The breath's resuscitating power is the exemplar that the authentic and the charlatan alike strive to imitate.[25] Coveted as it is, the breath is not so easily acquired, for "it is not any wind and breath that arises from joy and sorrow" (V:1319). It can revive and beautify only those who are willing to die in supplication and poverty (I:1909–10; IV:2165). Not until the screen of the body is removed can a spirit retrieve its original nature, whose very speech is the breath of Jesus (I:1598–99). Witness the experience of the Christian child who was thrown into the fire by the Jewish king: "In this fire I have seen a world wherein every atom possesses the breath of Jesus" (I:794). We can now say a word about Rumi's more specific references to the two sides of the coin of *dam-i masih*—healing and restoring life.

Healing: Celebrated and efficacious as were the medical arts of Galen, they were little more than a joke compared to the breath of the Messiah (I:528). Jesus, not Galen, is the archphysician and the model in Mawlana's story of the medics who were retained by a king to care for his hand-maiden (I:47). For Rumi, the lover is always the ailing patient, the beloved his "Jesus son of Mary" (VI:1998). He speaks often of Jesus' healing powers without mention of any particular physical ailment.[26]

When the poet translates the therapeutic breath into words Jesus addresses to the sick, two things become clear. First, God effects the cure, and second, healing is closely related to forgiveness (III:303–4). To the deaf Jesus restored hearing (D 189:12). To the blind, his breath was the shirt of Joseph.[27]

Restoring Life: Jesus' power over death appears in a variety of images and combinations. Sometimes Rumi speaks of the Messiah's bringing the dead to life in an otherwise unspecified manner, or by his mere presence, or by his "kiss" upon the soul.[28] Sometimes it is the breath of Jesus that revivifies.[29] Since the breath is actually love, one must first submit to being slain by it before one can receive new life (D 2719:5). On the other hand, Rumi warns that the breath of the Antichrist deals out only irremediable death (D 993:4).

Perhaps the single most frequently used image is that of Jesus' incantation of a life-giving word or name. Mawlana describes the nature and uses of the incantation in a two-part story based on 'Attar's *Ilahi Nama*. One of Jesus' companions asked the Messiah to teach him the name that makes the dead live, so that he might enliven a pile of bones lying in a roadside pit. When Jesus informed the man that the name was not for everyone to utter, he requested that Jesus himself pronounce the name. Jesus obliged, whereupon the bones became a lion which immediately sprang up and killed the man. The lion explained to Jesus that he had killed as a warning; he was not permitted to eat the man since that was not his allotted sustenance, and that was why the lion had been dead in the first place.[30]

Jesus had not taught the companion the name because the man's request was essentially unprofitable and he would only have abused the privilege (II:451–53). One must not casually put tools into the hands of those who do not know their proper use (II:307–9). Even if a fool should happen to learn the incantation, endless repetition would be useless to a person who has no love and whose folly is a disease resulting from God's wrath.[31] On the lips of Jesus the incantation was like the rod in the hand of Moses.[32] A human being is like the incantation: in form (i.e., only apparently) it is in the mouth of Jesus; in reality, it is in the hand of God. It is death's flight, not the form of word and sound, that matters (III:H.4258–62). Therefore the kind of life Jesus was able to restore to bodies was a pale imitation of the life to be obtained by one who abandons self utterly into the hands of a Friend of God.[33] Finally, 'Azar (Lazarus) appears as the only named individual whom Jesus raised to life. He is the type of the lover revivified by a word from the beloved. Jesus' raising of Lazarus is still inferior to the resurrection that occurs when a person accepts the gift of faith.[34]

The Table from Heaven: Another of Jesus' miraculous works finds a parallel in Moses' providing a boundless supply of food for his people. The table, after which Sura 5 of the Qur'an is named, descended from heaven at Jesus' request to assuage the hunger of those who are "fasting." Jesus continued to invite all and sundry to wash and share in the feast.[35] Because the original recipients of the Messianic bounty refused to believe, they were turned into apes and swine. Rumi cites them as an example of how breach of covenant is a cause of metamorphosis.[36]

Walking on Water: Mawlana makes several brief references to one more miracle based on a Gospel story. The Messiah walked on water as well as on land (II:1185; I:571–72); the "Spirit of God" danced on the sea like a waterbird (D 624:13). This miracle occurred as a result of Jesus' faith; but had his faith been greater, he would have become airborne as Muhammad was (VI:H.1186–88; AM 632).

The End of Jesus' Earthly Life

The Simulacrum: Rumi agrees with the traditional Muslim position on the Crucifixion, based on Q 4:156, namely that a substitute was crucified in Jesus' stead. Rumi believes the switch occurred as a "hidden grace of God." His account follows that of Baidawi. Jesus fled into a certain house to escape his enemies (D 598:6), and a Jewish amir followed him, hoping to seize Jesus and usurp his crown. Unable to find Jesus, the amir was himself seized and crucified because of his likeness to Jesus, a likeness which Baidawi says "God put upon him" (MCN VI:4367–70). In the *Diwan* Mawlana says in so many words that Muslims simply do not believe that the Messiah was slain on the cross (D 728:10).

The Ascension: Jesus, like the prophet Idris, ascended to the fourth heaven.[37] Ascension was possible for Jesus because, by virtue of his mind or reason, he was more akin to the angels than to the "donkey" of the body.[38] Unaided by reason, the ass is earthbound; but Jesus' donkey sprouted a pair of wings (D 1017:3/1172:6). "Reason gave Jesus wings," says Rumi quoting from Sana'i's *Diwan* (F 118/107) and the "celestial bird" (Gabriel) bore the prophet aloft.[39] Brother to all the prophets, Jesus shared in the light, which became his "ladder" (II:920).

Theological Dimensions

Jesus Was Not Divine

A Christian once claimed in Rumi's presence that he had heard some companions of Sadr ad-Din al-Qunawi agreeing that Jesus was indeed God. Of course, they could not assert that belief in public for fear it would divide the community. Rumi responded that it simply made no sense to insist that a form so frail and in such constant fear of the Jews could be the disposer and controller of all creation. Mawlana does call Jesus by the Qur'anic epithet "Spirit of God" (F 239/232; IV:H.113), and "pure spirit" (III:2581). Here the poet takes the occasion of his own discussion with the

Christian to clarify his use of those titles. The Christian's reply to Mawlana's first rebuttal was that Jesus was not all frail form, and that although his dust returned to dust, his spirit also returned to spirit. Against that tack Rumi marshaled two arguments. First, a spirit returns only to its Creator. If Jesus was the Creator, to whom could his spirit have departed? Second, if God sent a *nabi* greater than Jesus, one whom Jesus must therefore follow, Jesus could hardly be God. However, God has brought Jesus close to Himself, "so that whoever serves him has served the Lord, whoever obeys him has obeyed the Lord" (F 134–36/124–25).

Jesus' Intercession

In connection with the last point, Jesus' proximity to God allowed him to secure benefits for those to whom he ministered, through the prophetic privilege of intercession. In texts already cited, Rumi has stated that Jesus healed and raised the dead to life by prayer (III:H.298–304, 3504). Two additional passages talk of the intercessory nature of his prayer. Jesus made *shafa‘a* and God sent down an endless food supply for the table (I:83). Another story tells how an amir besought 'Imad al-Mulk to intercede with the sultan that the amir's horse not be confiscated. The amir said to 'Imad al-Mulk, "Since God has bestowed (on you) a (spiritual) connection (with Himself), stroke my head at once with your hand, O Messiah!" (VI:3380). Rumi says further that the 'Imad was a *shafi‘* (Intercessor) before the sultan (VI:3372) and was like a prophet (*payghambar*) in the sultan's eyes (III:3367). The connection with Jesus is clear.

The Religion of Jesus

Rumi's attitude toward Christianity appears chiefly in three stories about the followers of Jesus. Christians are in manifest ignorance when they persist in believing they can appeal to a crucified Lord for protection—especially since those from whom they are so often seeking refuge are the very Jews who undid Jesus in the first place. The implication of Rumi's argument is that the Muslim position, the doctrine of the "look-alike," makes much more sense in view of the historic durability of Christianity. The religion of Jesus has survived, and Christian prayers for protection have apparently been answered. That could be so only if Jesus were indeed still alive and, as Muslims believe, living in the fourth heaven (II:1401–04, MCN). Rumi's story of the Jewish, Christian, and Muslim fellow travelers puts this Muslim view of Jesus' present state in the mouth of the Christian, who boasts that the Messiah has visited him in a dream and taken him to the fourth heaven (VI:2453–54, 2487). It seems a trifle ironic, in view of all this, that Rumi would say that grape wine is for the community of Jesus, while the wine of Mansur (al-Hallaj, who was crucified) is for the community of Ya Sin (a title of Muhammad, D 81:3).

As the Jews were the archenemies of Jesus himself (D 3094:2), so they remained the nemesis of Jesus' followers. "The Messiah brings the dead to life, and the Jew tears his moustache in wrath" (II:420, 1863). Moses and Jesus were the "souls" of each other; but a certain Jewish king failed to recognize the accord of the two prophets and styled himself the defender of the faith of Moses as against that of Jesus. His crafty vizier devised a ruse by which to gain the confidence of the Christians. He then began to sow disaffection among them by jumbling their doctrines, and, finally, by appointing each of their twelve amirs as his own successor. When the vizier committed suicide, the Christians were left to squabble among themselves in hopeless confusion. Persecution was later renewed by a descendant of the first Jewish king. Mawlana identifies the wicked vizier as the Antichrist. The Antichrist of sadness reappears now and then, but in a world so full of Jesus, how can there be room for the Antichrist?[40]

One last characterization of Jesus' religion needs only a brief mention, since we shall treat it at greater length in the context of Muhammad's teachings. With their distinctive girdles (zunnar) to set them apart,[41] Christians tend to be "monkish" and withdrawn from the harsher realities of life. According to Rumi, "In our religion the right thing is combat and fear; in the religion of Jesus the right thing is cave and mountain."[42]

The Jesus of the Spirit

Two key texts, supported by several lesser references, develop the notion of Jesus' continuing relationship to the believer. Explaining how suffering can be a salutary experience and even necessary for growth, Rumi writes in Fihi Ma Fihi: "The body is like Mary. Every one of us has a Jesus within him, but until the pangs manifest in us our Jesus is not born. If the pangs never come, then Jesus rejoins his origin by the same secret path by which he came, leaving us bereft and without portion of him."[43] Jalal ad-Din also explores the more philosophical side of the relationship, in the Mathnawi. When the universal soul touches the individual soul, the latter becomes pregnant with a "heart-beguiling Messiah." In like fashion the whole world is impregnated and gives birth to another world, that of the Resurrection (II:1183–88). Both the shaykh and the mystic possess, or rather are, the Jesus of the spirit, for there are "many Messiahs inside the ass (of Jesus)" (VI:4584; IV:1065–68). In short, Rumi's advice is, "The Jesus of your spirit is present with you; beg aid from him, for he is an efficacious helper" (II:450).

Knowledge and Light

With the phrase "Jesus and the Ass," Rumi often refers to the antipathy between the authentic knower and the ignorant, the *'aql* and the *nafs*, the soul and the body.[44] The Jesus of soul sat on the donkey of body for the sake of humility (M 70/154; D 3426:9). Donkey is the enemy of knowledge and mystery, and the envier of Jesus, who possesses both *'ilm* and *ma'rifa*.[45] The donkey is able to benefit from the company of the intelligent (*'aqilan*) only when Jesus is firmly in control (II:1850–63). A person without intelligence, in whom the donkey dominates, is neither alive, that he might breathe like a Jesus, nor dead, that he might be a tool for demonstrating the life-giving breath. Such a person has no part with Jesus whatever (IV:2200).

Jesus possessed knowledge even before his time. God taught him before his birth (IV:3043), so that John's mother described the Messiah in the womb as *agahi* (endowed with knowledge, II:3603). As a babe in the cradle he was "old in understanding and knowledge" (*'aql* and *ma'rifa*, V:H.1271). So long as Jesus is master of the donkey, God and not barley will be his intoxication and he will be free from care (IV:2691; V:1094).

When Gabriel first spoke to Mary, the breath of his speech was a "wick of pure light" (III:3770); from that same light the Lady became pregnant (V:3856). As prophet, Jesus offered his light to all the blind who admit they are in need of spiritual guidance (VI:4115-18). Jesus' ladder to the fourth heaven (VI:920) was also the "dying vat of a single hue" through which Jesus rendered the vat of a hundred dyes superfluous, by making the hundred-colored garment the color of light.[46]

CHAPTER 7

The Muhammad of History

We will discuss Jalal ad-Din's extensive treatment of the Prophet Muhammad in two sections: the first on the Muhammad of History, the second on the Ahmad of Faith. Rumi probably did not think of the Prophet's significance as falling so neatly into halves this way,[1] but it seems clear enough that the poet was very much aware of Muhammad both as an historical figure and as a ongoing presence. We therefore use the distinction somewhat as Rumi might have used that between outward and inward meanings, except that Rumi always has the inward meaning in view no matter what his subject

The present chapter will relate the pertinent material in Rumi's works to the three major chronological divisions of Muhammad's life (the years before his prophetic mission, and the Makkan and Madinan periods), and then discuss the poet's interpretation of Muhammad's personality and teachings. In the next chapter we will investigate the key theological and traditional aspects of the Prophet's relationship with God, the various proofs of his prophethood, his names and titles, his place among the prophets, and his relationship to the individual believer.[2]

Muhammad's Personal History

Before the Call

Of the first forty years of Muhammad's life Rumi says very little. In his only extended reference to the time before Muhammad became the Prophet, Mawlana elaborates on a story included in Ibn Ishaq's *Sira*. He describes how Muhammad's nurse Halima brought the child back to Makka, to return him to his relatives after she had weaned him. As Halima entered the precincts of the Ka'ba, she was entranced by a voice that called out from the "unseen world" and addressed the holy sanctuary:

> . . .O Hatim [the area on one side of the Ka'ba partially enclosed by
> a low semicircular wall], a most brilliant Sun has shone upon you.
> O Hatim, today there will suddenly come upon you a hundred
> thousand beams from the Sun of munificence.
> O Hatim, today there will march into you with pomp a glorious
> King, whose harbinger is Fortune.
> O Hatim, today without doubt you will become anew the abode of
> exalted spirits.
> The spirits of the holy will come to you from every quarter in troops
> and multitudes, drunken with desire. (IV:919–23)

The nurse put the child down and went to find the voice's source. When
she returned the boy had vanished mysteriously.[3] Halima went distraught
from one person to another, seeking news of the lost Pearl. An old man
whom she encountered presented Halima to the goddess al-'Uzza and
made petition on the nurse's behalf. When the idols heard the name of
Muhammad they fell prostrate and besought the elder to leave and afflict
them no more with that name. 'Abd al-Muttalib, the child's grandfather,
received word of the boy's disappearance and went immediately to the
Ka'ba to pray. He said:

> "O You who know the secret of night and the mystery of day, I see
> no accomplishment in myself, that one like me should be your
> confidant.
> I see no merit in myself, that I should be welcomed at this auspicious
> door, Or that my (bowed) head and my prostration (in prayer)
> should have any worth, or that because of my tears any fortune
> should smile (upon me); But in the countenance of that unique
> Pearl (Muhammad) I have beheld the signs of your grace, O
> Bounteous One;
> For he does not resemble us, though he is from among us: we are the
> copper, while Ahmad is the Elixir.
> The wondrous things that I have seen in him I have not seen in friend
> or enemy.
> None, (even) with a hundred years' endeavor would (be able to)
> describe what your bounty has bestowed on him in childhood.
> Since I saw with (intuitive) certainty your favors towards him, (I
> know that) he is a pearl of your ocean.
> Him I bring (forward) to plead with you: tell me his plight, O you
> who know (every) plight!" (IV:986–95)

From within the Ka'ba came an encomium of the world's preeminent child and an assurance that 'Abd al-Muttalib would discover his grandson under a tree in a wadi.[4]

With this story Rumi reasserts an ancient parallel between Muhammad and the earlier prophets whose lives were imperiled in early youth, or who were declared even as infants to be marked for greatness, or whose very name could destroy idols: Moses, Abraham, Jesus, and John.

The Makkan Period

Muhammad's Inaugural Revelation: According to Ibn Ishaq (SN 105) it was Muhammad's custom to spend one month each year in seclusion on Mount Hira. During such a retreat he received his first revelation. Rumi does not always distinguish clearly, in his lengthier treatments of Muhammad's encounters with the revealing God, between the Prophet's vision of Gabriel on Mount Hira and his meeting with the angel on the night of the Ascension. One can attribute Mawlana's blending of the two experiences in several texts to his interpretation of Sura 53, an-Najm (The Star), which seems to place the two visions together. Here we shall be concerned only with the earlier of the two experiences; we shall consider the Mi'raj separately in the next chapter.

Muhammad's periods of solitude on Hira sometimes found him in severe distress due to Gabriel's delayed appearance. Rumi's language throughout his sections on the Prophet and Gabriel suggests that even before the night of the first definitive revelation, Muhammad had known the presence of God through, or otherwise in connection with, the presence of the angel. Whenever Muhammad's sense of separation and isolation became particularly intense, he would think of throwing himself from the mountain. At just such moments Gabriel would appear in person to dissuade the man from acting rashly. Mawlana speaks several times of the angel as the Prophet's comforter, the one who assured Muhammad that a special destiny was being forged for him and that it would soon become apparent. The poet seems to suggest that Muhammad had to endure a period of purification before at last "the veil was lifted, so that he gained the pearl (of his desire) from the bosom (of his inmost consciousness)." He notes, however, that it was only Muhammad's body, his "foam," that needed Gabriel's solace. As Rumi makes clear in the context of the Mi'raj, the Prophet's spirit, his "sea," was far greater than that of the angel.[5]

On the "Night of Power" (Qadr) Gabriel mediated the initial revelation to Muhammad. It was the night on which "all human the needs are granted" (D 1201:6), and from which all human attempts to communicate, and all other nights, take their meaning.[6] On that night, Muhammad's mission (*risala*) "came into the *mihrab* of his ear from the *qibla* of spirit" (D 645:7). On that night Muhammad also had a vision of a form traditionally said to have been Gabriel; the apparition came "two bows' length or nearer" according to Q 53:9. Rumi often recalls the events of the Night of Power by alluding to those words of the Qur'an.[7]

Thus began Muhammad's career as Prophet and recipient of revelation. Shortly thereafter, says tradition, Muhammad went to his wife Khadija and had her wrap him in a cloak, perhaps in the manner of the pre-Islamic *kahin*. We turn now to Mawlana's commentary on a very early Makkan Sura, one addressed to al-Muzammil, "the one wrapped up."

Commentary on al-Muzammil: Rumi interprets Sura 73 as a commissioning of Muhammad as Prophet. He interprets the "cloak" as a refuge from which the Prophet must be called forth, as a candle set in the sight of those who live in the dark. The poet has God entitle Muhammad a Noah and a Khizr, and the Lord cautions the Prophet not to practice the solitude of Jesus. He must lead the blind, dispel sorrow, raise the "sands of the dead" from the earth, and be himself a proof of the Resurrection (IV:H.1453–83). Such is the Prophet's mandate. However, Mawlana's interpretation and imagery, especially that of the moon (IV:1464–66), suggest that although the text is labeled *Tafsir-i ya ayyuha 'l-muzammil*, the poet may actually have had Sura 74 al-Muddaththir in mind as well. In the latter text, Muhammad is literally called forth to "Arise and warn"; in Sura 73, on the contrary, he receives instructions precisely on how to keep solitary vigil (Q 74:1ff.; 73:1–6). In the *Mathnawi* God tells the Prophet, "arise and blow on the terrible trumpet" (IV:1478); and Sura 74:8 reads, "For when the trumpet shall sound. . . ." Finally, Rumi's image of Muhammad as moon (IV:1464–66) is reminiscent of the striking Qur'anic asseverative, "By the moon . . ." which occurs in al-Muddaththir (v. 35).

Early Converts and Companions: Tradition generally identifies 'Ali, Zayd, and Abu Bakr as the first three male converts to Islam. Their order of acceptance of the faith is disputed; but we will follow the order just given, which is that of Ibn Ishaq. Two later converts, 'Umar and Muhammad's uncle Hamza, along with the Prophet's uncle Abu Talib— an important figure even though he never converted—also figure in Rumi's accounts.[8] Another uncle, 'Abbas, became a Muslim after the Battle of Badr and will appear later in the section on the Prophet's military engagements.

Muhammad's relationship to 'Ali, and its manifold interpretations, could quickly draw us beyond the scope of this investigation. Suffice it to note here only three images that pertain directly to the development of Rumi's prophetology. The Prophet once told 'Ali that even though he was a lion, he must not rely solely on his own ingenuity, but must seek to associate with God's "chosen servant." Rumi then proceeds to extol the virtue of the *pir*-pupil relationship.[9] 'Ali was cautioned further that he must know how to keep special knowledge secret; and if he absolutely could not contain it, he must sigh it into a well, lest the secret fall on unappreciative ears.[10]

Most importantly, Rumi views 'Ali as an extension of Muhammad's prophethood, and as the initiator of a new phase of the divine dispensation. The prophet said, "My cousin 'Ali is the protector and friend of every one who is under my protection" (VI:4539; AM 736). A protector (*mawla*) is one who liberates. One can therefore say that 'Ali participates in Muhammad's prophethood, for it is *nubuwwa* that leads people to freedom (VI:H.4538–41). 'Ali becomes, then, the model of those who wisely seek companionship with the holy, in virtue of his share in the mission and special knowledge of Muhammad. 'Ali was "the pride of every prophet and every Friend of God" (I:3723; I:3984–85).

Zayd ibn Haritha's conversion provides Rumi with a dual-purpose story. Through that story the poet first describes the exalted gift of discrimination that infuses the eye of every believer, and then elaborates on the point just made about 'Ali regarding the relationship of the Companions to the prophethood of Muhammad. One day the Prophet asked his freedman Zayd (MMec 86) how he was. Zayd answered that he had become a believer. When Ahmad asked him to present some proof of his newfound faith, Zayd went on to tell of a spiritual journey in which he had passed beyond time and space. As a "traveler's gift" the freedman had brought back with him an ability to distinguish believer from infidel, the saved from the damned, whether born or unborn. Though Zayd could scarcely contain his new knowledge and was most eager to tell everyone about the Resurrection, Muhammad advised him to "shackle his Buraq" for awhile. God wanted to keep the veil drawn, the Prophet explained, for the keeper of a border fortress (*ribat*) is all the more vigilant in watching the fort for his distance from the king (I:3635–37). He assured Zayd however, that his gift would not be without consequence. As Companion of the Prophet, Zayd would give starlike guidance, genuine but ephemeral; for stars give witness to the sun, but when the sun appears, no one will think to ask about the stars.[11]

Abu Bakr's acceptance of the faith was the result of the Prophet's looking at him and of his gazing back upon the face of Muhammad. Without insisting on a miracle, Abu Bakr believed spontaneously that the Prophet spoke only the truth (IV:351) and thus received the name *Siddiq*.[12] In Muhammad's face the *Siddiq* saw a sun "neither of East nor of West" (I:2367; Q 24:35) and became a prime witness to the Resurrection (VI:747–53). For that reason Muhammad paid Abu Bakr the supreme compliment of holding him up as the example of one who has "died before death" (VI:742–49). The older man conceived an affection for the Prophet that would make him Muhammad's spiritual kin and counselor (IV:2654), who would later support the embattled Messenger in his most difficult hour. Abu Bakr described his love for Muhammad with images of earlier prophets:

> I sought a Joseph comely and with limbs (white as) silver: in you I
>   beheld an assembly of Josephs.
> I was (engaged) in searching after Paradise: from every part of you a
>   Paradise appeared (to me).
> In relation to me this is praise and eulogy; in relation to you this is
>   vituperation and satire,
> Like the praise given to God by the simple shepherd in the presence
>   of Moses the Kalim—
> "I will seek out your lice, I will give you milk, I will repair your
>   shoes and lay them before you."
> God accepted his vituperation as an expression of praise: if you also
>   have mercy, it will be no marvel.
> Have mercy upon the failure of (our) minds (to comprehend you), O
>   you who are beyond (all) understanding and conception.
>   (VI:1088–94).

We shall return later to Abu Bakr's important supporting role during the Hijra.

Islam's second caliph, 'Umar, appears often in the *Mathnawi* as a personality in his own right; but we shall speak of him here only in relation to Muhammad. *Fihi Ma Fihi* tells how 'Umar, enraged at finding his own sister reading the Qur'an, set off to the Prophet's mosque planning to kill Muhammad. Gabriel meanwhile alerted the Prophet to 'Umar's intentions; 'Umar was coming to convert to Islam. An arrow of light pierced

'Umar's heart as he burst into the mosque, and he was hopelessly smitten with affection for the Prophet. Upon regaining his senses the future Commander of the Faithful asked that he might receive the faith.[13] 'Umar became an example of how sin can lead one to the door of belief and devoted service of the Prophet (I:77, 3832).

'Umar's *metanoia* prompts Mawlana to expose further the inner workings of the phenomenon of conversion. In the story of 'Umar and the Ambassador, the details of which are otherwise not germane to our topic, the poet fashions an ingenious play on words. Juxtaposing the spiritual quest with the intellectual, Mawlana writes:

> At the time when the intellectual quest was in keeping (with the
>   circumstances), this 'Umar was intimate with Bu 'l-Hakam
>   [Father of Wisdom],
> (But) when 'Umar went away from intellect towards spirit, Bu
>   'l-Hakam became Bu Jahl [Father of Ignorance] in searching into
>   that (subject) (I:1503–4).

The irony so cleverly heightened by the wordplay is yet further underscored by the prominent mention of Muhammad's constant prayer prior to 'Umar's conversion. "God assist my religion by means of 'Umar or Abu Jahl" (F 171/163). Abu Jahl, who will reappear shortly, and his nephew 'Umar had both been such formidable adversaries to Muhammad that either one would surely have made a redoubtable ally. Destiny selected the better of the two.

Muhammad was not so pleasantly surprised by his Uncle Abu Talib as he was by the abrupt reversals of Zayd and 'Umar. Rumi records a conversation in which the Prophet tried to move his longtime protector to a deathbed conversion (SN 191–92). Abu Talib declined, however, for fear that the Arabs would laugh and accuse him of confessing under pressure. Mawlana explains that Muhammad's uncle was one of those people who are in love with the Creator, but who are hindered by the evil eye or ear from trusting Him entirely. "But if the predestined grace had been (granted) to him, how should his faint-heartedness have existed (simultaneously) with God's pull (towards Himself)?" (VI:193–99). Mawlana's account mentions one feature of special prophetological importance, in agreement with Ibn Ishaq. Muhammad told Abu Talib that if he would profess the faith, the Prophet would plead with God for him (VI:196). Ahmad's intercessory role will catch our attention again in the final section of chapter 8.

Hamza, another of the Prophet's uncles, had a reputation for bravery in battle. Ibn Ishaq calls him "the strongest man of the Quraysh, and the most unyielding" (SN 131), and Rumi does not hesitate to call him a companion of the classic Iranian hero Rustam (D 738:9; 2141:3). Hamza submitted to God one day after he heard that Abu Jahl had insulted the Messenger of God without provocation. Seeking to redress the injury done his nephew, Hamza asked Abu Jahl, "Will you insult him when I follow his religion . . . ?" Ibn Ishaq notes that, notwithstanding Hamza's apparently ulterior motives, his Islam (surrender) was complete. Rumi has the uncle describe his own faith by saying, ". . . through the light of Muhammad, I am not subject to this city (world) that is passing away. Beyond (the realm of) the senses, I behold the camp of the king thronged with the army of the light of God" (III:3431–32).

Opposition in Makka: Muhammad was as out of place among the unbelievers as spirit in a rubbish heap (D 2400:6). God had warned the Prophet in a revelation to sit only among lovers, for though the world is warmed by fire, fire dies in the company of ashes (R 907). Rumi's imagery leaves no doubt as to his interpretation of a trying time in the Messenger's early mission. As the Makkans began to take Muhammad more and more seriously, they redoubled their efforts to discredit him. Some taunted the Prophet, saying, "Why does the Qur'an come down upon Muhammad word by word? Why not chapter by chapter?"[14] When the Prophet spoke with his Companions he became accustomed to speaking cryptically, so as to keep his adversaries ignorant of his real meaning (I:1052–54). To Muhammad's sole attempt to reach a theological compromise with his adversaries, now enshrined in the so-called Satanic Verses, Rumi alludes only in passing; but he does say explicitly that the Prophet's lapse was a momentary temptation from the Devil, and not part of revelation.[15]

Increasing pressure from his Makkan critics seems to have given Muhammad second thoughts about his mission. He needed reassurance; it came to him in the form of Sura 68, al-Qalam (The Pen), and other similar revelations. Commenting on this very early Makkan Sura, Mawlana speaks of the "evil eye" by which Muhammad's enemies tried to trip him up. They had apparently persuaded an *'ayyan* of the Banu Asad to cast the evil eye on the Prophet. Such an eye from the wicked could make even a mountain like the Prophet lose his footing. Verse fifty-one of Surat al-Qalam was revealed at that moment: "those who disbelieve would disconcert you with their eyes when they hear the Reminder. . . ." The opening words of the verse (*wa in yakad*) have thus become popular as a spell against the evil eye. For the Prophet, the revelation was an assurance that if the same evil eye had been cast upon anyone but him, it would have utterly destroyed that unfortunate person. As it was, Muhammad's "stumbling" was meant to be a sign "that none but God can preserve His creatures from being smitten by the powers of evil" (V:498–511; MCN V:504).

Nothing better epitomizes Ahmad's antipathy to the infidel Makkans than his relations with Abu Jahl and Abu Lahab (D 3061:3). Little love was lost between the Prophet and his acerbic uncle nicknamed Abu Lahab, the "Father of Flame." Rumi often plays off Bu Lahab's deceitfulness against Muhammad's sincerity.[16] The spiteful man "chewed thistles" when he saw Muhammad split the moon (II:420; III:2043). Rumi refers also to Sura 111, al-Masad, in which Abu Lahab and his wife enjoy an unenviable prominence—husband bound for the fire, and wife bound with a collar of palm-fibre and bearing the fire-wood.[17] Bu Lahab's entirely negative response to the prophetic message stands in marked contrast to the response of Abu Hurayra, on the one hand, and by comparison with that of Abu Jahl on the other. The poet writes:

> I saw Bu Lahab there biting hard his hand, Bu Hurayra putting his
>   hand in his own wallet;
> Bu Lahab was like the back (and no back sees the face), Bu Hurayra
>   turning his face to his own moon and seventh heaven;
> Bu Lahab plunged in thought, seeking proof and demonstration, Bu
>   Hurayra his own proof and his own demonstration.[18]

The strident "Father of Flame" was as much akin to the Father of Ignorance as he was different from the docile Abu Hurayra, and "Bu Lahab became the counsellor of Bu Jahl" (IV:2654).

As "general of the army of iniquity" (VI:2165), Abu Jahl became Rumi's second major example of opposition to the Prophet (D 704:14). Abu Jahl's friends were Muhammad's enemies (VI:1894–95). Though his own son was to become a firm believer (I:3401), Bu Jahl himself refused to be impressed by "a hundred cleavings of the moon," for he was not "in sympathy" (II:2060). Muhammad and Bu Jahl looked alike on the surface, but the similarity ended there. Divine grace elevated the Prophet (F 223/215; I:1019), while envy reduced an Abu l-Hakam to an Abu Jahl (I:808–9), leaving him fit only to be regarded as the paradigm of bodily existence. Muhammad was intellect and Jahl was the senses (I:782; II:1605). Consequently, when Ahmad entered the temple, the idols fell;

when Abu Jahl entered, he himself fell (IV:816–17). Finally, Bu Jahl was as adamant in his unbelief as Abu Bakr was receptive in his truthful witnessing. Abu Bakr needed no miracle; Abu Jahl never ceased to demand miracles (IV:350–51). Abu Bakr saw only beauty in Muhammad; Abu Jahl saw only ugliness, for he was unaware that Ahmad is a mirror (I:2365–68).

Commentary on Sura 80, 'Abasa: In the context of the Prophet's dealing with Makkans, and especially of his considerable interest in converting the more influential of the Quraysh, Rumi's interpretation of the early Makkan Surat 'Abasa ("He frowned") finds an appropriate place. While the Messenger was conversing with one of the Quraysh, a poor blind man approached and sought instruction in the faith. Muhammad was so "eager for the great ones to take the right way, in order that the common folk may learn from the rulers" (II:2069), that he frowned upon the blind man and said, "This gathering (of strangers) seldom falls out so opportunely, (whereas) you are one of my friends, and your time is ample. You are urgent with me at an inconvenient time. I give you this admonition, (but) not in anger and strife." [19]

Jalal ad-Din expands on the text of the Qur'an by giving the reader Muhammad's words to the blind man. Secondly, the poet embellishes God's rebuke of the Prophet; he softens the reproach by adding warm tones to the stark finish of the Qur'anic version. In addition, Mawlana allows the Prophet to defend his actions. Rumi has Muhammad respond to God's admonition by saying that he is not all that concerned with winning the approval of the high and mighty. On the contrary, he views their displeasure as proof positive of his prophethood. Let Mawlana's imagery in this prophetic self-defense speak for itself:

> . . . I am unconcerned with the acknowledgment of the world: what
> care (for the world) has one whose witness is God?
> If a bat receives anything agreeable (to it) from a sun, that is proof
> that that (sun) is not the (real) sun.
> The disgust of the wretched bats is a proof that I am the shining and
> glorious sun.
> If the beetle feels a desire for some (particular) rosewater, that is
> proof that it is not rosewater.
> If any false coin is eager for the touchstone, it casts uncertainty and
> doubt on its being a touchstone.
> The thief wants night, not day—mark this! I am not night, I am day,
> for I shine throughout the world.

I am discerning, I am exceedingly discriminating and sieve-like, so
   that the chaff finds no passage through me.
I make the flour distinct from the bran, in order to show that this is
   the (external) forms, and that the (inward) souls (essences).
I am the scales of God in the world: I distinguish every light thing
   from the heavy.
A calf deems the cow God; the ass (deems God) one who is fond (of
   it) and that which accords with its desires.
I am not a cow, that the calf should be fond of me; I am not thistles,
   that a camel should browse on me.
He (the unbeliever) supposes that he has done me an injury; on the
   contrary, he has wiped away the dust from my mirror.
   (II:2068–94, quoting 2083–94)

The Story of Bilal: Muhammad's early followers endured much for
their faith. Stories of their physical pains have no doubt been amplified,
since the Qur'an makes no obvious mention of followers' being killed or
tortured. But of those who are said to have been maltreated, none is more
important for Rumi than Bilal.[20]

Bilal's Jewish slave master sometimes flogged him. At each stroke the
slave would cry, "*Ahad, Ahad!*" (i.e., "one, one"). Imagining that Bilal
was praising *Ahmad*, the master's wrath mounted. Abu Bakr happened
one day to be in the vicinity and heard Bilal's shout. Shortly thereafter he
went to the slave and advised prudent silence, since God already knew his
heart's desire without his having to publicize it so boldly. Next day, the
Siddiq again heard the cry and again counseled Bilal, but to no avail;
"Love came and consumed his repentance" (VI:897) and the slave could
no longer conceal his affection for the Prophet. Ahmad would later return
the favor, and, after returning from his Ascension, say to Bilal, "How dear
to me (you are), how dear!" (VI:951).

In the meantime, however, Abu Bakr informed Muhammad of Bilal's
straits—the owls were tormenting the Sultan's falcon. Siddiq described
how he had advised Bilal to repent of his public confession, but how the
worm of repentance had been no match for the dragon of love. As Abu
Bakr told the story to the delighted Prophet, "Every hair of him (Abu
Bakr) became a separate tongue" (VI:985). Muhammad resolved to buy
Bilal and sent Abu Bakr as his agent to make the purchase. Siddiq offered
to trade one of his white Jewish slaves for the black Bilal. The Jewish
slave owner demanded two hundred dirhems over and above that, and they
closed the deal, with the Jew believing he had swindled Abu Bakr. That

Jew had the same undiscriminating eye with which the brothers had looked upon Joseph. When the emaciated (lit. "toothpick") Bilal came to Muhammad, the Prophet embraced him and addressed him with words that would turn night into day. So the toothpick "found his way into a mouth: he was hastening towards a man of sweet tongue." [21]

Bilal had a sweet tongue of his own, and thus became the Prophet's first *muezzin*. Muhammad would call, "Revive us, O Bilal!/ O melodious sweet-voiced Bilal, go up into the minaret, beat the drum of departure (for the spiritual journey)." [22] When he stopped for a respite from that journey, Muhammad became so beside himself at the sound of Bilal that he failed to perform the ritual dawn-prayer (I:1989–90). It is hardly surprising, then, that the Prophet was able to overlook a minor defect in Bilal's Arabic pronunciation and angrily defend the *muezzin* against his sour-grapes critics. Out of fervor Bilal was used to calling *hayya* rather than *ḥayya* (i.e., mispronouncing the "ḥ" sound, thus speaking unintelligible Arabic instead of *"be alive to* the ritual prayer, *rise* to success"); but "a fault committed by lovers is better than propriety from strangers" (III:H.172–79). Any lover who hears Bilal's call is enabled to grasp the cloak of Muhammad (D 1354:11). The same Bilal who had once professed his faith openly at great risk was now commissioned to shout it from the minaret (VI:1099–1101). Bilal, once thin as a *hilal* (crescent moon, VI:904), now became a *hilal* (new moon) to the sun of Ahmad (VI:1098). Weakness and age would again make Bilal a *hilal* of skin and bones, but he would die rejoicing: his body was only a cloud, his spirit the moon (III:H.3517–33).

The Hijra: In the Prophet's emigration from, and return to, Makka, Mawlana sees the model of the mystical journey. As such, wayfaring was also integral to the experience of prophets before Muhammad. As Joseph had to undertake the journey into the well of separation from his father, and Moses from his mother to Midian, so Muhammad had to journey to Yathrib from Makka. As Joseph was amply compensated for his pains with lordship over Egypt and ultimate return to his father, and Moses with leadership of Israel, so Muhammad at length gained victory over Makka and kingship of a hundred lands (D 1142:6; 214:10). Of the Hijra itself Rumi has singled out one detail and transformed it into an image of the lover/beloved relationship. Abu Bakr accompanied Muhammad on the road from Makka to Madina and is traditionally considered to have been the "second of the two" who spent time in a cave along the way. [23] Abu Bakr's loyalty and affection for Muhammad, as mentioned earlier, kept the Siddiq by the Prophet's side through the most trying circumstances (D 738:6; 2220:14). On the way to Madina the two stayed in the cave as in a heart, where a spider had spun its web as a concealment.[24] There the Sufi Abu Bakr was disciple to the Master Muhammad (D 2275:17). Mawlana often alludes simply to the "Friend" or "Friends of the Cave." "Friend" always refers to Abu Bakr, but occasionally, in a reversal of roles, Abu Bakr is the image of the shaykh.[25] For keeping the Prophet's secret in the cave, Abu Bakr is with him in the seventh heaven (D 859:7).

The Madinan Period

Muhammad and 'A'isha: Rumi tells of two dialogues between the Prophet and his young wife 'A'isha. Both stories play on the hidden meanings of sight and vision.

Muhammad went to a burial one day. When he returned, 'A'isha was amazed to find her husband's clothes still dry, for she had "seen" rain fall that day. When she revealed to Muhammad that she had that day used a garment of his as her head covering, the Prophet explained that she had experienced the "rain of the unseen" (I:H.2012–34). That rain, Muhammad continued, was a trickle of intelligence sent down to quench the fires of grief and selfish desire and forgetfulness (I:H.2060–70). Another day a blind man paid a visit to the Prophet's home. 'A'isha quickly went into hiding as the guest entered. Later Muhammad asked her why she had run away to avoid being seen by a man who was unable to see. 'A'isha responded with an inverted version of one of Muhammad's own hadiths, "If you do not see Him (i.e., God), He sees you." 'A'isha said, "(If) he does not see (me), yet I see him." In other words, 'A'isha felt there was still reason to suspect her husband might be jealous. As Rumi explains, reason is jealous of spirit no matter how hidden the spirit may be (VI:H.670–91).

Muhammad's Relations with the Factions of Madina: One of the first tasks facing the Prophet upon his arrival in Yathrib was that of orchestrating a working truce among the city's many feuding parties. Several of those factions are featured in Rumi's portrait of Muhammad, notably the Helpers, the Hypocrites who built the Mosque of Opposition, and the Jewish and Bedouin Tribes.

The Prophet enjoyed his most notable success in enlisting the support of a group that came to be known as the Ansar, the Helpers. By the light of Islam the Messenger managed to pacify the inimical Aws and Khazraj tribes to such an extent that, "First, those enemies became brethren like the units of grapes in the garden; and (then) at the admonition given in the words, 'The true believers are brothers,' they dissolved and became one body."[26] So steadfast were the Ansar in their loyalty to Muhammad that Rumi does not hesitate to associate their name with "the everlasting light" (I:1545).

Muhammad's dealings with the Munafiqun, the "hypocrites," appear to have been rather like a game of cat and mouse. The image is doubly appropriate here, since the word *munafiq* originally connoted a "cowardly rodent" (MMed 184). Quoting 59:14, Mawlana writes that,

> God has said of the unrighteous Hypocrites, "Their valor amongst
>   themselves is a great valor."
> Among one another they are courageous, (but) in a warlike
>   expedition they are as the women of the house. (III:4002–3).

Muhammad and the Munafiqun waged a cold war against each other, but never a pitched battle. The Hypocrites used sarcasm and withdrawal of support at crucial moments as their chief weapons. Not unlike the Pharisees of the New Testament, the Hypocrites seem always to appear conveniently at meetings of the Prophet and his Companions, with criticism at the ready. They disliked Muhammad's designation of 'Ali as a *mawla*, for they were angered at the suggestion of subservience to a "snivelling child" (VI:H.4538). Attempting to undermine the faith, "they used to put on the prayer-robe, in order to make those who imitated the ritual slack in the way of religion" (F 97/85; VI:2234). Even when they praised the Prophet, or perhaps especially then, Muhammad became suspicious of their motives. He was wont to instruct his Companions at such time, by a sort of code, to "conceal wisdom from strangers, and in their presence stop your mouths and tongues, for they are mice and are not worthy of this wisdom and grace" (F 82–83/70).

In their game of "odd and even" against Muhammad, the Hypocrites' boldest ploy was their construction of the "mosque of opposition." Rumi's story is an embellishment of Q 9:108–11, of which the first verse says: "And as for those who chose a place of worship out of opposition and disbelief, and in order to cause dissent among the believers, and as an outpost for those who warred against God and His Messenger, they will surely swear: We intended only good. God witnesses that in fact they are liars." Approaching the Prophet with fraudulent intent, the Hypocrites praised him and begged him to come visit their newly completed mosque. Their guile was as conspicuous as "hairs in milk," but Muhammad preferred to

be courteous and accept the invitation, saying "bravo to the milk"
(II:2852). As the Messenger was preparing to set out for the mosque, God
warned him not to go because the mosque was part of the Hypocrites'
scheme to rend the community and bring in a Syrian Jewish preacher who
would inflame the Madinan Jews. Muhammad decided to postpone his
visit until after he should return from a planned military action at Tabuk.
When the Hypocrites came back to restate their invitation, Muhammad
was prepared to expose their treachery. They vehemently denied the
Prophet's allegations, swearing oath upon oath. Each time, the Prophet
called them liars. Mawlana concludes the story by likening the Munafiqun
to the Christian Abyssinians who had tried to lure Muslims away from the
Umma by building a Ka'ba in San'a (Yemen) to compete with the Makkan
sanctuary (II:H.2825–2905).

Jalal ad-Din alludes only infrequently to Muhammad's relations with
the Jews of Madina. As mentioned above, Rumi quotes from Q 59:14,
which Nicholson believes referred to the tribe of Nadir as well as to their
allies, the Hypocrites (MCN III:4002). One text specifically mentions
Nadir and Qurayza together, and describes how Muhammad conquered
them as he retreated from Hudaybiya. Rumi attempts there to explain how
one could still interpret the action at Hudaybiya as a victory for the
Prophet. Rumi appears, however, to have erred in his chronology, for
Muhammad had defeated those tribes before Hudaybiya. After Hudaybiya
it was "Khaybar and other Jewish settlements in the north" that fell to the
retreating Messenger. Aside from two explicit mentions of Khaybar, Rumi
says nothing specific about Jewish tribes.[27]

Two brief stories describe one instance of Muhammad's treatment of an
unspecified group of Jews. They illustrate in a general way Muslim-
Jewish relations in the Prophet's day. The first story is based on Q 2:88–90
and 62:6–7:

> They (the Jews) said, "Our hearts are the covers of the book," but
>   God curses their unbelief; they believe little. And when a book
>   comes to them from God . . . they refuse to believe it. . . .
> Say (O Muhammad): O Jews! If you claim that God has chosen you
>   above all other persons, then long for death if you speak the truth.
>   But they will never long for it because of all that their own hands
>   have brought about.

In Mawlana's story, the Prophet gave some Jewish captives the option of
asking to be killed immediately. If they chose death they would give proof
of their alleged belief in Paradise; but if they refused death, they would

testify to the emptiness of their faith (I:3967–73). They preferred to become *dhimmis* ("protected community") and remain alive. This account illustrates the poet's belief that "a star (of divine illumination) appeared in Muhammad, so that the substance of (the beliefs of) Zoroastrian and Jew passed away" (V:3397).

Ahmad among the Jews and Zoroastrians was like a Friend of God hidden in the body of the world (D 940:8, MPR1 122). Muhammad's treatment at the hands of the Jews was like that which the prophet Salih had received in the prison of Thamud (III:406). Jews and Zoroastrians (Gabr) are not, however, entirely excluded from the Prophet's light (D 792:4), even though the acknowledgment of Muhammad's light is precisely what distinguishes a Muslim from a Jew (D 1506:6). Conversions from Judaism were not unheard of in the Prophet's own time, as Mawlana suggests in the following story. A Jew lived next door to one of the Companions. Dirt from the Jew's upper room was continually falling through into the Muslim's house. But whenever the Muslim met the Jew, he thanked him. One day the Jew came to visit the Muslim. When he saw how much dirt fell through the ceiling, he asked why the Muslim kept thanking him. Muslims were taught always to be grateful, replied the Muslim. The Jew was so impressed that he became a believer.[28]

As the Prophet gained influence over more territory, he had to deal diplomatically with more and more special interest groups. A delegation of Arab amirs once came to Muhammad and asked him to share his kingdom with them, since their amirate was as much a gift of God as his was. Muhammad agreed, but added that his amirate was given as a possession until the Resurrection, whereas theirs was merely on loan to them. The amirs were incensed and insinuated that the Messenger had no grounds for his grandiose claim. To provide a setting for a test of the respective claims, God raised a cloud and flooded the area so that the town was endangered. Each amir threw his lance at the torrent, but the flood swept the lances away as though they were bits of straw. Then Muhammad threw his wand. It prevailed against the water, and this Moses *redivivus* established an unchallenged hegemony among the Bedouins (IV:H.2779–2801).

The Prophet and Jihad: Mawlana gives considerable attention to Muhammad's involvement in combat, both military and spiritual. All of his bellicose activities were wholly justified in that they were done on God's behalf and thus, in the final analysis, became the "pivot of peace" (VI:64–65; I:3866–67). However much his antagonists might goad him to justifiable anger, the Prophet would not counsel war without God's inspiration to do so. Muhammad was most patient and lenient with the unbelievers (M 102/205) even though

> They put their hands to the sword and continued to come and molest and insult his Companions. The Prophet . . . said, "Be patient, so that they may not say that they have prevailed over us. They desire by force to make the religion manifest. God will make manifest this religion." For some time the Companions prayed secretly and pronounced in secret the name of Mustafa. . . . Then after a while the inspiration came: "You too unsheathe the sword and make war." (F 151/142)

In every case Muhammad's actions were justified because he was always the wronged party (F 64/52). When Muhammad had to face terrifying odds, God would cause the enemy to seem insignificant to him so that he would not shrink from the conflict (II:2292–2300). Outward warfare, the lesser jihad, was ultimately only an obstacle to be removed before one could concentrate more fully on the inward warfare, the greater jihad (I:1387). This emphasis shaped Muhammad's most characteristic attitude toward Christianity. One must wage jihad; but Christianity, with its "monkery," attempts to remove the enemies of lust and desire, thus voiding jihad of its significance, since "heroism cannot be displayed against the dead" (V:H.574–78).

Rumi speaks often of various episodes in Muhammad's lesser jihad but he emphasizes always the inner meaning of the episodes. The Battle of Badr went in favor of the Muslims because Iblis in disguise had convinced the Makkan Quraysh that they could win easily (III:H.4036, MCN). After the battle the victorious Muslims took a number of captives. Mawlana finds great significance in the episode and refers to it often. Against the wishes of many of his Companions, Muhammad chose to let the prisoners live; and as he surveyed the band of fearful infidels, the Prophet laughed. The prisoners immediately supposed Muhammad was taking delight in their bad fortune. He must indeed, they thought, be an ordinary man, ruled by his passions as all human beings are. Ahmad knew what the captives were saying among themselves and assured them that his laughter was not prompted by *Schadenfreude*, but by the humor of watching people struggle so hard to keep from being rescued from the Fire.[29]

Rumi also gives two slightly different interpretations of a saying that belongs in this context, "I laugh as I slay." His first exegesis relates obliquely to the story of the captives. Muhammad "kills the unbeliever in one way, so that the unbeliever may not kill himself in a hundred ways. So of course he laughs as he slays" (F 138/127). Another explanation para-phrases the hadith and gives its meaning a twist: "'My laughing in the face of him who is harsh to me is a slaying of him.' The intention of laughter is gratitude in the place of complaining."[30]

Even though Muhammad detected a certain humor in the condition of the prisoners, he also ached for them in their unbelief. God therefore instructed the Prophet to offer them the faith. Rumi paraphrases the words addressed to the infidels in Q 8:70: "In your present state of bondage and chains, if you resolve upon righteousness God will deliver you out of this and will restore you to that which has gone, and many times more, and will give you forgiveness and blessing in the next world—two treasures, one that has gone from you, and one the treasure of the world to come" (F 64/52). Among the captives of Badr was Muhammad's uncle 'Abbas, who had long opposed the new faith (I:2794). On the uncle's captivity, Rumi notes that Muhammad had felt a pain in his own hands because of the pain he had inflicted by binding his uncle's hands (F 77/66). Now at last 'Abbas accepted Muhammad's long-standing offer of the faith. Muhammad told the repentant 'Abbas that he would have to surrender all his possessions to the army of Islam as a token of his sincerity. When 'Abbas insisted that all his goods had already been taken in plunder, Muhammad read his thoughts and disclosed the place in which his uncle had in fact hidden his wealth. At that sign, 'Abbas was definitively persuaded and became a true believer. Muhammad then "heard the snapping of the girdle of doubt" within his uncle.[31]

In about the year A.D. 628, Muhammad set out for Makka with the inten-tion of performing the lesser pilgrimage ('*umra*).[32] Nine miles outside of Makka, the Prophet met a force of Makkans who threatened to fight if the Muslims proceeded on their pilgrimage. The two parties struck a compro-mise and concluded a treaty by whose terms the Muslims could return the next year and have Makka to themselves for three days. Muhammad returned to Madina without achieving his goal, but Rumi nevertheless views the incident as a clear victory. His opinion follows ancient tradition and several times he quotes from the first verse of Sura 48, al-Fath. The Sura is thought to relate to the Treaty of Hudaybiya, of which God said to Muhammad, "We have given victory. . . ."[33] Mawlana holds that the Prophet was granted victory over a segment of Arabian Jewry in lieu of victory in pilgrimage (III:H.4503–5). He bases his judgment on Q 48:24–25, which suggests to Rumi that God preferred to give a nonmili-tary or psychological victory to the Muslims for the sake of those believers in Makka who would doubtless have suffered unfairly from a battle

(III:4573–75, MCN). Rumi quotes another verse from the Hudaybiya Sura (48:10 in I:2972) in an entirely different context, thereby radically reinterpreting the verse as shall be noted later. For the present context, the poet gives the entire Hudaybiya incident a curious significance relating to the person of the Prophet: "to have been present at Hudaybiya" appears as an image of intimacy with the Messenger. In other words, to love the Prophet is to have been at Hudaybiya when the treaty was made, for one is present to one's beloved (V:742–47).

Another story of military action is more difficult to locate chronologically, but may have occurred on the eve of the Prophet's last illness. According to the account in the *Mathnawi*, one of Muhammad's soldiers raised a vehement objection to the appointment of Usama son of Zayd as commander of an expedition into Syria. Usama was much too young to lead a force full of veterans, the objector argued. The Prophet's ire was kindled at the man's insubordination and disrespect toward "one who knows the hidden" (i.e., the Prophet himself). Rumi excuses the objector partially by explaining that the man had been intoxicated by the Prophet's presence and had therefore lost his normal sense of propriety. At length Muhammad explained that he had chosen the young man as commander because he was old in understanding, not unlike the child Jesus. Age and appearance matter little.[34]

Muhammad had explained to the infidel prisoners of Badr that his purpose in waging war was not merely to conquer the world, but to deliver humankind from destruction. He was not interested in dominion, for "this world is a carcass" (III:4550–53; AM 705). Turning to a discussion of the Prophet's campaign to reconquer Makka, Mawlana again quotes the hadith just cited. His purpose is to demonstrate the absurdity of the accusation that one who has experienced the seventh heaven, as Muhammad had, could be motivated by desire to possess the mundane likes of Makka (I:3948–57). Since people must be beguiled into receiving gifts from God's intimates, Muhammad had first to retake Makka for the Muslims before he could bestow light on Makka's people (F 37–38/25–26). The chiefs of Makka multiplied sacrifices for victory over Muhammad; but their efforts were in vain because the chiefs were not united with the Prophet and did not understand the command of God (I:2226–33).

When at last Muhammad reoccupied Makka, he went immediately to the Ka'ba. His first task was to repeat what the mere mention of his name had done sixty years before, when the old man had brought Halima before the goddess al-'Uzza. He prostrated the idols of the sanctuary (IV:950–63). By destroying the gods and cleansing the Ka'ba, Muhammad was fulfilling his inmost nature. Like Abraham and all the other prophets, Muhammad was essentially a breaker of idols. All idols bow to the prophets (IV:814–15).

In the context of jihad, Muhammad's sword, later bequeathed to 'Ali (D 985:6), takes on a special significance for Jalal ad-Din. Dhu 'l-Faqar was the actual weapon of the Prophet. God deceived his enemies by making them perceive the sword as a harmless dart, when in fact it was the defense of Muhammad's religion (II:2300; M 138/264). More importantly, Dhu 'l-Faqar became the paradigm and touchstone of spiritual maturity. One who submits to the tutelage of a Friend of God begins as a mere needle and becomes a Dhu 'l-Faqar.[35] Proof of the Friend of God, in turn, is ability to turn a wooden sword into Dhu 'l-Faqar (V:2506). Rumi exhorts one who is like the sword to behead selfhood (D 2965:2), and slash the neck of sorrow with intoxication (D 1985:7). The seeker can thereby "become a selfless naughted one like the dervish" (VI:1522).

Rumi makes a similar point several times in the *Diwan* by punning on the words *faqar* and *faqir* (dervish).[36] A Friend's breath, or speech, is as sharp as the sword of Muhammad in order that it might bestow "a beneficial perplexity" on listeners (VI:3313). As the weapon of love[37] in the sheath of patience (D 588:8), Dhu 'l-Faqar becomes in the hand of the beloved, like death, a cutter of secondary causes (M 128/246). Shifting his metaphorical field slightly, Rumi makes Dhu 'l-Faqar the image of the self hidden in the sheath of the body (D 2840:12). Finally, four allusions in the *Diwan* associate the sword more explicitly with the history and function of prophethood. Like the staff of Moses the sword is a "water-giver" (D 3496:5; 871:1), and like the staff for the journey, it must be transformed from the stick of *taqlid* (blind acceptance of authority) into the Dhu 'l-Faqar of *'aql*.

Muhammad's Death: As the Prophet became aware that his death was imminent, he reflected on the purpose of his life. He had desired to make all the world Muslims, and had lived only to call people to God. He was keenly disappointed at falling so short of his desire, but his Lord gave him hope:

Do not grieve. In that very hour when you pass away, provinces and cities that you would conquer by armies and by the sword I will convert to obedience and to the Faith. . . . The sign of that is, that at the end when you are dying you will see people entering in throngs and becoming Muslims. When this sign comes, know that the time for

your departure has arrived. Then give praise, and seek forgiveness,
for thither you shall come. (F 90–91/78)

That, according to Rumi, is the exoteric meaning of Sura 110, an-Nasr.

Gabriel had informed the Prophet that he would die during the month
of Rabi' al-awwal. As Muhammad became more desirous of death, he
prayed to the "Most High Companion on the Way" all night long. He
promised God that the first person to inform him of the ending of Safar,
the month before Rabi' al-awwal, would be assured of the Prophet's
intercession and would gain Paradise. A Companion named 'Ukkasha
brought the news and Muhammad fell in love with the moment of his
approaching journey.[39] He could rejoice at the prospect of his earthly
demise because he had lived out his own most famous hadiths on death:
"Die before you die," [40] and "As you live so shall you die; as you die so
shall you be sent forth (at the Resurrection)" (M 48/115; AM 40). He
knew that God had made death the prophet (*payambar*) from whom he
would receive the message (*payam*) of Life (D 1284:2). Taking his cue
from Idris, who led the way to Paradise (VI:H.723), the "twice-born"
Prophet was a hundred Resurrections (VI:752).

Mawlana comments on the hadith "Die before you die" in several
texts. A good person who has "passed away from the sense of personal
identity so that his self no longer remained, having been consumed in the
light of God" (F 24/12) will attain genuine happiness all the sooner for
having died spiritually before dying physically (V:H.604). A wicked person who does the same gains the advantage of lessening his wickedness.
In either case, when one must at last "shuffle off this mortal coil," one's
only grief will be at not having lived up to one's full potential
(V:H.604–5; VI:1450–53). Hence the Prophet counsels believers both to
leave good deeds behind and to be buried in good company, that is, to
take along good deeds as well. One's deeds are, for good or ill, one's
companions on the journey (IV:1203; V:H.1051–52). A slightly more
technical exegesis of the hadith also comes from the Prophet's mouth in
the *Mathnawi*:

> Hence Mustafa said, "O seeker of the mysteries, (if) you wish to see
>   a dead person living—
> Walking on the earth, like living human beings; (yet he is) dead and
>   his spirit is gone to heaven;
> (One) whose spirit has a dwelling-place on high at this moment, (so
>   that) if he should die, his spirit is not translated,

Because it has been translated before death: this (mystery) is
  understood (only) by dying, not by (using one's) reason;
Translation it is, (but) not like the translation of the spirits of the
  vulgar: it resembles a removal (during life) from one place to
  another—
If any one wishes to see a dead person walking thus visibly on the
  earth, Let him behold Abu Bakr, the devout, (who) through being
  a true witness (Siddiq) became the Prince of the Resurrected.
  (VI:742–48)

Muhammad died. That is, says Rumi, "his form passed away," and the
world cried "Allahu Akbar" (D 1052:7). He "slept" but "his fortune and
prosperity slumbered not." The Prophet's eyes slept, as did those of Moses
(D 478:20), but his heart remained awake; and his "light in heaven" continues to wage the jihad (III:1210–4). Muhammad's corporeal senses are
buried at Madina, but again as in the case of Moses, "that mighty-natured
part of him" is in "the abode of truth" (IV:3786–98).

Muhammad's Personality and Teachings

Personal Qualities of the Prophet

God's last and greatest Prophet emerges from Rumi's writings head and
shoulders above the generality of humankind. Mawlana does not regard
Muhammad as more than human, but as fully human, as one who has actu-
ated and realized his full human potential. That complete humanity the
poet describes as "purged of this fire and smoke" (of human passion,
I:1397); "free from (creaturely) existence" (I:3824); "shadowless"
(V:672); yet still "composed of flesh and skin" (V:1323). Muhammad
exhibited in his genuine humanity a wide range of characteristics, the
more prominent of which warrant special mention here.

Despite his high fortune, the Prophet sought the gift of tears from God
(VI:2338–42; II:2766–67). "Sweetnatured" Muhammad (V:746) was
remarkably sympathetic and compassionate, and Rumi delights in spotlighting the Messenger's solidarity with other human beings. Muhammad
felt pain in his hand when his uncle 'Abbas felt pain from his prisoner's
manacles after Badr (F 77/66). He was also quite capable of anger, arrogance, and vexation.[41] Most of all, however, it is Muhammad's compas-
sion that stands out, principally in two stories of his visiting the sick.

Mustafa once went to visit a sick Companion, for "his nature was all
kindness and generosity" (II:2141). He dealt with the man "sweetly and

tenderly" (II:2252), so that his "light-giving presence" allowed the suffering man to realize the source of his ill health—he had been careless in prayer and had asked for the wrong thing (II:H.2456–81). Another story tells of the Prophet's concern for the slave Hilal who had been underestimated and neglected by his master, as had Joseph and Bilal. Muhammad received an inspiration as to Hilal's plight and went immediately to inquire of the master where the slave was kept. He found Hilal in a foul stable and "laid his face against (Hilal's) face and kissed his head and eyes and cheeks" (VI:H.1110–85).

Muhammad did not shrink from associating with the down and out because he himself was preeminently humble. "Mustafa seeks a blessing from the lowly poor," because "he knows that the King deposits the royal treasure in ruined places" (VI:1632–34). Muhammad never spoke in an elevated tone to those who would not understand. His aim was to communicate the message to people whatever their level of comprehension. He therefore counseled his followers, "Speak to people according to the measure of their understanding ('uqul), not according to the measure of your understanding, so that God and His Messenger may not be given the lie" (IV:H.2577; I:3810–11). Mawlana explains the Prophet's humility:

> All the fruits of this world and the next were gathered upon him, so of course he was humbler than all people. He said, "No one ever preceded the Messenger of God in making a greeting." No one was able to precede the Prophet in offering greetings because the Prophet would outstrip him out of extreme humility and so would greet him first. Even supposing that he did not greet the other first, even so he was humble and preceded the other in speaking, for they learned the greeting from him and gave heed to him. (F 116/105)

Rumi's concept of humility is that what is brought lower is more humble. Hence, the branch of the fruit tree that is most heavily laden will be the humblest.

The Religion of Muhammad

The Community: Noah preached for a thousand years and gained only forty followers. Muhammad preached only a few years and yet his community encompassed countless lands and peoples.[42] The Qur'an instructed him to "follow the religion of Abraham," and told him, "Truly you have a good example in Abraham."[43] Abraham's religion began with a breaking

of idols, as did Muhammad's, thanks to the Prophet's fearlessness in origi-
nating Islam (M 56/131).

Though the likes of Bu Musaylim (usually called Musaylima al-
Kadhdhab), the false prophet of the Banu Hanifa, might rise up to con-
found the new Faith, their efforts could only fail miserably (IV:1695–97).
"God most Glorious desired that the religion of Muhammad . . . should be
high honored and spread abroad and should abide for ever and ever" (F
115/130). Bu Musaylim might take the name of Ahmad, but his true name
would remain "*Kadhdhab*" (liar, I:321–22); and since "the religion is sincerity" (III:3945; AM 282), such an imposter would be immediately
exposed.

Islam makes undeniable demands on the believer. A man once com-
plained to the Prophet that he no longer wanted the religion because it had
caused him to lose his money, wife, family, respect, strength, and even
lust! Muhammad replied:

> Wherever our religion has gone, it comes not back without uprooting
> a person and sweeping clean his house. . . . For this reason you have
> not peace and do sorrow, because sorrowing is an evacuation of those
> first joys. . . . You say, "O Muhammad, take away religion from me,
> for I cannot find rest." How should our religion let anyone go, before
> it brings him to the goal? (F 125–26/114–15)

On several occasions Jalal ad-Din comments on the hadith "Islam is a
stranger in this world," and variations on that Tradition. One explanation
finds in it a "description of the chosen servant of God amongst worldlings
and those addicted to passion and sensuality" (V:H.833; M 73/159).
Another passage employs the hadith as part of a sinuous defense of the
Prophet's military campaigns (F 64/52). Only once does Rumi refer the
saying specifically to the individual believer as member of the religion,
and there he gives this description of the Muslim: "Islam is a stranger in
this world"

> . . . Because even his (the true Muslim's) kinfolk are fleeing from
>   him though the angels are in harmony with his essence.
> The people deem his form homogeneous (with theirs) but they do
>   not perceive in him that (spiritual) fragrance. [Allusion to
>   Jacob/Joseph]
> He is like a lion in the shape of a cow: behold him from afar but do
>   not investigate him!
> And if you investigate, take leave of the cow, (which is) the body;

for that lion-natured one will tear the cow to pieces. (V:925–29; AM 489)

Muhammad's classic description of Islam vis à vis Christianity is the oft-quoted hadith, "There is no monkhood in Islam: the congregation is a mercy." He wanted to insure the mutual support and solidarity that monastic solitude did not afford.[44] Life in community also provides two other benefits. It allows the believer to associate more freely with people of proven holiness and to consult with them, thus minimizing the false steps one might take on one's own (VI:2611–21). Secondly, if a believer only runs from the enemy, he cannot join the jihad (V:H.574–78), part of which involves the refinement of character that results from interaction of male and female. But if one cannot survive in the Muslim community, following the way of Jesus would be preferable to remaining entirely outside the religious fold and its values (F 98–99/86–87).

Unity among this "people on which God has taken mercy" was a primary value for the Prophet. He made "one soul" out of the warring factions of Madina.[45] The *Umma* is an "Ark" of unity and safety and, said the Prophet, "amidst the sea of cares (my) Companions are (as) stars in respect of guidance."[46] A star does not need to speak; it guides merely by being visible, and thus do all the Friends of God exercise wordless influence over the believer (F 140–41/129). Now "the stars, every one, are all part of the moon" (I:2926), and thus the Companions become the trustees of the Prophet's guiding presence in the *Umma*; they are the guardians and guarantors of the Sunna of the Prophet.

Following the Sunna is, along with trust in God, a primary means to guidance (I:912–13; V:163). The Sunna is the safe road on which believers walk together, working and earning along the way. One who leaves that road has "drunk his own blood."[47] Rumi also gives a more philosophical image of the Sunna:

The Sunna is a road trodden by the feet of the prophets. . . . On the right hand of that road lies the desert of determinism [*jabr*], where one (the determinist) regards oneself as having no power of choice and denies the command and prohibition and employs (false) interpretation [*ta'wil*]; (this in turn leads to all manner of straying from the basics of the faith). . . . And on the left hand of that road lies the desert of freewill [*qadar*] where one (who holds that doctrine) regards the power of the Creator as over-come by the power of the creatures; and thence arise the corruptions (vicious opinions) that

have been enumerated (in preceding story told by a Magian determinist). . . . (V:H.2963)

In very practical terms, adherence to the safe road involves the fundamental Muslim observances, the Five Pillars.

The Five Pillars: Though Mawlana seldom mentions specifically the
Muslim's first duty of the profession of faith or *Shahada*,[48] his entire work
is clearly an elaboration of the doctrine of God's unity as revealed through
Muhammad.

Of fasting *(sawm* or *siyam* or *rawda)* the poet has more to say. In the
Mathnawi and *Fihi Ma Fihi* Rumi scarcely mentions the practice. He
appears there to take fasting more or less for granted, saying only that fasting took on a new form at the time of Mustafa.[49] In the *Diwan,* however, he
places fasting squarely in the midst of Muslim life and, significantly, of
prophetology. Mawlana has devoted several entire odes to fasting in general and to the month of Ramadan.[50] Most important for present purposes
are several texts that speak of fasting in relation to Prophethood. The poet
likens fasting to the Seal of Solomon—that which gave the king power
over all creation (D 1602:14; 1739:8)—and to the well in which Joseph
experienced both the pain and hunger of separation and an abundant garden (D 2344:9). In a similar vein Rumi records a saying in which the
Prophet calls fasting a garden.[51] Finally, the blackness of fasting is in reality golden; for only in such blackness can one find the white hand (D
3390:9). Gift of dominion, patient suffering of separation and denial by
one's own people, and more, fasting is the very setting in which the God
bestows that Mosaic proof of prophethood, the white hand.

Mawlana views almsgiving as founded on the Prophet's teaching that
"munificence is a gainful trade" and that poverty is both treasure and a
source of pride.[52] Because God first gives generous alms of light and water
of life (D 1652:17; 1280:9), believers can and must be generous according
to their means. Rumi records three variants of a hadith in which the
Prophet exhorted his people to seek their needs from the generous members of his *Umma*.[53] Two angels pray constantly that God will be abun-
dantly generous to those who give freely of their substance.[54] All cries of
the poor for assistance are in reality the voice of the Prophet saying, "Give
me something. I am in need. Either give me your cloak, or your wealth, or
your clothes." Muhammad asks, not because he himself has need of those
things, but "to lighten your garment so that the warmth of the sun may
reach you" (F 234/227). Ultimately, it is the hope of the Resurrection that
will make people generous. As Muhammad said, "Whoever knows for

sure his recompense on the day of Resurrection—that his compensation will be ten for one—at every moment a different munificence will issue from that person."[55] If that is not enough, God makes Himself a beggar and says, "Give God a loan" (D 909:2 quoting Q 53:18).

Pilgrimage is formally a visit to the House (Ka'ba), but in reality it is a visit to the Lord of the House (IV:15) Mawlana develops two pilgrimage images at considerable length. One of the odes pictures the beloved as the Ka'ba of souls (or of the spirit) around which all make *tawaf*, the circum-ambulation.[56] Another text tells of Bayezid al-Bistami's pilgrimage to Makka. As the famous mystic journeyed, he met a shaykh. When the old man learned that Bayezid was bound for the Ka'ba, he told Bayezid:

> Make a circuit around me seven times, and consider this better than the circumambulation (of the Ka'ba) in the pilgrimage;
> And lay those dirhems before me, O generous one. Know that you have made the greater pilgrimage and that your desire has been achieved;
> (That) you have (also) performed the lesser pilgrimage and gained the life everlasting; (that) you have become pure [*safi*] and sped up (the Hill of) Purity [*safa*, one of the two mounds between which Hagar ran in panic while baby Isma'il cried of thirst].
> By the truth of the Truth (God) whom your soul has seen (I swear) that he has chosen me above His House.
> Even if the Ka'ba is the House of His religious service, my form too, in which I was created, is the House of His inmost consciousness.
> Never since God made the Ka'ba has He gone into it, and none but the living (God) has ever gone into this House (of mine).
> When you have seen me, you have seen God: you have circled around the Ka'ba of sincerity.
> To serve me is to obey and glorify God: beware lest you think that God is separate from me.
> Open your eyes well and look at me, so that you may behold the light of God in human form. (II:2241–49)

The shaykh functions as a type of the Prophet, and he even paraphrases the hadith "Who has seen me has seen God."[57] Rumi says elsewhere that Muhammad is the "Amir of the Hajj of love" (D 3377:6) and that one must make the journey of love to catch a glimpse of the Prophet (D 199:2). Putting together the texts cited here, one can make the following conclusion: the pilgrimage made ostensibly toward the House (i.e., Muhammad) is actually the journey to the Lord of the House (God) through love. It is, then, a simple matter for Mawlana to expand the metaphor so that "seeking the aid of a *pir*" is both modeled on, and a model of, the pilgrimage.

Prayer had existed, along with fasting, from the time of Adam; but with the advent of Mustafa the form of prayer changed (F 86/75). Formal prayer (*salat*) had been invented by the prophets. Muhammad then invented Muslim prayer. He taught that the soul of prayer (interior prayer) was a "way nearer to God" than the "body of prayer" (ritual) (F 24/11–12). Rumi nevertheless considers the "ritual prayer and rosary and observances" to be very much a part of the "way of the Prophet and his Companions" (VI:2067). Mawlana quotes a hadith on the necessity of ritual ablutions (F 196/187; AM 253) and even likens the ablutions to the fire of Khalil (V:231). On the need for public, formal prayer, God had declared to Muhammad: "Your companions out of weakness and fear for their lives and because of the envious, used to pronounce your name secretly into the ear. I will publish your greatness abroad to such a point that people will shout it aloud in sweet intonations five times daily on the high minarets in all regions of the world. . . ." (F 155/142). At the call to prayer (D 915:4) the Muslim turns to Makka. In the presence of the Prophet, however, one who turns away so as to face the prayer-niche has in fact turned away from Makka. "For God's light is the 'soul' of the Makka-ward direction . . . it was the Prophet who made the Ka'ba to be the place of turning for all the world. How much more is He the place of turning, for whose sake Makka was appointed" (F 25/12).

We will discuss Muhammad's personal practice of prayer, and the content of his prayer, shortly. For the present we shall note briefly how the Prophet's teaching and example related to the prayer of the Muslim community (R 875). Muhammad prayed with his Companions and conferred the blessing as the Imam.[58] He also performed the *namaz* "anywhere, without a prayer-carpet," for "God makes impure pure for the great. On that account the grace of God has made my place of worship to be pure up to the seventh tier (of heaven)" (II:H.3424–25, 3427–28).

By his example the Prophet taught that tears of repentance for missing the time of formal prayer more than made up for the lost ritual.[59] Rumi also includes some of Muhammad's verbal teaching on prayer. In the story of the poor man who began to pray when he became empty, the poet recalls the hadith that "the true believer is a lute (that) makes music (only) at the time when it is empty" (VI:4213; AM 728). The Prophet taught that the *salat* was the delight of his eye; that formal prayer is never complete "without presence of heart"; and that one should be persistent in private prayer.[60]

Fundamental to Muhammad's example and teaching on both ritual and private prayer was his belief that "whosoever makes all his cares a single care, God will suffice him as to all his other cares." [61] Finally, as we shall later see in greater detail, companionship with the Prophet in prayer, even though he be in the company of only "two or three poor people," is far better than the pursuit of riches and apparent securities (III:421–29). We turn now to those interior qualities and values that describe Muhammad in his essential relationships.

CHAPTER 8

The Ahmad of Faith

In chapter 7 we examined those aspects of Rumi's treatment of Muhammad most directly associated with the Prophet's historical existence. Here we move to the less easily discernible interior dimensions of his person and meaning. The chapter treats the material in three sections: the Prophet's relationship with God, the various proofs of his Prophethood, and Ahmad's prophetic attributes.

The Prophet's Relationship with God

"You Did Not Throw . . ."

God was Muhammad's friend and "taught him the way" (II:2297); and in the Prophet's own words, one is united with one's friend (V:745–47; AM 482). In other words, God is "contained in the true believer's heart" (I:2655; AM 63). By the divine grace of such a presence, Ahmad became as different from Abu Jahl as a hearing ear is from a deaf ear. Both ears look the same; but as we shall see shortly, Ahmad was the very essence of ear (F 223/215). Muhammad's intimacy with God was not the result of his own initiative. Journeys on the she-camel of the body occur as a result of human effort; but the journey of the spirit to union happens only under the influence of the divine attractive power to which Ahmad awarded preeminence.[1]

Rumi underscores the divine initiative by repeated allusions to Q 8:17: "You did not throw when you threw. . . ." When the Muslims and the Quraysh joined battle at Badr, an ancient tradition says the Prophet routed the enemy merely by throwing a handful of gravel in their faces. The Qur'an attributes the action ultimately to God and not to Muhammad. Mawlana then transforms the words of Q 8:17, "*ma ramayta (idha ramayta)* . . ." into a topos that sums up succinctly this most basic feature of Ahmad's union with his Lord; Ahmad is the bow, God the Archer.[2]

Ahmad is like the (the Arabic letter *a*) *alif* in the word *bism* (In the name of
. . .): he is there, but the correct sound of the word requires his silence
(VI:2239–46).

Mustafa enjoyed unique and exclusive union with the Beloved. He
shared his state with neither prophet nor angel.[3] Ahmad is separated from
Ahad (one, i.e., God) only by a *mim* (the Arabic letter *m*). Mawlana bor-
rows the *Ahmad/Ahad* pun from 'Attar and uses it in connection with the
name of the Governor (Parvana) of Rum, *mu'in ad-din*; the m is added to
the Governor's first name because he has not yet become *'ayn ad-din* (the
essence of the faith). Similarly, the poet continues, "*Ahad* is perfection and
Ahmad is not yet in the state of perfection; when that m is removed it
becomes complete perfection" (F 226/219). Rumi transforms the play on
words into another *topos* with which to recall to his reader the second
major facet of Muhammad's friendship with God. Ahmad and his Lord are
so close that "praising Muhammad is praising God. It may be compared
with a person saying, 'God give the king a long life, and him who showed
me the way to the king, or told me of the king's attributes!'"[4] The petition
of one so united with God is like the petition of God to Himself
(V:H.2243). Extending the notion still further, the Prophet himself had
said that "whoever knows himself knows his Lord" (V:2114; AM 529).

Night vigil was a special time for Muhammad as the hadith says, "I pass
the night in the presence of my Lord, who provides me food and drink." At
those times his prayer was totally absorbing, "a state of unconsciousness
excluding and not finding room for all these outward forms" (F 24/12; D
1402:2). God assured Muhammad, however, that even outside those privileged moments, even in the thick of less exalted concerns, their union
would not be disturbed. Mawlana tells of Ahmad's worry over the matter
and God's consoling response:

> Mustafa . . . He occupied at first wholly with Himself; thereafter He
> commanded him, "Call the people, counsel them and reform them."
> Mustafa wept and lamented saying, "Ah my Lord, what sin have I
> committed? Why do you drive me from your presence? I have no
> desire for people." God most High said to him, "Muhammad, do not
> sorrow. I will not abandon you only to be occupied with human
> affairs. Even in the midst of that occupation you shall be with me.
> When you are occupied with human affairs, not one hair of the head
> of this hour you spend with Me, not one will be taken from you. In
> whatever matter you are engaged, you will be in union with Me. (F
> 78/66–67)

Muhammad nevertheless continued to pine for the days before his embroilment in worldly affairs. Notwithstanding the fame and greatness of the Prophetic office, he would have preferred to be totally free from distraction, so much so that he said, "Would that the Lord of Muhammad had not created Muhammad" (F 211–12/203).

Ahmad's Prayer

Ahmad was truly a contemplative in action. Whether keeping vigil, sometimes so long that his feet became swollen,[6] or swamped with community business, the Prophet was equally in God's presence and sending prayer to heaven (D 898:5). Even when he judged that sleep was better than prayer, still he remained alert to his Lord: "My eyes sleep, (but) my heart is not asleep to the Lord of created beings."[7] Muhammad once said that "(Whoso knows God), his tongue falters" (II:3013; AM 179). In his own prayer, however, he was not always at a loss for words. He asked pardon of God "seventy times every day."[8] He likened genuflection and prostration, the prescribed actions in ritual prayer, to "knocking the door ring of (mystical) attainment to the divine portal," which inevitably opens to the persistent (V:2048–49; III:4782). When Mustafa visited the sick Companion who had foolishly prayed to receive the next world's punishment in this world, he instructed the man in a better way to petition God:

> Pray this way:—"O you who make the difficult easy,
> Give us good in this dwelling place, and give us good in the next!
> Make the path as pleasant as a garden: You indeed, O Glorious One,
>   are our goal." (II:H.2552–53)

Perhaps the foremost of Muhammad's prayers can be heard in the Tradition, "Show me things as they truly are." Although the hadith is not contained in the standard collection, it became very popular among later Sufis. Rumi alludes to various forms of the hadith, sometimes as quoted above and sometimes as "Let the false appear false, and the true as true."[9] Mawlana pays special attention to it in *Fihi Ma Fihi*. Because of the veils and darknesses that hamper true knowledge of the self, within which all things are written as in a "mighty volume," one must follow the example of the Prophet in praying for clarity. Ahmad prayed, "You show a thing as fair, and in reality it is ugly; You show a thing as ugly, and in reality it is lovely. Therefore show us every thing just as it is, that we may not fall into the snare and that we may not go astray perpetually" (F 18/5). If such clarity of vision were not remarkably difficult to attain, Muhammad would not have had to seek it in prayer. He asked, in effect, to see with the eyes of God. As Rumi paraphrases the prayer elsewhere, "Show (unto me) each part from above and below such as that part is in Your sight" (IV:3567–68). Only God's "lawful magic" can open and close the eye of the heart (VI:3512).

Alam Nashrah: *The Nature of the Revelation*

Even as he prayed for vision, Muhammad was gradually allowing God more and more to open him, to "expand" him, to make him more receptive. According to Mawlana, "petitioning from God most High and persistence thereat is more beneficial for the supplicant than the thing requested" (III:H.1484). In the instance of Muhammad, the "actual petitioning" and the thing asked for were identical; the one reinforced the other. At the heart of the matter lies the commentary (*sharh*) that God wrote within Muhammad when He "expanded" (*sharaha*) the Prophet's *sadr*, spiritual center. Since the heart is the astrolabe of the seven heavens, the commentary on Muhammad's heart is in seven volumes (D 882:4). Several times Rumi refers to Q 39:22, "He whose spiritual center God has expanded" (F 66/54; M 43/107). Rumi also makes more general allusions to "expansion of the *sadr*" as a desideratum in prayer or as a thing wished for as blessing upon another person.[10] Most important of all are the poet's several quotations of Q 94:1, "Have we not expanded your *sadr*?"[11] Commenting on the Qur'anic verse, Mawlana remarks that "the expansion of the spiritual center is infinite. Once that expansive commentary has been read, from a hint a person understands much. . . ." (F 123/112). Sura 94, al-Inshirah is traditionally associated with the story of two individuals who threw the child Muhammad to the ground, split him open, removed and discarded a clot from his heart, and then washed the boy with snow from a golden basin.[12] If indeed the text carried such an association for Rumi, it would support the poet's affirmation that Muhammad was possessed of revelation even as a child.

Related to Mawlana's understanding of Sura 94 is his interpretation of Qur'an 15:9, "It is we who have sent down the Reminder" (*dhikr*). Speaking of the source and beginnings of the revelation, and indirectly describing the two classes of seekers in relationship to God—the wayfarer (*salik*) and the one drawn (*majdhub*)—Rumi writes in *Fihi Ma Fihi*:

There are certain servants of God who proceed from the Qur'an to God. Others more elect come from God, find the Qur'an here, and know that God has sent it down. "It is we who have sent down the Remembrance, and We watch over it." The commentators say that this (the word *dhikr*) refers to the Qur'an. This too is good; but it can also mean, "We have placed in you a substance, a seeking, a yearning. We watch over that, not letting it go to waste but bringing it to a definite place." (F 125/114)

One may argue convincingly, in view of Rumi's proposed alternative meaning of "Remembrance," that "substance, seeking, yearning" constitute a prevenient grace that predisposed Muhammad for capacity to be the prime recipient of revelation. In other words, "we have sent down the Remembrance" would be for Mawlana equivalent to "we have expanded your *sadr*."

Rumi characterizes the Prophet as responsive (V:925). By itself, such a qualification of Ahmad would be sheer understatement; but the poet proceeds to multiply images of Muhammad's unique suitability for perceiving the word of God. All of creation "tells a tale" to Ahmad (V:2819; VI:4289–90). He is "entirely ear and eye" (III:103), who hears and sees through God (V:H.498). "He is an ear" that draws out the hidden meaning of words. More than just a hearer, as his critics claimed, he was a hearer of good news for his people, discerning "subtle discourse from clod and brick."[13] The ear of Ahmad's soul perceived the sound of conversion, "whenever any one breaks the girdle of doubt and polytheism and unbelief" (F 17/4), and the sound of hypocrisy as well (III:H.790–91). Muhammad heard the voice of God as Moses had heard it (II:2883) and so was never daunted by envious criticism, for the barking of dogs never reaches the ear of the moon (II:422). By contrasting Muhammad with the "deaf ear," Abu Jahl, Rumi underscores the extent of the Prophet's sensitivity (F 223/215). Finally, Rumi rounds off the image by saying that this ear even had an ear-ring in the person of the martyr Husayn (VI:791).

Muhammad's was the "station of seeing" (F 103/91–92). By means of the "collyrium of *alam nashrah*" (VI:2863) he saw a world "filled with love and bounty" and alive at every level (IV:3533). His eye saw the end of all things (VI:3475), the whole chain of destiny past and future, as a result of his selflessness.[14]

Ahmad also possessed a Jacob-like olfactory sensitivity. He was ever aware of the "breathings" of God, which are like Spring, giving new life (I:H.1951–52; I:2054). The Prophet said, "I feel the Breath of the Merciful

from the direction of Yemen."[15] His sense of smell shared with his hearing
the power of discrimination between true and false.[16] Imagery of scent and
breath in Rumi is so extensive that it could easily become a separate topic
in itself. Here it must remain part of the larger picture of the responsive
Prophet in whom God had become his very senses, according to the
famous *Hadith an-Nawafil*.[17] That Tradition suggests that God was not
only Ahmad's ear and eye (and nose), but his tongue and hand as well. A
separate section on the proofs of Muhammad's prophethood will discuss
the works of the Prophet's hand, but before considering more specifically
his knowledge, a word about his tongue seems in order.

"Recite!" God commanded Muhammad in Qur'an 96:1. From then on
Ahmad's speech became that of the "sea" and his words pearls (VI:815).
Even those who could not recognize the Prophet with their eyes would
know him as a kindred spirit when he spoke (F 177/167). Rumi says that
Muhammad received the gift of speech "without struggling"—and even
the precociously talkative Jesus had to struggle to speak—(F 66/54), but
not, evidently, without praying. Ahmad had long desired eloquence of the
kind so celebrated among the Arabs. When God introduced him to the
unseen, his desire waned. God nevertheless gave him the gift and told the
Prophet not to worry over his sudden indifference to the gift, for indifference to such things would not harm him. Ahmad thenceforth became so
eloquent that after countless volumes of commentary on his words, people
still understand them only imperfectly (F 154–55/142).

Mawlana further explores the vexing issue of who actually was speaking when Muhammad "was transported out of himself" and began the various revelations with "God says" (IV:2122). Rumi's own words on the
question will then take us still deeper into the phenomenon of *wahy* (inspiration) and the problem of what Muhammad actually knew. The poet
quotes part of God's admonition to the Prophet not to anticipate the revelation by moving his tongue (V:H.1430, quoting Q 75:16), and then elaborates in *Fihi Ma Fihi*:

> From the standpoint of form it was his (Muhammad's) tongue that
> spoke, but he was not there at all, and the speaker in reality was God.
> Having at first perceived himself ignorant and knowing nothing of
> such words, now that such words are being born from him he realizes
> that he is not now what he was at first. This is God controlling him.
> Mustafa . . . reported about past individuals and prophets who lived
> so many thousands of years before him, and even unto the end of the
> world, what should come to pass; as likewise about the Throne and

the Footstool, the Void and the Plenum. His being was a thing of but yesterday, and a being newly created but yesterday assuredly does not speak of such things. How should a creature born in time give information about the eternal? Hence it became realized that it was not he who was speaking; God was speaking. "Nor speaks He out of caprice. This is naught but a revelation (*wahy*) revealed."[18]

On the "Night of Power" Ahmad had experienced his initiation into the mysteries of the Unseen. As Rumi reads the text, Sura 97, al-Qadr speaks of Muhammad's awakening from the "Sleeper's Dream" that is this world, to find himself privy to the secrets of the other world. Ahmad suddenly became endowed with understanding, possessing secret, esoteric knowledge.[19] Thus taking his place beside the mysterious and inscrutable Khizr, Muhammad's teaching became "wholly revelation within revelation within revelation" (*gushad andar gushad andar gushad*, VI:174).

Mustafa received inspiration for a variety of reasons and occasions. By *wahy* he was told to "unsheathe the sword and make war" on the infidels (F 151/142), to offer to the captives of Badr the option of conversion (F 64/52). He knew by inspiration that 'Ali would be slain by the hand of his own stirrup-holder (I:H.3844–46), that the pain he felt in his hand issued from that of his uncle 'Abbas (F 77/66), that 'Umar was coming to the mosque to convert (F 171/163), that Hilal was in need of solace (VI:H.1110–85), and that the Hypocrites who proposed to build the mosque were not acting in good faith (II:2885). Muhammad firmly insisted in public debate with unbelievers that he was indeed the recipient of *wahy*, informing them that such a recipient ". . . has certain marks and signs, in his actions and in his words, in his mien and in every part of him the token and mark may be seen. Since you have seen those tokens, turn your faces towards him and hold firmly to him, that he may be your protector" (F 151/142). Part of the problem, as Rumi sees it, is that while all could see the Prophet's intelligence, only a few perceived his inspiration (II:3259). Some of those "marks and signs" we will treat in the section on the proofs of Muhammad's prophethood. Here we look at two more key aspects of Ahmad's relationship with God.

Wa 'd-Duha: *Muhammad the Light of God*

God's expansion of the spiritual core is intimately connected with the imagery of light in Rumi's prophetology. Mawlana says that the *sharh* fills the heart with light (*diya*). Rumi counsels the believer to "contemplate the expansion of the *sadr* within (yourself), lest there come the reproach, 'Do you not see?'" (V:1066–72; Q 51:21). Again alluding to Q 39:22, which calls Muhammad "he whose spiritual center God has expanded for surrender, so that he follows a light from his Lord," Rumi also quotes from a hadith in which Muhammad spoke of the sign of the entry of light into the heart when it is expanded.[20] Another text speaks of God's creation of light in the dark core of the heart. It is not unlikely that the poet is here alluding to the already-cited story of the splitting of the child Muhammad's heart and the removal of the clot. As already suggested, that story is often associated with Sura 94, al-Inshirah.

Mawlana's attention to the subject of God's light in the Prophet leads him to comment extensively on several other Qur'anic texts as well. Speaking of Ahmad as the model servant of God, Rumi gives an exegesis of a text that was a favorite of Sana'i's and to which Rumi himself refers occasionally.[21] Sura 93 begins, "By the morn" (*wa 'd-duha*). Mawlana explains that whether one takes the words to refer immediately to the "hidden mind of Mustafa" (*damir*) or literally to the morning, one must conclude that they refer ultimately to the Prophet. In other words, if "morning" is taken literally, it must still be understood to be a reflection of Muhammad; otherwise, God would be swearing by a transient phenomenon, and such an oath would scarcely be appropriate to God. According to a parallel logic, "and by the night" (Q 93:2) must refer to Muhammad's "occultation and his earthen rust-dark body." In a slight variation on the theme, Rumi says elsewhere that the oath "by the afterglow of sunset" of Q 84:16 is likewise swearing by the body of Ahmad (VI:1498–99). Muhammad's "sun," the light, rose. When it set, it reassured the "night of the body" with the words of Q 93:3, "Behold, he has not forsaken you."[22] Elaborating on the meaning of Ahmad's dawn to dusk cycling, Mawlana has the "hundredfold sun" say:

> I have thrown my orb over Saturn: beware, O stars and cover your faces!
> Be annihilated in my incomparable radiance [*sha'a'*], lest you be put to shame before my light [*nur*].
> For kindness' sake I disappear every night; (but) how should I depart? I only make a show of departing,
> That for a night you may fly without me like bats, flapping your wings, around this flying place;
> And that like peacocks, you may display a wing, and then become intoxicated and haughty and self-conceited. . . .

At dawn I may show my face to reprimand you, lest from egoism you
 become among the people of the left hand. . . .
This sun goes with face uncovered: His face is veiled by the excess of
 His light (*nur*) (VI:677–82, 684, 691)

According to Rumi's more usual de facto linguistic practice, the word *nur*
most often refers to the sun itself, and the word *diya* to its radiance.
However, on the basis of Q 10:5, "He it is who appointed the sun a splendor (*diya'an*) and the moon a light (*nuran*)," Mawlana also makes a theoretical distinction. Here *nur* is the light of the moon while *diya* remains the
light or radiance of the sun, as in the poet's normal usage. Rumi's theoretical exegesis of the Qur'anic text is only a momentary aberration, for
shortly thereafter the poet explains, using sun imagery, how the Prophet's
nur rose and made it possible for traders to distinguish true coin from
counterfeit (IV:18–24; II:2733–34).

Rumi reserves the poetic right to shift image fields at will; but the
import of even such a temporary distinction between lunar and solar illumination becomes clear from other texts of the *Mathnawi*. In those passages Mawlana does not attempt conscious and explicit distinctions, but
the following conclusion seems warranted. God's light is to the Prophet as
the Prophet's light is to the Friends of God and all who are illumined by
Muhammad. When Rumi calls God the sun, then Ahmad is the moon. If
Ahmad is the sun, then the Friends are moons.[23]

Ahmad the "Sun of the Arabs" (D 634:11), the "Sun of Mystery," nulli-
fied the multiple shadows of the world's contending faiths (VI:1861–64;
D 882:1). His light is the *qibla* (F 25/12) in relation to which one can
learn to pray aright, as did the sick man whom Muhammad visited
(II:H.2456ff.). Ahmad made war in order to give light to people (F 37/25)
by keeping guard over them with that light (I:737). He nourished them
with light and caused people to see and hear through that light/intellect
that is the prophetic heritage.[24] Though Ahmad postdated the other
prophets in time, he was the light by which they all saw (D 3212:8) and
from whom all other lights issue (R 149). In his efforts to unify all the
world, Ahmad was aided by the Ansar of the light (I:1545), a light without limit, "neither of East nor of West."[25]

By the lamp of Muhammad's face Abu Bakr and 'Umar received the
faith.[26] Recalling the image of source/reflector, or sun/moon, Rumi quotes
the hadith, "Happy the one that has seen me and the one who looks at a
person who has seen my face." Who sees the lamp also sees the source of
its light, the candle (I:1946–50; AM 25). It is therefore necessary and effi-

cacious to relate to a saintly shaykh as though to one who is a moon to Ahmad's sun. About the effect of his own relationship to the believers, Muhammad once expressed some concern and was comforted by a revelation that clarified the matter for him:

> ... the Prophet remained in astonishment, saying. . . . "How are the
> people not seeing the light of my face, which has borne away the
> prize from the orient sun?
> And if they are seeing (it) wherefore this perplexity?"—until a
> revelation came, saying, "That face is in concealment.
> In relation to you it is the moon and in relation to the people it is the
> cloud, in order that the infidel may not see your face for nothing.
> In relation to you it is the bait, and in relation to the people it is the
> trap, in order that the vulgar may not drink of this chosen wine."[27]

For the believer's eye of faith, the final proof of Muhammad's prophethood was made possible by the gift of light when the "sun split the moon" (I:921). A separate section will shortly be devoted to the signal miracle of Ahmad's cleaving of the moon. Here in the context of the light and of what has been said regarding Rumi's clever use of words, the image of sun splitting moon is a perfect capsule, both playful and serious, of the importance of God's light in Mawlana's prophetology.[28]

Law Laka: *Muhammad's Cosmic Mission*

God so exalted Ahmad (III:1788) that the Prophet became the very raison d'être of all things; or in the words of Nicholson's translation, "(the final cause of) the command 'Be!'"[29] Rumi elaborates on the "final causality" of Ahmad chiefly in two ways; first, from the side of the Prophet, employing an epistemological model; and second, from a theological perspective, speaking in terms of God's motivation. Let us examine this dual aspect of Mawlana's treatment briefly.

Ahmad prayed for clear vision, and God responded by expanding the Prophet, becoming his very senses, thus fashioning him into a fitting receiver of revelation. According to the famous *hadith qudsi*, God was a hidden treasure and so created the world in order that He might be known (D 3426:2; AM 70). Rumi explains, however, that:

> If there were no ears to receive (the message from) the Unseen, no
> announcer would have brought a revelation from heaven;
> And if there were no eyes to see the works of God, neither would the
> sky have revolved nor would the earth have smiled.

> The declaration *Lawlaka* means this, that the affair (of creation) is
> for the sake of the piercing eye and the seer. (VI:1659–61)

The sacred hadith, "But for you (*law laka*) I would not have created the
heavens" means that everything is related to the Prophet as the actions of a
hand are related to the mind. Mind prevents the hand from becoming atro-
phied, so that the hand remains the mind's instrument (F 117/105–6).
Thought is the beginning and action is the end, but the thought is always of
the end product. A tree's roots and boughs and leaves must come first, but
the tree exists for the sake of the fruit. "Hence that hidden thought that was
the brain (core) of those (nine) heavens was in the end the lord of
lawlak."[30]

Because of the Prophet's complete union with the Lord, God's saying
"*law laka*" is equivalent to His saying, "I created the heavens for Myself"
(F 57–58/46). Another side of God's motivation likewise issues from
Muhammad's utter oneness with pure love. God elevated Ahmad above
the other prophets because he had become the ultimate goal in love. Rumi
explains the divine favoritism in two texts, the first spoken by God
Himself, the second delivered by the poet: "Had it not been for pure love's
sake, how should I have bestowed an existence on the heavens? I have
raised up the lofty celestial sphere, that you may apprehend the sublimity
of love" (V:H.2734, 2737–40).
And elsewhere:

> The object of God's regard in both worlds is the (pure) heart, for the
> king's gaze is fixed upon the favorite.
> God's love and the mystery of His dallying with His favorite were
> the origin of all His veil-making (creation of phenomena).
> (It was) on that account, then, (that) in meeting (the Prophet) on the
> night of the Ascension our (Lord who is) fond of dalliance said,
> "But for you. . . ." (VI:2882–84)

Proof of Muhammad's Prophethood

The Qur'an

Ahmad's foremost "miracle" was the Qur'an. Muslim tradition beginning
with the Qur'anic text itself teaches that the Prophet was "unlettered"
(*ummi*). Rumi argues that Muhammad must be considered *ummi*, not
because he was unable to write and learn, but because those skills were
innate and not acquired. About this important distinction the poet writes:
"He who inscribes characters on the face of the moon, is such a man

unable to write? And what is there in all the world that he does not know, seeing that all people learn from him?"[31] Nevertheless, the Qur'an did have to be "sent down" (F 125/114) as God spoke it.[32] Even though the body of Ahmad was spirit, the Qur'an was taught to the Prophet (III:593–94). The revelation came down upon him word by word, lest the Prophet should be dissolved by having to receive it all at once. Piecemeal revelation was no drawback, however; for when one already knows the entire story from firsthand experience, one needs only a hint to recall the full significance of the story (F 41/29). As it was, even the safeguard of gradual revelation did not prevent the Prophet from being consumed by the light; as the kernel of knowledge increases and the rind becomes thinner, at last the pistachio nut (the lover) is consumed by the beloved (III:1389–90).

Muhammad had a scribe to whom he dictated the revelation as he received it. When the scribe began to discern wisdom within himself, he failed to realize that it was reflected there by the Prophet as he dictated. In his pride the secretary attributed the Messenger's light to himself. His supposed illumination was shown up as false when the scribe turned against Muhammad and against the faith (I:H.3228–36, 3355–56). Any one who has the true light for food "becomes the Qur'an" (V:2478), which in turn is like the rod of Moses, devouring all infidelities like a dragon (III:1208).

From the very beginning, unbelievers criticized the Qur'an as merely a composition of "legends and paltry tales" that even children could comprehend. How could anything so shallow and obvious be worthy of serious consideration? Rumi answers the attack by quoting a hadith which, by extension, doubles as a defense of the *Mathnawi* as well. The Tradition says that under the exterior meaning of the Book are hidden seven interior senses. Mawlana then proceeds to enumerate a total of four senses, including the exterior meaning. The first interior sense is "exceedingly overpowering"; in the second "all intellects become lost"; and the third only God perceives (III:4230–47; AM 227, 289). Muhammad resembles the Qur'an in that he, too, appears to be of ordinary constitution; but "in that constitution there appeared evidentiary miracles (*mu'jizat*) by which all constitutions were vanquished" (III:4248–49; V:1323–28). Of the Prophet's evidentiary miracles, this hundred tongued wonder whose name is *umm al-kitab* (mother of the Book) is the first. "None dares either steal a single letter thereof or add to the plain word."[33]

The Splitting of the Moon

Qur'an 54:1 alludes to a second miracle overlooked by those who regarded only the Prophet's exterior aspect: "the moon was cleft asunder" (II:1605–6; I:1478). Ahmad's sincerity, so great that it even stopped the course of the sun, split the moon effortlessly (V:2776). His light was such that it became a hundred moons and easily put the earth's moon to shame;[34] but even in its shame the moon became truly blessed. Ahmad performed this miracle by a mere sign, a nod, so that Rumi sees the miracle as a symbol of the Prophet's unchallenged authority against all foes.[35] Because God's hand worked beneath appearances (II:1917–19; IV:2831), the moon's shield gave way to Ahmad's spear (D 938:9). As a touchstone of belief, the splitting of the moon serves to highlight the obstinacy of unbelief. Rumi singles out Bu Jahl and Bu Lahab for their denial of this miracle (II:420, 2060). Even though the moon would be split if the prophetic message were to descend upon it, the heart of one who is "veiled" remains untouched (VI:4278–79,1303–6). In the heart of the believer, by contrast, the moon is cleft every moment (D 462:6, 8). Mawlana interprets the miracle as a last-straw effort to persuade those who were too obtuse to recognize the greatness of the Prophet as a person (VI:2446; II:1921). As in the Prophet's own time, so in later times, if one cannot believe the Prophet, even the cleaving of the moon will not effect a conversion (I:1076–77). As for the moon itself, it could scarcely have been more fortunate than to have stepped outside of its own cycle and intruded upon the "cycle of Ahmad."[36]

The Mi'raj

Rumi uses the story of the Khwarizmshah's steed as an occasion for telling of Ahmad's Ascension. Swift as the moon, the Shah's horse could travel through the whole zodiac in one night. Surely, the poet exclaims, the Prophet's Ascension is not less credible than that (VI:3444)! Developing the two stages of Ahmad's mystical experience suggested in Q 17:1 and 53:13–18, Mawlana recounts Muhammad's journey to the "uppermost sphere" and the seventh heaven.

As a recompense for "breaking his foot on the path of exertion," Mustafa was invited to ride on Buraq so that the "bearer of the religion" became "one who is borne" (I:1073–74). Rumi refers to the first stage of the Prophet's journey, the Isra', in the Diwan and has devoted one entire ode to it, ending each verse with the words of Q 17:1: "Glory to Him who carried (His servant by night . . .)" (D 2538; D 213:6). From the "Farther Mosque," already made famous by Solomon, the Prophet was taken to the seventh heaven.[37] Mawlana says once that Ahmad's spirit hurled a lasso on high and rode up on it (VI:2834), but in general the Prophet rides the Pegasus-like hybrid mount called Buraq. On that horse of Paradise, Ahmad raided and seized with a long hand whatever he desired (D 941:9). The same mode of conveyance awaits every believer at the moment of departure from this world (VI:3878–79; IV:1210). Buraq is the symbol of spirit's victory over the ass of the body (D 709:14; 1997:4), and of the believer's death to self, which alone can send one on the journey that is like the *mi'raj* of cane to sugar or of an embryo to rationality (V:4134; IV:552–56). Jalal ad-Din speaks of Buraq as heart, as spirit, as unity and union; but most frequently, Buraq is desire and love.[38]

On his journey, the Prophet glimpsed the heavens and the angels. His purpose, however, was to obtain the vision of God Himself;[39] and on that night God disclosed Himself to the "form" of the Prophet (D 1052:4, MPR1 134). Several texts attempt to describe Muhammad's ineffable encounter. It was a day of trial for Ahmad: would he prefer the "treasury of the seven heavens" to union with God? Alluding to Q 53:17, "The eye neither turned aside, nor did it wander," Rumi has the Prophet himself answer the question with a marvelous play on words—an Arabo-Persian compound—that recalls our falconry image indirectly. "We are *ma zagh*" (i.e., "our eye did not rove"), he said; "we are *ma zagh*" (i.e., "we are not crows"—*zagh*, creatures that search for carrion treasure).[40] Muhammad preferred the Dyer to the dyed and regarded even the heavenly intellects as mere straw (I:3949–55).

So perfect was the Prophet's communion with his Beloved that he left Gabriel behind, keeping station at the Lotetree on the marge of Paradise. Just one of the guiding angel's seven hundred wings[41] covered east and west, and stunned the Prophet when the angel first appeared. Nevertheless, Gabriel "cut his hand" like the women of Egypt bedazzled at the sight of Joseph (D 1275:5). The spirit of Ahmad far surpassed that of the angel, and the most persistent urging of the Prophet could not persuade the guide to accompany him further. Gabriel feared, with good reason, that he would be consumed instantly, for the Messenger comes from the kitchen where angels are cooked (D 225:4). Gabriel judged it prudent to remain at his appointed station outside of the immediate presence of God, at the Sidra tree.[42]

Mawlana includes in one of his letters a brief conversation in which Mustafa asked Gabriel about his "state"—relationship to God. Gabriel replied that at times he felt so grand that all the world could not contain his feathered wings, while at other times he felt no bigger than a finch. The angel explained God's absolute control over his angels, who, powerful as they are, are nothing before the Creator (M 103/207). Rumi further emphasizes the superiority of the Prophet over the angel when he notes that the "guarding tablet" (the heart of the seeker) had become the "guarded tablet" (source of all divine knowledge and the archetype of the Qur'anic revelation), and the intellect that had formerly been Ahmad's teacher became his disciple on the night of the *Mi'raj*.[43]

Jalal ad-Din explicates the inner meaning of the Ascension by means of numerous one-line images in the *Diwan*, as well as in his exegesis of a pair of hadiths relating to two earlier prophets. Rumi likens the Ascension to patience and wisdom; a journey of a hundred thousand years telescoped into a single night, on which only those may embark who are poor and pure of heart.[44] Faith makes one a candidate for Ascension. Even though Rumi has already said that Jesus, too, ascended to the fourth heaven, he proceeds to mention a hadith that says that if the faith of Jesus had been greater he would have ridden not only the water, but the air, as Muhammad did (VI:H.1186; AM 632). Clearly the most important facet of the *Mi'raj* was that it brought Muhammad near to God. Accordingly, Rumi quotes another Tradition: Ahmad's Ascension does not rate above that of Jonah simply on the grounds that the Prophet went up and Jonah down. Nearness is beyond directional calculation. "To be near (to God) is not to go up or down: to be near to God is to escape from the prison of existence."[45] Muhammad's exemplary, but unequaled, proximity to God means, finally, that the Ascension is love, and it is the intoxication that accompanies the wine of *mi'raj*. Rumi regards that Ascension as the "time" of Muhammad's reception of revelation; Sufis have used the term to suggest paradoxically the timeless essence of an individual's experience of God. It is the theological center of Mawlana's thought on revelation. Because of *alam nashrah*, the Prophet's eyes were opened even wider than Gabriel's, so that Ahmad became the "Witness." Because his eye "did not rove," he became the "Intercessor;" and it was on the night of the Ascension that God said to Muhammad, "*law laka*."[46]

The Moaning Pillar

When he preached in the mosque in Madina, Muhammad was in the habit of leaning against a certain palm trunk that served as a pillar. One day a woman of the Ansar offered to have a carpenter-slave of hers build a proper pulpit for the mosque. Ahmad accepted her offer. The forsaken pillar wept when the Prophet preached the following Friday. As Ahmad descended from the *minbar* to comfort the pillar, it began to moan softly. Rumi describes how the pillar's sadness arose from the separation from the Prophet. Conversing with his former resting place, Muhammad asked the pillar what it wanted. Everlasting life, it replied. Thereafter the Prophet buried the pillar so that it might rise at the Resurrection.[47]

Mawlana explicitly regards the pillar's "coming into the way of righteousness" (III:1017) as one of the Prophet's miracles (I:2141–44). The pillar felt the pain of separation because it possessed knowledge (*khabar*) and the "eye of the heart" that Nimrod's fire and Hud's wind also possessed (IV:2418). Attachment to Ahmad radically transformed the pillar (F 145/135). Likewise the believer who has become enamored of the Prophet by hearing the song of his light will moan if the Prophet does not enter his heart (D 1649:12; 2131:10). Let no one take the Prophet's attention for granted, however, or "be puffed up by reason"; for "many a well-trusted master who was a pillar of the world has become more lamenting than the Moaning Pillar" (D 526:6, MPR1 62).

Not least among the pillar's miraculous qualities is that it is a touchstone of the seeker's faith. Anyone who disbelieves in the moaning pillar Rumi deems a closet philosopher (i.e., one who is skeptical of the action of God, I:3280–85). Only those in touch with the spiritual mysteries will hear the "complaining of inanimate things" (I:2122). To the unbelievers "the pillar of the mosque is a dead thing; to Ahmad it is a lover who has lost its heart" (VI:859).

Other Miracle Stories

Rumi pays less attention to a number of other miracles; but they are a part of the lore that the poet inherited, and so we include them here.

The Water Skin: Mustafa once happened upon a caravan whose water skins had all gone dry. The caravaneers were staring death in the face when the Prophet appeared and told them to keep lookout on some nearby dunes for a black camel rider who would bring help shortly. Apprised that a prophet awaited him in the camp, the black man balked for fear the prophet might actually be a wizard, so the caravaneers had to bring him by force. The Prophet then instructed the Arabs to drink their fill from the visitor's water skin. After all the people and camels had quenched their thirst, the skin was still full. At that the black man converted. He clasped the Prophet's hands to his face to kiss them and his face turned white: he became a "Joseph in beauty" as a result of his relationship with Ahmad (III:H.3130–74; V:707).

Two Stories Confirming Ahmad's Prophethood: When Halima brought the child Muhammad into the precincts of the Ka'ba, a voice from the unseen spoke to the sanctuary to announce the presence of the exalted child prophet. Many years later a most unlikely witness again confirmed Ahmad's prophethood. An infidel woman came to Muhammad to put him to the test, but her two-month old suckling child spoiled her design. Speaking precociously as Jesus and John had done, the baby delivered a eulogy of the Prophet. Gabriel had taught the child the qualities of prophethood and had thereby freed the child from the power of al-'Uzza to become the servant of God. In the first story, Muhammad too had broken free of al-'Uzza when the mere mention of his name brought the idol crashing from its pedestal. Hearing the child's advanced wisdom, the infidel mother followed her offspring into the ranks of believers. Rumi concludes the story, "As for that one whom God endows with knowledge, things inanimate and growing (living) utter a hundred expressions of belief in Him" (III:H.3220–36).

The Eagle that Snatched the Prophet's Boot: "As for the one whom God protects, birds and fish become his guardians" (III:3237), the above story continues. When the Prophet was preparing one day to go for the ritual prayer, an eagle swooped down and snatched away the boot he was about to put on. From the overturned boot there fell a black snake. Ahmad would have been aware of the serpent's presence, except that he had been momentarily preoccupied with himself. Fortunately, the reflection of the light of Ahmad opened the eagle's eyes to the danger. Returning the boot, the eagle bade the Prophet proceed to the place of prayer (III:H.3238–54).

The Talking Gravel: Abu Jahl once tested Muhammad by asking him to reveal what Bu Jahl had hidden in his closed palm. Ahmad asked him, "Shall I say what those things are, or shall they declare that I am truthful and right?" Bu Jahl preferred the latter. Immediately every pebble in his hand began to recite the *Shahada* and Bu Jahl angrily threw the stones to the ground (I:H.2154–60; VI:858).

Mawlana alludes to a similar story in which the stones and trees made *salaam* to Ahmad (III:1018; IV:2832). Ibn Ishaq records that, as Muhammad journeyed toward solitude outside Makka, "not a stone or tree that he passed by but would say, 'Peace to you, O Messenger of God.' And the Apostle would turn to his right and left and look behind him and would see only trees and stones" (SN 105).

Muhammad's Staff: In a story that clearly parallels the accounts of Moses' rod and its effect on the Nile and Red Sea, Mawlana tells how God provided a flood as a test to convince the disaffected amirs that Ahmad's amirate was not to be questioned. Like so many hapless magicians of Pharaoh, the amirs hurled their lances at the torrent. Ahmad threw his wand and the flood turned aside (IV:H.2779–2801; F 145/135).

Muqawqis' Cornfield: One very cryptic reference appears to hint at a story in which Muhammad turned stony ground into a fertile cornfield for a certain Muqawqis (II:1648). Muqawqis' identity is disputed. According to Nicholson (MCN), he may have been the Coptic ruler of Egypt to whom the Prophet wrote a letter in 6 A.H.; or he may have been a poor Companion of the Prophet. Of the two possibilities, the latter seems more likely in view of the action in the story.

The Unburnt Napkin: A miraculous relic story tells of a napkin that was impervious to fire because Ahmad had once wiped his face with it. The traditionist Anas ibn Malik used to clean the napkin by throwing it into a fire. Rumi views the napkin as an example of how one must rid oneself of fear of the fire of purification by seeking the company of the likes of Ahmad (III:3110–27).

Ahmad's Prophetic Attributes

Here we examine the various names by which Rumi knew Ahmad; Ahmad's role as definitive prophet; and the Prophet's relationship to the believing Muslim.

Names and Titles of the Prophet

Had Rumi not supplied so much specific data about Muhammad, one could still glean a large part of his prophetology merely from a careful study of the Prophet's names and titles. Many of those aliases of Mustafa, "the chosen one," have already appeared or will in the last two sections of this chapter, either explicitly or by association. Here we shall gather up some of those names that would otherwise find no place.

"The name," either alone or with "of Ahmad" or "of Mustafa," occurs in Rumi as a prayer in its own right. At first the name was pronounced in secret or "into the ear" by the Prophet's embattled Companions; later it would be broadcast from minarets as a call to prayer.[48] The man who called the name in derision, however, had his mouth permanently distorted as a punishment (I:H.812–15). Long before the time of Muhammad, his name was celebrated in the Gospel. Here Mawlana seems to have in mind the ancient Muslim tradition that the word *parakletos* (advocate) of John 14 and 15 should be read as *periklutos* (much praised), and therefore refer to Muhammad, the highly praised. Mawlana recounts how one party of Christians would stop and kiss the name when they came to it in their scripture reading. Another party of Christians, however, held the name in contempt because their texts had been corrupted. The readers of the true text were protected by the name in time of the persecution by the Jewish king, whereas the other party remained vulnerable. If the Prophet's name could afford such protection, how much more protective must his essence be (I:H.727–38)? Long after the time of Muhammad, the name is still stamped forever on coinage minted by royalty whose names have come and gone.[49]

Mawlana occasionally calls the Prophet by names taken from the beginnings of Qur'anic verses. In addition to al-Muzammil (Q 73:1; IV:H.1453ff.), for example, he is entitled "Sultan of 'Abasa" (Q 80:1; IV:2082; V:73); the "King of wa 'n-Najm" (Q 53:1; IV:2082); and "O la 'amruk" (Q 15:72; V:112). "Ya sin" is one of the seven names given the Prophet by the Qur'an itself; and in Traditions that Rumi probably knew, the name had come to mean "The Lord of Humankind."[50]

Regal and military epithets abound. Muhammad is the "King,"[51] the "Sultan,"[52] the "Emperor,"[53] the "Commander in Chief of Things Unseen" (*sepahdar-i ghuyub* III:4004), the "Commander of Destiny" (*'mir-i qada* VI:2886), the "Captain of Mankind" (*sepahdar-i bashar*, VI:1450), the "Goodly Hero" (*khush pahlawan*, III:4079), the "Chief" (*mihtar*, V:125; VI:3475), the "Caliph" (V:112), the "Lord of Justice" (II:3021), the "Majestic" (VI:2620), the "Pole" (III:2196), and the "Leader of Our Caravan" (D 463:5). Rumi even uses a Turkish honorific to call Muhammad the "Great Hero" (*alp ulugh*, VI:1862). In stark contrast to all of these glowing titles, the Prophet is, perhaps most importantly of all, God's Servant (V:3111).

Some of Muhammad's names have already been mentioned in association with his light and knowledge. A few others like those are "Master of All Sorts of Knowledge" (*dhu funun*, IV:526), the "Candle" (I:3982; IV:1697), the "Lamp,"[54] the "Sea of Light" (I:3985), the "Light of Light" (I:1087), and the "Ruler of the Stars" (I:1076). Names such as "Assembly of Josephs" (VI:1088), "Orphan Pearl,"[55] "Pride of the World" (D 463:5), and "Jewel of the Eye and Heart" (D 1290:6) emphasize Ahmad's beauty.

Numerous other titles assist Rumi in coloring his description of Muhammad's relationship to the other prophets and to the believer; we shall treat some of them in the remaining sections of this chapter.

The Seal of the Prophets

Ahmad's intimacy with God was the foundation and cause of his preeminence among God's Messengers. Paradoxically, the utterly exclusive nature of the Prophet's communion with his Lord made possible his global relationship to all creation.[56] God singled him out from among the messengers (V:2738), and refined him "by salt" above all others (I:2004). Ahmad became superior in respect of security, Rumi explains in an allusion to Q 43:31, "And we have raised some of them above others in rank" (F 60/48); so that God addressed Ahmad as "my greatest prophet" (IV:1477). A hadith says that although Muhammad was the last in time, he was the foremost in excellence.[57] Among the prophets Muhammad is therefore entitled the "Head" (I:727), the "King" (IV:3358), the "Chiefest of the Chief" (*sadr-i sudur*, I:381), the "Glory of the Prophets" (VI:2497; D 1113:8), the "Heart of the Prophetic Mission" (*risala*, M 1/34), and the "Sovereign of 'We have sent as Messenger.'"[58] Contrary to appearance, Adam was in fact born of Mustafa, the "Forefather of (every) Forefather" (IV:522–30; F 116-17/105–6). Jalal ad-Din explains how Muhammad became the Seal, as follows:

> The seals that the (former) prophets left were removed by the
> religion of Ahmad [allusion to Q 36:65, "We seal their mouths. . . ."].
> The unopened locks had remained (as they were): they were opened
> by the hand of "Behold, We have opened (unto you)" [Q 48:1]. . . .
> He has become the Seal for this reason that there never was any one
> like him in munificence nor ever shall be.
> When a master surpasses (all others) in his craft, don't you say (to
> him), "The craft is sealed on you"?
> In the opening of seals, you (O Muhammad) are the Seal. . . .[59]

Muhammad's relation to certain specific prophets emerges several times by comparison or contrast. Abraham's religion set an example for Ahmad to follow (V:H.1265). "There is a flood in every age," according to a Tradition, and Muhammad is a "second Noah," "Captain of the Ark of the Umma."[60] As the "Khizr of his Time" he brings every ship home safely and is "Lord of the Water of Life" (IV:1461; VI:671). Though Muhammad's Ascension was not superior to that of Jonah, the Prophet's faith was greater than that of Jesus.[61] Ahmad equaled or surpassed Moses as desert guide and master of the waters (II:2284–94; IV:H.2779–2801). As close to God as he was, Moses nevertheless yearned for the "cycle" of Ahmad; for God allowed Moses to glimpse the new age and opened for him the way to communion with Mustafa (II:355–60). In short, "The name of Ahmad is the name of all the prophets: when the hundred come, ninety is with us as well" (I:1106).

The Prophet and the Believer

Rumi thought of himself as living in the "cycle of Ahmad" in the sense that the Prophet remained spiritually present in his community. Believers could thus relate to the "Pride of Humankind, the Best of Created Beings" (III:3140) in a personal manner, looking to him for guidance, intercession, and blessing. Ahmad is present also in the Friends of God and shaykhs who arise in every age (I:813, 2005). Great as many of Muhammad's successors have been, however, Rumi points out that no one would ever mistake one of them for the Prophet himself. To underscore that important point, Mawlana tells the story of how Abu Bakr used to sit on the second step of the Prophet's pulpit, and 'Umar on the third, while 'Uthman sat on the top in the Prophet's place. The third caliph explained that if he were to take a lower position he might be taken for Abu Bakr or 'Umar; but no one would think him like Mustafa.[62]

Ahmad extends a twofold influence on the believer, both disruptive and comforting, for the Prophet is both the "Heart-Ravisher" (I:3867) and the "Lord of Relief" (VI:2252). When 'Umar entered the mosque, intent on slaying Muhammad, an arrow of light from the Prophet pierced his heart. Stunned by affection, 'Umar wished only to dissolve into his new beloved (F 170–72/162–63). Another story tells of how a man came to Mustafa and professed his love for the Prophet. Muhammad cautioned the man to beware of what he said. When the man reiterated, Muhammad warned him again. After the man's third profession of love, Ahmad said, "Now stand

firm, for with my own hand I am going to slay you, woe upon you!"
(F 125/114). Muhammad conquers only to give life and light and security
(F 37/25; I:3867). One who would achieve union with this Beloved must
be willing to rediscover his poverty, experience *fana'* , and become "shadowless" like the flame of the candle (Muhammad) (V:672ff.). True
believers must allow the "breaker of idols" to deliver them from the idols
of their hearts (II:366–71; D 1492:6).

Painful as it may be to take the cure from this elixir,[63] one can find no
other sure way. He alone is the guide who risked his own life to blaze a
trail. Recalling the image of the Sunna quoted earlier (V:H.2963),
Mawlana describes how Ahmad discovered the road and posted markers
along the way. No one can come to God who does not first come to
Muhammad the guiding reason.[64] Along a journey fraught with possible
wrong turns and pitfalls, the Prophet is also the "Protector," the "Guard,"
the "Warner," and the guarantor of the journey's goal.[65] As the solicitous
shepherd, Ahmad tends his own flock sometimes without speaking
(II:1915), sometimes speaking low according to the measure of their
understanding.[66] He counsels and commands and witnesses to the faith.[67]
As the Mirror, Muhammad is the source of true self-knowledge for all who
are willing to behold themselves in him, and who become in turn mirrors
for one another.[68]

Ahmad shares with the other prophets the prerogative of intercession.
The "Hatim in the world of givers of spiritual life" gives his gifts to the
believer both in this world and in the next, for his prayer is efficacious
always (VI:167–73; Hatim at-Ta'i is the paragon of generosity among the
ancient Arabs). Ahmad flows between the sinner and God like the water of
life (D 821:9; 398:5). He promised to intercede for 'Ukkasha as a reward
for bringing news of the Prophet's imminent demise (IV:2590); and
Muhammad urged Abu Talib to profess the faith that he might plead with
God for his uncle (VI:194–96). The Prophet's intercession is not restricted
only to the obedient. He intercedes wholeheartedly for the disobedient and
will deliver them from their misdeeds. In intercession Ahmad's scent
comes to the sinner (II:1204; VI:2861), while the righteous do not need
Muhammad's help. On the contrary, they themselves become interces-
sors.[69]

Companionship with the Prophet is possible because he has come from
among the people.[70] Therefore, when God said to Muhammad, "Peace be
upon you, O Prophet," God was bestowing peace also on all who are kindred spirits of the Prophet. Those with an affinity to Muhammad know the

Prophet as a tree knows its own sweetest fruit. Through Ahmad all blessings and gifts come to those of his kind.[71] They who are one with the Prophet in nature and aspiration behold him by the same light with which the Prophet sees them (I:3462–63). Ahmad himself warned that closeness to him could be risky, saying, "If you pretend to be sick beside me, you will become sick" (III:1580; AM 217). Still, companionship with him is one of the highest goals to which one can aspire (III:429). In the absence of Muhammad, the next best thing is the company of a Friend of God: "Either behold the light from the lamp of the last (Friends of God), or behold His light from the candle of those who have gone before," for a shaykh who has achieved perfection is "born of Mustafa" and is like a prophet to his people.[72] One of Rumi's favorite images of the seeker's association with the Prophet is that of the banquet in which the believer shares the Prophet's wine.[73] In the context of that imagery Jalal ad-Din tells the story of Muhammad and the greedy infidel, which seems a most appropriate final summary of Ahmad's apostolic concern for, and relationship with, the individual.

One evening a group of infidels arrived at the mosque after a long journey. Tired and hungry, they sought hospitality from Muhammad. The Prophet asked each of his Companions to take one guest along home for dinner. When all the Companions had gone, the least attractive of the infidels was left unchosen "like the dregs in a cup." He was enormous and an obvious threat to any larder, but the Prophet took him home. The man devoured enough food for eighteen men and drank the milk of seven goats. As the hadith says, the infidel eats with seven stomachs. That night the man became ill and befouled his sleeping quarters because the door had become jammed when he tried to get out. Even though he had not been present, Ahmad had become aware of the infidel's plight; but he did not move to alleviate the guest's embarrassment by loosening the door, for God desired that the infidel feel shame and confusion. In the morning someone brought the soiled bedclothes to Muhammad. Against the protestations of those present, the Prophet began to wash the bedclothes. Just then the infidel came into the house, momentarily overcoming his embarrassment, to search for an amulet he had left behind. When he saw Ahmad washing, he was enraptured and astonished at the all-encompassing cosmic reality of Mustafa. Muhammad embraced the man, imparted knowledge to him, and the infidel became a believer. There is in Rumi no finer illustration and proof of Ahmad's first and last title, a "Mercy To All Created Beings."[74]

Afterword

What, in the final analysis, does Rumi really think about prophets and revelation? The answer to that question depends on how one identifies Rumi himself and in what context one situates his writings. This broad survey has viewed Mawlana from the perspective of Islamic religious studies, regarding him as a major teacher of Muslim tradition and a strong link in the chain of the Islamic religious heritage. We have used the image of the Royal Falcon in much the same way that Rumi, from our chosen perspective at least, has employed the imagery of the prophets in general, namely as an organizing and pedagogical device.

Though these chapters have in several instances seemed to proceed as though one could reconstruct the stories of the prophets in Rumi's words, it seems clear that Rumi cares as little about prophetic biography and personality as about the historical contexts in which the messengers found themselves. He considers the prophets and emblematic elements of their stories his most important pedagogical *topoi*, weaving them into all of his work much as the Qur'an itself does; but his purpose in doing so differs significantly from that of the scripture.

Where the Qur'an employs the prophetic stories chiefly as moral exempla, Rumi the teacher uses the prophets and their stories as a convenient reservoir of familiar and attractive images with which he catches the ear of his listener, and as the come-on with which he entices the prospective buyer into his shop. Leaving himself open to the charge of bait-and-switch merchandizing, what Rumi is really selling is a vision of the relationship of the divine to the human and of a way homeward. Prophets and their deeds thus become metaphorical guideposts and reminders that function somewhat as does Rumi's celebrated reed flute: as a hollow tube capable of hauntingly plaintive song, but only when inspired not with wind but with fire.

One could of course single out dozens of major metaphors and image clusters that Rumi uses to serve his larger religious purposes as viewed

151

from this angle. But Rumi's use of explicitly prophetic imagery, along with his penchant for creating unexpected twists in already familiar tales by overlaying new images on the old, makes that imagery as reliable an index of the poet's thought processes as one can hope for. For sheer frequency of occurrence alone, for example, few classes of image can approach that of prophet metaphors.

In addition, one could read Mawlana's interpretation of prophets and revelation through a number of other filters. A biographical-developmental model, for example, might approach Rumi as a fascinating personality whose own life experiences provide an essential key to his writings. This method might study the imagery chronologically with an eye to possible correspondences between changes in his personal life and variations in his development of prophet imagery. Offering a clue as to what such an approach might turn up, Annemarie Schimmel points out that Joseph's rejection by his envious brothers gave Rumi a way of interpreting both his own relationship to Shams and the bitter jealousy of Rumi's family and friends.[1] One could observe something similar in his views of other prophetic figures as well. Prophets are, from this perspective, in a sense also psychological *topoi*, and prophetic revelation the larger framework within which Rumi understands all important human relationships.

Another approach might identify Rumi chiefly as a mystical poet, situating his work within the history of Persian mystical literature, or even more broadly, of Islamicate literatures. Such a perspective might highlight the continuity, or lack thereof, in the mystical development of these themes so central to the Islamic tradition as a whole, perhaps expanding on chapter 1's capsule description of mystical prophetology.

A third point of view might identify Mawlana primarily as a deft wordsmith, a literary artist capable of crafting highly specialized uses of different types of imagery for finely nuanced purposes. Such an approach might investigate comparatively variations in the complexity or density of certain kinds of imagery employed in certain contexts. For example, as Fatemeh Keshavarz suggests, when Rumi is speaking directly and clearly about God's dealings with humankind—especially through the Messengers—he tends to use rather simple metaphors, such as those drawn from nature. One needs little or no technical savvy to appreciate them. When he delves into the vagaries of human interrelationships, by contrast, the poet seems to gravitate to more complex images, such as astrological allusions or references to the intricacies of backgammon. One needs a more specialized and often highly technical knowledge of the conceptual system and its rules to catch the drift of the imagery.[2]

Finally, from the perspective of the history of religion or, more narrowly, of Sufism, one might characterize Rumi as an important communicator of specific major religious concepts through his prophetology. A prominent example is that of the function of shaykh or spiritual guide. As we have mentioned in several contexts already, Mawlana does not concern himself with expounding the theory and practice of any particular mystical school, and often uses the technical language of Sufism with less than technical precision. Still the poet clearly regards the role of shaykh as at least generically crucial and as an extension of the prophetic function of guidance from darkness into light. To illustrate how one might look at Rumi's prophet imagery through a lens or filter other than that of a prophet's life story, let us conclude with a brief glimpse, first, at how three prophets not previously discussed function as models of the spiritual guide, and second, at how the same lens reframes our picture of Muhammad in Rumi's writings.

Taking his cue from a hadith that likens the shaykh to a prophet among his people (III:4319, 1774), Rumi often uses the authority of such prophets as Adam, Noah, and David to give added substance to the role of the shaykh. Adam models the prophetic struggle to remain in tune with true knowledge, and to impart that knowledge as a shaykh would. He teaches creation the names and "melodies" of God, the inner truth of things. Because that knowledge was infused from creation in all beings and then gradually forgotten, the role of the prophet shaykh is to reactivate humankind's faulty memory. At the moment of Adam's creation, God sowed 'aql into the water and clay. In an allusion to the greater jihad, Rumi says that the angelic 'aql thus paid homage to Adam while the nafs of Iblis refused. Iblis won a temporary victory by blocking Adam's inspiration and insight (wahy and nazar).[3]

Pure light is the source of Adam's ma'rifa (intimate knowledge); hence his defeat was only temporary. Rumi plays on the irony of Iblis' inability to discern that light even though he was fashioned from fire. Iblis was too impressed by his own form and its apparent superiority to that of Adam. Angelic 'aql discerned in Adam the child of earth illumined like the moon by divine rays, and to its own surprise, acknowledged its debt to dust.[4] That light then becomes the thread that binds together in timeless succession all the prophets, Muhammad's Companions, and all the subsequent great mystics (II:905–30).

On the other side of the coin, Adam also models the experience of the *murid*, whom the poet seems to regard as the untutored falcon. Rumi likens Adam's forty-day development to the *murid*'s formation: "It is not surprising that the Sufis made attempts to designate Adam as the first Sufi; for he was forty days 'in seclusion' . . . before God endowed him with spirit; then God put the lamp of reason in his heart and the light of wisdom on his tongue, and he emerged like an illuminated mystic from the retirement during which he was kneaded by the hands of God."[5] Adam's forty tearful years of exile from the garden is likewise compared to the *chilla* from which the seeker emerges as a fully initiated mystical adept; the *safi* (pure) is therefore also *sufi*. Unlike Iblis, who blames God for leading him on, Adam accepts responsibility for his fall and thus models repentance as the first stage on the Path.[6]

Rumi uses the image of taking refuge in Noah's ark as a metaphor for seeking the tutelage of a shaykh. In that context the flood is a metaphor for the greater jihad. Rumi often speaks rather generally in that vein, as in this reference in one of his letters, quoting a hadith: "In the flood of Noah . . . there was no refuge except to turn to Noah. . . . And the Messenger said . . . , 'O Umma, in every age there is a flood and a Noah and a Qutb of that time who is the caliph of the age. The ship of Noah exists in that time and whoever grasps his hem is saved from the flood.'"[7]

Sometimes the poet likens the ark to the intimate knowledge toward which the shaykh assists the seeker: "The tablet of *ma'rifa* is the ark of Noah; the storm will drown whoever does not enter his ship."[8] Though Noah had never read Qushayri's *Risala* or Makki's *Qut al-Qulub*, he possessed all the requisite qualifications of a guide and merits a place in the company of such great mystics as Karkhi, Shibli, and Bayazid.[9] As a type of the mystic, Noah rode heavenward on the Buraq of the Ark (VI:2208). Finally, Rumi makes his most direct and explicit connection with Noah as shaykh. Alluding to a second hadith, in which Muhammad first calls himself the ship in the "flood of time" and then includes his Companions in the image, the poet says, "While you are in the presence of the Shaykh evil is far from you, for night and day you travel in a ship. Life-giving spirit shields you: asleep in the ship, you travel the path."[10]

In one of his lengthiest prophet tales, Rumi has David display his divinely inspired justice and skill in arbitration and discernment that make him an outstanding paradigm of the shaykh. The story uses the theme of animal as *nafs*. A poor man prayed earnestly that God would grant him livelihood without effort. Next day a cow battered down his door and allowed the man to slaughter it. The owner of the cow took the man before David to plead his case. At first the judge sided with the plaintiff. But when the poor man appealed, David reversed his decision after prayerful seclusion, and he ordered the plaintiff to give all his possessions to the defendant.

After this Khizresque action, David revealed to an angry crowd the reason for his decision. He showed the people a tree beneath which the plaintiff had long ago murdered his master. He then ordered the plaintiff executed with the very weapon he had buried beneath that tree. Rumi explains that David is the shaykh whose judgment aids the *murid* to kill the cow of *nafs* with the weapon of intellect. He can then render justice upon the *nafs* (the plaintiff) and secure unearned sustenance for the *murid*. "With the shaykh to help it, the intellect pursues and defeats the lower self; the *nafs* is a dragon with immeasurable strength and cunning; the face of the shaykh is the emerald that plucks out its eye."[11]

Luqman then becomes a model of the *murid* to David's shaykh. The sage watched David at his blacksmith's furnace making chain mail. Luqman was unacquainted with the armorer's art and wanted very much to ask what David was making, but he refrained, telling himself that patience was better. Asking too many questions merely hampers the shaykh's efficiency. David rewards Luqman's virtue with a fine coat of mail, for patience defends against pain (III:1842–54). Luqman's patience as embodied in an ascetical separation from all attractive morsels (*luqma*) teaches seekers to seek the hidden game rather than the game that attracts by appearance only.

Finally, Muhammad naturally strikes the poet as the ideal spiritual guide. Rumi's most extended allusion to Muhammad as shaykh occurs in a story of how the Prophet went to visit one of his sick Companions. Rumi leads up to the story with a long series of interwoven frame like tales, each emphasizing the need for the kind of spiritual insight in which only a shaykh can provide instruction: "if you do not want to lose your head, become a foot, under the tutelage of the discerning Qutb" (II:1984).

In the stories that precede the segments on Muhammad's visitation, the underlying pattern is that one character comes to the aid of another in trouble: the man who woke a person into whose mouth a snake had crawled; the man who rescued a bear from the dragon's mouth and did not recognize the bear for what it was—the *nafs*; and Moses trying to open the people's eyes to the falsehood of the golden calf. In those that come after and/or recur intermittently within the visitation story frame, images of the greater jihad appear and Rumi speaks more explicitly of the role of shaykh and *pir*. Muhammad as shaykh helps the sick man to realize the cause of his malady, and instructs him in the greater jihad. With imagery that recalls the first two stories—of the serpent swallowed and the dragon swallowing the bear—Rumi takes the metaphors a step further by conjuring up the image of how Moses transformed the snake-become-dragon into a potent rod against Pharaoh the *nafs*.

Before bringing the story of Muhammad's visitation to a close, the poet introduces several more stories exemplifying the greater jihad. Finally Muhammad discovers that the man has been praying inappropriately, asking God to inflict upon him now the pain of the next life's possible punishment, so as to let him avoid it hereafter. The Prophet, whom Rumi again likens to Moses leading out of the desert of the first stages of spiritual wayfaring, warns him not to be so arrogant as to think he could bear such a thing. He should ask rather for good and ease both here and hereafter. After concluding that frame sequence, Rumi nevertheless continues the jihad theme, returning to feature Muhammad as shaykh battling the *nafs* symbol called the Mosque of Opposition. The entire complex of stories (II:1778–3026), in turn, sits between a set of stories of Moses and Jesus as shaykhs and a series, running virtually to the end of the Book, continuing the themes of the role of the shaykh in discernment and spiritual combat.

Various aspects of Muhammad's shaykh-hood emerge from this cycle, especially, but from elsewhere as well. Not only is Muhammad a shaykh, but he is the model for shaykhs. As leader in the greater jihad, Muhammad wields his famous twin-tipped sword, Dhu 'l-Faqar. Rumi uses the sword as metaphor for spiritual maturity: the seeker who submits to spiritual tutelage is transformed from a mere needle into a Dhu 'l-Faqar, thus giving a dervish power to behead his selfhood—Dhu 'l-Faqar makes the seeker a *faqir*. Rumi often likens the sword to the staff of Moses.[12] The shaykh who has achieved perfection is born of Mustafa and is like a prophet to his people; and Rumi explicitly calls the model *pir* a *nabi*.[13]

Prophetology is not merely a thing of the past in the world of Islam. The sultan's jewel-encrusted scimitar on view in the Topkapi Museum is a work of enduring beauty and fascination, but it is also encrusted with nostalgia. Belief in God's revelation through prophets is a living reality on many levels of Islamic culture. Muslim presses continue to turn out pamphlets and books that recount the stories of the prophets, full of folkloristic details for the entertainment and edification of large numbers of people. In the villages of Iran and other Shi'i areas, plays in memory of the protomartyr Husayn reenact annually scenes from the lives of all the great prophets. For the better educated readers, "modernist" prophetologies focus on the figure of Muhammad as the ideal leader, man of prayer, husband, and as a sign of hope. Polemical prophetologies develop the notion of Muhammad as the Seal of the Prophets and of Islam as the final revelation, as a way of promoting Islam as the one religion for all people. Twentieth-century Islam has its poets with a distinctly mystical orientation as well. Echoing Islam's sure belief along with its hopes for the future, Muhammad Iqbal wrote earlier this century:

> From Prophethood is in the world our foundation,
> From Prophethood has our religion its ritual,
> From Prophethood are hundreds of thousands of us one,
> Part from part cannot be separated.
> From Prophethood we all got the same melody,
> The same breath, the same rain. . . .[14]

Appendix

Other Prophets in Rumi's Works

Adam

I: 316; 430; 540–41; 613; 1012,20; H1234ff.; H1480ff.; 1633ff;
1731; 1943–44,88; 2063; 2140ff.; 2272; 2426ff.; 2663;
2790ff.; H3893ff.; 3991.

II: 15; 18; 19; 67; 129; 229; 257; 696; 910–11; 1614ff.; 1824;
2058; 2119ff.; 2507ff.; 2708–39; 3268–69; 3330; 3773.

III: 591; 1080; 1276; 1470; 2299; 2407; 2759; 2853; 3196ff.; 3268;
3535; 3632; 3902; 4247; 4543.

IV: 324ff; 525–27; 736; 809; 1036; 1402; H1497; 1502ff; 1617;
1713; 2406; 2969–70; 3042; H3189; 3343; 3414.

V: 157; 520; 563; 941,62; 1219; H1556; H1581,90; H1621;
H1649; 1922; 2103; 2610–11; 3983.

VI: 260; 404; 1216; 1341,45; 2077; 2155; 2264; 2478; 2648; 2801;
3134,38; 3710; 4470; 4549; 4786.

D   15:6; 59:7; 65:6; 150:8; 187:2; 201:2; 227:3; 236:2; 280:7;
328:5; 335:7; 478:4; 527:2; 533:13; 678:8; 786:12; 804:5;
841:14; 859:5; 1012:2; 1048:11; 1062:2; 1203:2; 1243:10;
1290:5; 1401:2; 1443:4; 1468:7; 1500:1; 1505:3; 1514:5;
1520:22; 1534:3,4; 1542:1; 1576:6; 1597:7; 1615:4; 1623:5;
1655:12; 1671:7,8; 1705:6; 1717:3; 1737:14; 1752:5; 1787:3;
1794:8,9; 1875:6; 1876:7; 1905:3; 1908:5; 1965:4; 1967:8;
2006:8,9; 2041:10; 2061:7; 2068:3; 2082:2; 2168:7; 2170:16;
2276:6; 2282:4; 2300:3; 2317:2; 2371:9; 2408:3; 2447:1,2;
2500:11; 2512:7; 2514:1,2; 2529:4; 2583:5; 2608:10; 2627:8;
2632:3; 2781:5; 2889:7; 2938:10; 2947:4; 2971:5; 3032:8,9;
3112:7; 3121:10; 3141:10; 3209:5; 3212:6,12,17; 3214:3;
3222:2; 3340:5; 3369:10; 3393:6; 3422:3; 3500:4,5; 3502:3.

F   10/22, 14/27, 27/39, 67/79, 68/80, 73/85, 75/86, 80/92, 101/113, 102/113, 105/116, 202/210, 210/218, 231/238.

M   8/54, 22/75, 30/85, 37/93, 40/101, 55/133, 55/135, 68/150, 69/152, 84/174, 101/202, 129/249, 143/270.

R   68, 521, 799, 1073, 1310, 1331, 1498, 1590.

David

II: 493, 915, 1074, 1483, 1916, 3781.
III: 703, 1014, H1450ff., H1842–49, 1954, H2306ff., H2376–89, H2390ff., H2415–92, H2504ff., 2832, 4268ff.
IV: H388, H406, 787, 2416.
V: 3432.
VI: 856–57, 1842, 2182, 2285–87, 2657–58.

D   632:5, 660:7, 738:3, 914:2–3, 1086:5, 1100:19–20, 1144:17, 1369:4, 1411:9, 1421:5, 1792:6, 2074:5, 2120:9, 2524:16, 2529:8, 2608:13, 2945:3, 2953:1, 2962:5, 3121:11, 3130:4, 3149:6, 3212:5,7; 3442:7.

F   135/145.

M   37/94.

R   1179.

Ezra

III: H1763; IV: H3271ff.

D   491:5.

Hud

I: H854; II: 3056; IV: 133; VI: H2191, 4680, 4817ff.

Idris

IV: 2672; VI: H723, 2985.

D   1082:7; 1988:1; 2601:7.

Job

I: 2096–7; III: 452; V: 2903, 3689–91; VI: 876, 4836.

D   613:3; 624:8; 895:7; 1058:10; 1279:1; 1793:9; 1863:11; 2276:5; 2299:4; 2945:3; 3172:8; 3196:4.

F   233/241.

M   1/33, 117/228.

R   87, 739, 979, 1046, 1279.

Jonah

II: 3135,40; III: H4512; V: H1242, H1608ff.; VI: 2304–5.

D   507:15; 1215:15; 1247:6–7; 1700:6; 1839:14; 1863:14; 2058:5; 2550:2; 2598:8; 2821:6; 3016:7; 3119:2; 3194:2; 3327:5; 3381:4; 3418:3; 3424:12; 3481:15.

F   103/114.

Lot

II: 2663; III: 87; IV: 788; V: 1469.

D   60:5, 61:5, 879:15.

F   73/85.

Luqman

I: 1961–65; H3584ff.; II: H1462ff., H1510ff.; III: 52, H1842ff.; VI: H1111.

D   729:4; 788:11; 1250:7; 1390:17; 1471:5; 1665:5; 1925:5; 2204:6; 2228:7; 2347:4; 2896:16; 3109:1,3.

Noah

I: 403, 1404, 1841, H3124ff., 3402.
II: 352, 455, 912, 2661, 3057.
III: 86; 333; 1308,31,55; H2795; 2820; 3586; 3642ff.

IV: H538–39, 1410ff., 1458, 1946, 2153, 3357ff., 3584.
  V: 2344, 2504, 2655.
VI: 10; 20; 792; 844; 2043,2084–85; 2110ff.; 2208,25; 2359; 2652; 4471.

D   10:6; 36:11; 37:2; 129:12; 148:2,3; 369:9; 402:13; 483:10; 536:7; 539:10; 541:3; 668:9; 729:3; 876:3; 879:15; 880:8; 895:2; 935:6; 1020:2; 1130:3; 1250:5; 1301:5; 1302:5; 1343:4; 1369:6; 1644:10; 1674:5; 1712:5; 1840:2; 1889:14; 2017:3,4; 2034:5; 2090:2; 2347:4; 2388:13; 2391:6; 2473:19; 2646:4; 2684:4; 2747:3; 2830:7; 3057:11; 3090:3; 3351:9; 3354:17; 3434:7.

F   226/234.

M   22/74, 68/150, 72/157, 101/202, 128/243.

R   159.

Salih

  I: H2509ff.; III: 406; IV: 2648–49;

D   546:6, 1344:6, 1493:11, 2864:10, 2888:8.

F   227/234.

Seth

  I: 2272;
 II: 911.

Shu'ayb

 II: 1646; H3364–66; 3388; V: H1242.
D   3:11, 3081:14, 3408:8, 3423:10.

Solomon

  I: 956ff.; 1030; 1202ff.; 1576; 2604ff.; 2741; 3575,8; 3618–20,3682.
 II: 916; 1037; H1601–02; 3700ff.

  III: 1015, 1448, 2609, H4624ff.
  IV: 329; H388; H406; 467ff.; H563ff.; H614; 649; H653; 718ff.;
        H812ff.; 843ff.; H904–8; H1113ff.; 1251; H1263ff.; 1315,55;
        H1373,1379; H1897; 1901,1906.
   V: 839, 1442, 3184–85.
  VI: 810; 1532; 2660ff.; 4012ff.; 4674,4694.

D   23:4–5,15–16; 58:5–7; 64:8; 82:2; 90:3; 102:1; 103:10; 239:6;
          326:3; 332:6; 413:4; 415:6; 426:7; 441:24; 457:2; 504:2; 535:4;
          544:5; 598:7; 633:9; 640:6; 646:9; 679:3; 710:7; 765:7; 776:7;
          836:15; 838:5; 870:2; 882:16; 895:1; 956:3; 1012:6; 1053:10;
          1058:10; 1223:2; 1250:2; 1271:11; 1273:1; 1281:1; 1297:5;
          1364:4; 1426:7; 1427:11; 1460:9; 1466:1; 1564:9; 1602:15;
          1628:2; 1651:7; 1652:16; 1671:9; 1730:7; 1739:8; 1747:2;
          1765:7; 1792:10; 1849:4; 1889:11; 1894:6; 1902:4; 1940:60;
          1959:8; 1988:1; 2042:9; 2073:8; 2131:11; 2162:2; 2167:9;
          2175:13; 2184:6; 2240:8; 2298:9; 2333:8; 2365:6; 2408:7;
          2411:4; 2428:1; 2455:6; 2509:3; 2529:8; 2534:7; 2570:1;
          2593:2; 2609:2; 2622:5; 2643:8; 2655:10; 2674:8; 2832:4;
          2840:5; 2878:11; 2925:2; 2935:6,13; 2953:7; 3018:13; 3027:1;
          3042:1; 3076:6; 3092:3; 3093:11; 3117:5; 3130:4; 3135:8;
          3149:6; 3153:2; 3164:4; 3177:5; 3256:3; 3285:8; 3291:2;
          3296:6; 3299:11; 3329:3,4; 3368:5; 3425:10; 3502:7.

F   126/137, 233/241.

M   8/51,54; 37/94; 41/102; 118/229; 135/261,2.

R   95, 377, 406, 558, 580, 1006, 1179.

Abbreviations

AM	*Ahadith-i Mathnawi*, B. Furuzanfar, with his Hadith number
AMM	*And Muhammad Is His Messenger*, A. Schimmel
AS	*Sufism*, A. J. Arberry
CIA	*Creative Imagination in the Sufism of Ibn 'Arabi*, H. Corbin
D	Rumi's *Diwan*, poem : verse, Furuzanfar's one volume edition
DDH	*Dieu et la Destinée de l'Homme*, L. Gardet
EI2	*Encyclopedia of Islam*, Second Edition
F	Rumi's *Fihi Ma Fifi*, Arberry/Furuzanfar pages
FA	*Fusus al-Hikam*, A. Affifi Arabic Edition
FB	*Bezels of Wisdom*, R. W. J. Austin, trans. of *Fusus*
IPS	*Idea of Personality in Sufism*, R. A. Nicholson
ISD	*Introduction to Sufi Doctrine*, T. Burckhardt
KPC	*Key Philosophical Concepts of Sufism and Taoism*, T. Izutsu
LWR	*Life and Work of Rumi*, A. Iqbal
M	Rumi's *Maktubat*, letter/page number, Jamshidpur edition
MCN	*Commentary on Mathnawi*, R. A. Nicholson
MDI	*Mystical Dimensions of Islam*, A. Schimmel
MMec	*Muhammad at Mecca*, W. M. Watt
MMed	*Muhammad at Medina*, W. M. Watt
MM	*Mystique Musulmane*, G. C. Anawati and L. Gardet
MMF	*Mohammed, the Man and His Faith*, Tor Andrae
MP	*The Mystical Philosophy of Muhyi' Din Ibnul-'Arabi*, A. Affifi
MPR1	*Mystical Poems of Rumi*, A. J. Arberry trans.
MPR2	*Mystical Poems of Rumi 2*, A. J. Arberry trans.
MR	*The Metaphysics of Rumi*, K. Abdul Hakim
MW	*The Muslim World*
ND	*Divani Shamsi Tabriz*, selections, R. A. Nicholson
Q	Qur'an sura : verse number
QK	*Qisas al-Anbiya'* of Kisa'i, Eisenberg edition
QKT	*Tales of the Prophets of al-Kisa'i*, W. Thackston trans. of QK

QT   *Qisas al-Anbiya'* of Tha'labi, Dar Ihya' 'l-Kutub al-'Arabiya
         edition
R   Rumi's *Ruba'iyat*, quatrain number, Furuzanfar's edition
RPM   *Rumi, Poet and Mystic*, R. A. Nicholson
SDR   *The Sufi Doctrine of Rumi*, W. Chittick
SIM   *Studies in Islamic Mysticism*, R. A. Nicholson
SN   *As-Sirat an-Nabawiya* of Ibn Ishaq, A. Guillaume trans.
SPL   *The Sufi Path of Love*, W. Chittick
TM   *Themes Mystiques* or *Mystique et Poesie*, E. Meyerovitch
TS   *The Triumphal Sun*, A. Schimmel
TV   *As Through a Veil*, A. Schimmel
WF   *I Am Wind, You Are Fire*, A. Schimmel

I, II, etc. Rumi's *Mathnawi*, book : verse, Nicholson edition and
           translation

Notes

Chapter One: Rumi in the History of Islamic Prophetology

1. For a fuller treatment of Qur'anic prophetology, see Fazlur Rahman, *Major Themes of the Qur'an* (Minneapolis: Bibliotheca Islamica, 1980): 80–105.

2. F. Rosenthal, *A History of Muslim Historiography* (Leiden: Brill, 1952): 454, quoting Tashköprüzadeh; also 114ff. on the Universal Histories, and 190–93 on Kafiji's view of prophetic history in the larger task of the historian. On Mas'udi's Histories, see Tarif Khalidi, *Islamic Historiography* (Albany: State University of New York Press, 1975): 60–65.

3. F. Rosenthal, *Historiography* 358, quoting from *The Open Denunciation of the Adverse Critics of the Historians*. On the work of Tarafi of Cordova (d. 1062) who "stressed prophetic admonitions and moral counsels rather than the historical and legendary sides of their characters," see QKT xvi.

4. F. Rosenthal, *Historiography* 216.

5. *Ibid.*, 220–21; see also the "Introduction" to QKT for a history of the development of the genre of "tales of the prophets."

6. F. Rosenthal, *Historiography*, 122–23; Rosenthal adds, "For this reason, the 'idle talk' of the prophets—one cannot fail to be reminded of the extremist Shi'ah literature on the 'charlatanry of the Prophets'— was barred from Miskawayh's history." See also M. S. Khan, "Miskawaih and Arabic Historiography," *Journal of the American Oriental Society* 89:4 (1969): 710–30.

7. II:906–33; for other texts in which four or more prophets appear in a single ghazal, for example, see: D 214; 598; 1250; 1369; 1792; 1863; 1889; 2220; 2840; 2953; and 3434. See QKT "Introduction" and notes on continuity in the stories.

8. Fazlur Rahman, *Islam* (New York: Doubleday, 1966):142. In the sections on philosophical and theological prophetology, I have used the following sources: A. J. Arberry, *Revelation and Reason in Islam* (London: Allen and Unwin, 1957); Osman E. Chahine, *L'Originalité créatrice de la philosophie Musulmane* (Paris: Librairie d'Amerique et d'Orient, 1972): 74–82, on Farabi's theory; H. Corbin, *Avicenna and the Visionary Recital* (London: Routledge and Kegan Paul, 1960); M. Fakhry, *A History of Islamic Philosophy* (New York: Columbia University Press, 1970); L. Gardet, *Dieu et la destinée de l'homme* (Paris: J. Vrin, 1967): 143–230; al-Ghazali, *al-Munqidh min ad-Dalal* ("Deliverance from Error")—the best translation is in *Freedom and Fulfillment* (Boston: Twayne, 1980) by Richard McCarthy, S.J., with excellent notes and five appendices summarizing or translating five works to which al-Ghazali refers in the *Munqidh*; F. Rahman, *Prophecy in Islam* (London: Allen and Unwin, 1958); E. J. Rosenthal, *Studia Semitica*, Volume II (Cambridge: Cambridge University Press, 1971); Richard McCarthy, S.J., edition and English summary of Baqillani's *Kitab al-Bayan* (Beirut: Imprimerie Catholique, 1958) and "Al-Baqillani's Notion of the Apologetic Miracle," *Studia Biblica et Orientalia* III (1959):247–56.
9. E. J. Rosenthal, *Studia Semitica*, 81.
10. R. Walzer, "Al-Farabi's Theory of Prophecy and Divination," in his *Greek into Arabic* (Oxford: Bruno Cassirer, 1962): 206.
11. E. J. Rosenthal, *Studia Semitica*, 98.
12. Ibn Sina, *On the Proof of Prophethood*, M. Marmura, ed. (Beirut: Dar al-Mashriq, 1968): xii–xiii. See also M. Marmura, "Avicenna's Theory of Prophecy in the Light of Ash'arite Theology," in W. S. McCullough, ed., *The Seed of Wisdom* (Toronto: University of Toronto, 1964):159–78.
13. Two centuries after Ibn Rushd, Ibn Khaldun (d. 1406) produced what has often been called the world's first "philosophy of history." His views on the role of prophets are available in F. Rosenthal's translation of the *Muqaddima* ("Introduction to History") (Princeton: Bollingen Series, 1967), Three Volumes. See also Muhsin Mahdi's *Ibn Khaldun's Philosophy of History* (Chicago: University of Chicago Press, 1964), *passim*.
14. Qamaruddin Khan, "Ibn Taymiyah's Views on the Prophetic State," *Islamic Studies* III (1964): 521–30, quoting 527.

15. MR 100–107. For further comparison between Rumi and Ghazali, see LWR 75–90.

16. I have used the following sources in this section: FA, the best translation of which is FB, with excellent introduction and introductory notes to each chapter; MP; Shah Wali Allah, *Tawil al-Ahadith*, G. N. Jalbani, trans. (Lahore: Sh. Muhammad Ashraf, 1973); J. M. S. Baljon, "Prophetology of Shah Wali Allah," *Islamic Studies* IX (1970): 69–80; idem, *A Mystical Interpretation of Prophetic Tales by an Indian Muslim* (Leiden: Brill, 1973); Fazlur Rahman, *The Philosophy of Mulla Sadra* (Albany: State University of New York Press, 1975); William Chittick, *The Sufi Path of Knowledge* (Albany: State University of New York Press, 1989); James W. Morris, *The Wisdom of the Throne: An Introduction to the Philosophy of Mulla Sadra* (Princeton: Princeton University Press, 1981).

17. Rahman, *Mulla Sadra*, 5.

18. *Ibid.*, 242.

19. In *Kashf al-Mahjub*, Hujwiri employs a very similar image in the earliest such instance I have found, speaking of the pedestrian uses to which some thoughtless individuals put great works on Sufism: "The Royal Falcon is sure to get its wings clipped when it perches on the wall of an old woman's cottage," in *Kashf al-Mahjub of Al-Hujwiri*, R. A. Nicholson, trans. (London: Luzac, 1976): 8. The *Fihi Ma Fihi* citation with which our second chapter begins is reminiscent of a text from Sana'i: "When people trap a wild falcon, they bind it neck and talon, blindfold it, and teach it to hunt. Once the falcon gets used to the company of strangers it no longer looks for its former companions; it is satisfied with minimal food and no longer remembers what it ate formerly. The falconer, its new companion, lets the falcon see only him, so that it will become attached to the one who provides all its sustenance and who is always with it. Eventually, the bird's full gaze can fall without fury on the trainer . . . and the bird is ready for the king's hand. . . ."; *Hadiqat al-Haqiqa*, J. Stephenson, ed. (New York: Samuel Weiser, 1972), Persian text, 80–81.

20. See the section on Muhammad's Mi'raj in chapter 8 regarding the pun on Qur'an 53:17; here Rumi puns on the "crow" (*zagh*, the old hag) who harasses the falcon, and the falcon as *ma zagh* (i.e., the one who was both "not the crow" and the one whose eye was fixed on his goal, like that of Muhammad, and "did not wander"—*ma zagh*). Rumi

switches back and forth between the Arabic and Persian meanings of the words. Story appears in II:H.323–49, IV:H.2628–56, ND 48.

21. II:H.843–1130 for the story of the two slaves, similar in purpose to the stories of Hilal and Bilal; see II:1131–37, and D 728:9 for the falcon and the owls.

22. II:3731–65, quoting 3743, 3746, 3747, 3752; again punning, with the other side of "did not wander" meaning "was not a crow."

23. D 1353:3, MPR1 167, ND 29. Further references in D 26:4; 239:9; 441:3; 508:15; 649:2; 727:5; 1201:9; 1372:19; and many others. In III:H.432ff., almost as if to turn the tables on a reader who thinks Rumi has become predictable, he turns the falcon momentarily into the Devil himself, who tries to lure the ducks from their pond onto a dry plain. Rumi's point: God is in charge; Adam could have been Iblis, Moses could have been Pharaoh.

Chapter Two: Flight of the Royal Falcons

1. *nubuwwa* or *payhambari* or *risala*, F 184/176; VI: 1420.
2. I:982; D 2437:8; 3283:2; 3408:12; AM 23; I:1542; III:3973; VI:4541.
3. II:283–87, 2733, 2943; IV:230ff.
4. VI:164; IV:525; II:3056.
5. I:678–79; IV:449–50, 1652.
6. VI:2444; cf. FB 251–66 on Moses as "corporate" personality.
7. Heaven, I:640–41; cf. Q 83:7–9, 18–20.
8. II:1399; IV:2008; VI:1642, 4863; M 73/159; 131/252.
9. V:1982, H.2050, H.2080.
10. I:3307–8; IV:310; e.g., re: Moses I:3832–35.
11. F 80/68; III:4301–19; IV:3473–79; F 37–38/25–26, 60–61/49–50.
12. E.g., III:H.4258–64; IV:2200, 1065–72; I:3486.
13. "Substitutes," III:3106; VI:4139.
14. "Pole, axis," II:3325; V:2430, 2444.
15. F 65–66/53, 90/78, 177/168, II:2114, 2163–64. AM 635. MR 108–9 says, concerning the relationship of saint to prophet, "Rumi stands on a hill all by himself. For him there is no fundamental difference between sainthood and prophethood and both represent a stage of development realisable by every individual. The facts of positive religion have value only in so far as they represent eternal truths present at every point." On Ibn 'Arabi, MCN I:237 notes that saintship is the inward aspect of prophecy. As an institutional office, prophecy is infi-

nite. "The prophet *qua* saint is superior to the prophet *qua* apostle and lawgiver"—a distinction typified by the Khizr/Moses relationship. Cf. further MP 93–101, KPC 253–63.

16. I:1609–13, 1621. Allusion to AM 42 in v. 1610.

17. On this much discussed question, TM 237ff. goes so far as to say, "The theme of the Perfect Man is at the center of all Rumi's doctrine." MR 97–98, along with Nicholson, in MCN I:1679 and SIM, places Rumi in the line of Ibn 'Arabi, even though Rumi never actually uses his precise terminology. MR 109–12 summarizes the qualities of the ideal man, as mentioned in ND 8. About terminology, SDR 49–51 says that Ibn 'Arabi was the first to use the term "universal man," but that the doctrine predated him; and that although Rumi came later he used the "earlier terminology" of macrocosm/microcosm. Affifi's detailed exposition of Ibn 'Arabi's "Doctrine of the Logos" in MP 66–101 shows the Shaykh's idiosyncratic elaboration of this Hellenistic theme which appeared in Islam as early as Hallaj. Ibn 'Arabi develops the "indwelling logos" concept into a threefold theory with a metaphysical aspect (logos as reality of realities), a mystical aspect (logos as reality of Muhammad), and a human aspect (logos as perfect person). Affifi also indicates that the Shaykh "seems to confuse two different issues: the philosophical and the mystical aspects of the question" (81), and describes the perfect man as the "microcosm, cause of the Universe." Further on Ibn 'Arabi, cf. ISD 74ff.; KPC 208–52, 264–72. Finally, MDI 282 offers a welcome clarification of Rumi's thought in this regard: "Rumi probably did not think of the implications of a cosmic power embodied in this ideal man or of the possible relations between this perfect human being and gnostic concepts of the Primordial Man. . . . When reading his statements, one should remember that the Sufis frequently regarded the common people as something 'like animals'. . . . relying upon Koranic statements like that in Sura 7:178 about those who do not hear or see the signs of divine power and grace. Only the true 'man' can experience the vision of God through and behind His creation."

18. E.g., F 186/179ff., 207/199f.

19. III:1537–45, H.2900ff.; V:H.461ff.; VI:1903–5.

20. II:3366; III:2338; I:1919.

21. V:3935; III:3973; D 1058:5, 2990:2.

22. Cf. also D 1172:3/1178:2, quoting Q 17:41.

23. V:1226–31; VI:2926; I:1008–9; MCN I:223. Q 16:70 also quoted in D 3452:5.
24. D 228:6; 233:17; 1847:31; 1860:7; 3203:7.
25. F 172–74/164–65; D 303:9; IV:1416, II:1773–74; IV:2921.
26. III:1390. Further references to *wahy* in D 175:3; 573:2; 864:9; 985:10; 1715:5; 1847:30; 1860:4; 3030:16; 3276:20; R 907.
27. V:3914; F 155/146; F 80/68, 141/129, 216/207.
28. VI:2093; D 235:11. Further references to *kashf* in various forms in D 227:5; 248:8; 280:2; 400:2; 581:19; 1172:27/1178:13; 1279:3; 1772:6; 2239:11; 2425:5; 3127:8; M 82/172.
29. F 47/36; D 2953; alluding to Q 7:139.
30. As in I:3642, where God shows forth His knowledge (*'ilm*).
31. II:356. Many other references, often with light imagery, appear in D 33:24, 27; 264:6; 268:8; 271:3; 306:12; 414:7; 475:1; 518:4; 643:8; 649:4; 1141:6; 1966:13; 2073:3; 2083:9; 2100:11; 2346:8; 2464:15; 2519:38; 2524:17; 2593:6; 2630:11; 2655:13; 2814:14; 2935:14; 2960:5; 3133:7; 3142:12; 3167:8; 3229:14; 3234:4; 3291:7; 3358:2; 3397:5; 3398:5; 3452:13; R 130; 340.
32. III:3771–76. Vs. 3775's mention of the false dawn (*afili*) is an allusion to Q 6:79 in which Abraham repudiated all false gods.
33. IV:3331–32; D 2714:18. *'aql* and *khirad*, I:819; III:1515; VI:4138–39.
34. Called Gabriel by name in D 68:6; 117:11; 643:9; 844:6; 887:13; 1063:7; 1411:4; 1533:3; 1700:5; 1752:7; 1755:5; 1818:7; 2022:8; 2140:15; 2224:3; 2276:1; 2327:4; 2447:6; 2656:3; 2781:5; 2944:25; 2894:9; 3280:8/3489:9; R 1863; called the Trusted Spirit in D 16:3; 24:18; 1793:2; 1885:4; 1972:5; 2116:10; 2125:6; 2452:8; 3234:8; 3419:6; called the Holy Spirit in D 513:2; 732:8; 924:1; 934:5; 937:4; 1048:34; 1143:10; 1179:7; 1662:4; 2417:4; 2827:3; 3280:8; 3292:3; R 879; M 27/82; 49/120; 37/94; 94/188; 135/261.
35. F 139/128; hadith also in I:1331, 3520; IV:1852–55, 3400; M 33/89; 47/114 (3 times); 118/230; AM 33.
36. F 174/165; other comparisons and allusions to Q 24:35 in III:3406; IV:424–61, 695; VI:2069; and especially VI:3066ff.
37. Above summarized from II:1286–99, quote from II:1293; quote from Q 24:35 also found in D 565:6; 1166:11.
38. VI:4830; III:3907; F 107/96; D 836:5; 2781:13.
39. F 44/33, 156/147; III:3295; II:1299–1302.
40. V:786; III:2685; VI:3236ff.

41. *dhikr*, Q 15:9, F 125/114; *nadhr*, I:3824; *furqan*, Q 25:1, II:852; D 2119:32.
42. *muqallid, muhaqqiq*, II:493; VI:2617–18.
43. F 152/142–43; IV:3254; D 2122:8.
44. *hushmand*, I:3167, 3309–I0. *Kiyasa*, V:H.4025.
45. *'ilm, ma'rifa*, II:3603, 1851.
46. The fierce wind that destroyed the tribe of 'Ad upon their rejection of the prophet Hud; I:860; VI:4831.
47. VI:4567–69, 4584, II:H.3240.
48. Elsewhere Rumi calls God the *'allam*, the Knower, IV:3694.
49. D 132:2–3, 5–7, MPRl 16; see also D 182; 1955; 1957; 2366. Cf. MR 43ff. on love as mediator between the two worlds and on important differences between Rumi and Plato; LWR 244–53 on love in the *Mathnawi*.
50. IV:2921; on prophet as love see also D456:8; 1081:16; 1130:1; 1380:5; 1480:12–13; 1840:10; 2084:10; 2216:5; 3123:21; 3280:8/ 3489:9; R 57, 995, 1092.
51. F 127–28/116–17; 155–56/146–47; AM 33.
52. *salat*, IV:1181, quoting Q 2:148.
53. Sarraj, *Kitab al-Luma'*, R. A. Nicholson, ed. (London: Luzac, 1914) and Qushayri, *Das Sendschreiben al-Qushayris uber das Sufitum*, R. Gramlich, trans. (Wiesbaden: Franz Steiner Verlag, 1989), both *passim*; and AS 74ff.
54. F 66/53, 77/66, 213/204; *tawakkul* I:H.912–13, 956; V:1106; *fana'* I:575; III:4658; V:672ff; *baqa'* IV:445; *raja'*, *khawf* III:1965; VI:1855, 3235.
55. Punning on *aman* (security) and *iman* (faith), F 177/168; I:3866–67; V:3397–98.
56. VI:876; VI:2043; V:2903–4; III:1842–52.
57. I:515, 3308; IV:310, 789, 2852ff.; V:1540; VI:518, 4346–51; D 1298:6.
58. Also on *mu'jiz*, D 1975:10; 2338:4; 2992:5; 3419:6; 3465:10; 3452:3.
59. I:811; IV:2178. M 1/33; 45/110; D 2237:6; 2473:12.
60. F 231/205; III:3794; I:3605–6.
61. I:574–76; cf. especially the story of the Merchant and the Parrot in I:H.1547ff.; II:2943; III:3100; VI:886, 996; D 2057:3.
62. F 165/157; III:2700–2704, 2730–32; IV:H.3189; V:236–40.
63. I:1543–45; cf. M 97/193; D 3283:2; F 177/168; 227/220; I:1002–4; VI:3770; AM 23.

64. III:4146–48; VI:4394–96; VI:3288–91; AM 703.
65. IV:H.3311; F 151–52/142–43; II:2266–71.
66. F 172/164, IV:753, 1138; VI:861ff., 4672; IV:476, H.1113ff.
67. F 174/165; III:3109–11; IV:1383.

Chapter Three: Abraham and Sons

1. Principal extra-Qur'anic texts are in QT 63–88, QK 128–42, QKT 136–63; and FA 80–84, FB 90–95. Qur'anic citations will be given in subsequent notes.

2. Arberry's translation of D 824:19, MPRl 104. However, the word that Arberry translates as "lion" (shiri) can also mean "milk." Although Kisa'i's mention of "lions and wild beasts at the entrance of the cave" might make Arberry's translation seem plausible enough, another set of details in QKT 138 suggest that the verse ought to be translated "sucked milk from (his own) fingertips," for, according to Kisa'i, "When he sucked his fingers, his thumb flowed with honey, his index finger with wine, his middle finger with milk, his ring finger with cream and his little finger with water."

3. Quoting Q 6:79 in I:426; II:298, 564; III:1429–30; IV:1526; V:2650–53; VI:95, 1415; D 2:2; 402:2. The main features of the Qur'an's account of Abraham's repudiation of idolatry are found in Q 6:74–82; 19:42–49; 21:52–70; 26:69–104; 29:15–24; 37:81–96. Further see Y. Moubarac, *Abraham dans le Coran* (Paris: J. Vrin, 1958).

4. On sun and moon cf. D 185:9; 2894:6, MPR2 372. "I am free from you" is a near quote of Q 6:78 and/or Q 59:16, found in M 73/159. "I have surrendered" in D 2447:3 is quoting Q 2:125 .

5. II:74; D 772:5–6; 1959:4; 2006:6; 2190:2.

6. For the Qur'anic accounts of the sons of Abraham, cf. especially Q 11:72–78; 37:100–113; 51:24–34. There the prophet is promised a son, twice named Isaac explicitly; and an unnamed son is ordained for sacrifice. Rumi focuses entirely on the sacrifice theme's implications for spiritual growth. The *Qisas* accounts give more attention to the births of the two sons and to stories relating to the construction of the Ka'ba (QT 69–90; [Ishmael] QK 142–45, QKT 151–54; [Isaac] QK 150–53, QKT 160–62). Ibn 'Arabi focuses on the sacrifice of Isaac and on Ishmael's being loved by God especially (FA 84–94, FB 96–110). The mention of Isaac in context with Jirjis (George) in D

2092:14–15 seems to be a way of reinforcing the theme of sacrificial offering, for George "was a prophet who according to the Islamic traditions was slain seventy times by his people and again came to life"; MPR2 262, note 119.

7. D 565:3; 728:5; 1810:13; 2543:7.

8. D 1183:5/1237:4, 1665:12/2204:10.

9. II:283; III:4101, 4883.

10. D 1792:7; 2092:15 (*qurban*); 6:9; 151:3; 2092:20; 2213:3; 2375:5.

11. Concerning Ibn 'Arabi's interpretation of the sacrifice scene, Toshihiko Izutsu notes that even though Abraham was a prophet, he made the serious error of not "interpreting" his dream aright and of taking the dream to be a this-worldly reality rather than a symbol of a higher reality; see KPC 9–10.

12. II:379, following the story of the indebted Sufi. Allusions to Abraham's hospitableness in D 822:6; 3033:8; for related allusions cf. III:2519; VI:2285, 3711.

13. III:400; D 24:5; 1793:13; 2809:2. Because the Qur'an says the anonymous messengers refused to eat the meat offered them, tradition assumes they must have been angelic. See FA 84, FB 95 for Ibn 'Arabi's interpretation of how food is related to the name Khalil because food "permeates" (punning on the Arabic root) all parts of the one who is fed. Corbin attributes Abraham's hospitality to his being intimate with God, CIA 130–31 and notes.

14. III:H.1762–65, 1768; IV:H.3271–78.

15. V:333ff., 393ff., 764ff., 938ff.

16. D 1318:4; 1347:5; 1348:11; 1951:6; 2120:9; 2453:3; 3304:6; M 16/63.

17. D 1850:5; 3434:8; 2840:16. Also D 1249:6–7; 1696:5.

18. F 67/55; VI:2009; D 994:5/3478:5. Also D 2109:4; 2058:4.

19. Cypress and jasmine I:790; roses III:1016; F 80/69; sweet basil VI:4291. See also D 468:7; 528:5; 1665:13/2204:4; 1850:5; 1889:15; 2037:2; 2043:6; 2508:3.

20. I:547; VI:173ff., 3570–72. For more fire imagery, see: D 458:6; 470:7; 368:6; 567:16; 704:10; 751:5; 854:6; 994:4/3478:4; 1395:3; 1613:4; 1655:3; 1727:13; 1915:11; 1992:16–17; 2257:4; 2524:14; 2840:6, 16; 3234:17; 3418:3.

21. I:3700–3702; II: 1248–60; 2554ff.; IV:2709ff.; VI:4608ff.; D 2043:7; 2037:2—all ref. to the hadith commented on further in AM 134.

22. *Mantiq at-Tayr*, Persian text ed. by M. J. Mashkur (Tehran, 1353/1974), 231.
23. F 174/165; IV:1138; D 1214:11; 1747:3; 3232:4–5.
24. *Hadiqat al-Haqiqat*, Book I, Major J. Stephenson, trans., *The Enclosed Garden of the Truth* (New York: Samuel Weiser, 1972) 44–45.

Chapter Four: Joseph and His Family

1. It is worth noting by way of contrast that Ibn ʿArabi concentrates (FA 99–106, FB 119–27) exclusively on Joseph's inaugural dream of the celestial bodies bowing to him, and on its ultimate "interpretation" when Joseph receives his family in Egypt. The Shaykh uses the dream to extol the wisdom of the hadith, "the people sleep, and when they die they awaken"; and to discuss the epistemological qualities and deficiencies of this world of shadows in relation to authentic prophetic revelation and inspiration. (See KPC 5 where Izutsu gives Qashani's summary of the crucial differences between Joseph and Muhammad in the context of dream interpretation.) Ibn ʿArabi overlooks virtually every other aspect of the Joseph story. For Rumi, the dream holds less interest than other details that abound in both QK 155–79/QKT 167–92 and QT 94–126. For different approaches, see Annemarie Schimmel, "The Figure of Yusuf in Rumi's Poetry," in Leonard Lewisohn, ed., *The Legacy of Medieval Persian Sufism* (London: Khaniqahi Nimatullahi Publications, 1992), 45–59; and James Roy King, "Jesus and Joseph in Rumi's *Mathnawi*," *The Muslim World* 80:2 (April 1990): 81–95.

2. Here Rumi draws almost exclusively on Sura 12, to whose central features he gives distinctive poetic expression, with no noteworthy input from the *Qisas*. Thaʿlabi does not treat Jacob separately, but only in connection with Joseph; see QT 94ff. and QK 153–55/QKT 163–66; see also FA 94–99, FB 111–18. For various interesting approaches to the Qur'anic material, see: M. A. S. Abdel Haleem "The Story of Joseph in the Qur'an and the Old Testament," *Islam and Christian-Muslim Relations* 1:2 (December 1990): 171–91; Marilyn Waldman, "New Approaches to 'Biblical' Materials in the Qur'an," *The Muslim World* 75:1 (January 1985): 1–16; Mustansir Mir, "The Qur'anic Story of Joseph: Plot, Themes, and Characters," *The Muslim World* 76:1 (January 1986): 1–15; and M. S. Stern,

"Muhammad and Joseph: A Study of Koranic Narrative," *Journal of Near Eastern Studies* 44:3 (July 1985): 193–204.

3. II:609; V:3933; D 1845:10; 3280:5/3489:6.
4. II:1450ff.; D 511:7; 1743:5.
5. I:1904,08; III:3031; VI:2795; D 226:4; 441:8 (both quoting the "Alas" of Q 12:84);1252:5; 1990:8/2003:10; 2164:2; 2515:2; 2557:3; 2647:12; 2779:6; R 1046.
6. On Joseph's return cf. D 16:1–2; 236:3; 261:2; 624:9; 1035:13; 1279:1; 1293:6; 1645:2; 1680:5; 1793:9; 1805:5; 2559:1; R 739, 979.
7. II:3235; D 2896:17; 895:7; AM 195.
8. III:3034; further imagery on return of sight in I:1903; IV:1815; II:1205, 3233–34; III:3037, 4529; IV:1815; VI:4069–70; D 35:1; 76:3; 237:1; 261:3; 432:5; 483:7; 598:3; 631:4; 687:4; 704:11; 914:10; 1153:8; 1250:3; 1439:9; 1458:13; 1734:8; 1826:13; 1889:17; 1891:8; 2083:9; 2109:4; 2498:12; 2759:7; 2855:7; 2870:2; 3065:2; 3196:3; 3211:6; 3448:7; R 734, 1846, 1981; M 101/203, quoting Q 12:94.
9. D 214:7; 226:4; 1142:5; 1432:2; 2164:2; 2557:3; 2581:1; 2932:8.
10. D 75:1; 667:6; 2608:8/3121:8; 3276:9.
11. IV:3257; II:2008; VI:1422.
12. II:127; III:218, 3438; D82:13; 335:2; 458:7; 511:7; 672:3; 887:3; 895:5; 1048:10, 14; 1374:8; 1638:3; 1743:5; 1845:10; 1988:3; 2056:8; 2371:5; 2455:5; 2548:7; 2614:8; 2659:5; 2756:4; 2980:3; 3272:3; 3475:8; 3280:5/3489:6; M 72/158.
13. D 376:3; 849:2; 2029:6; 2133:2; 2938:5.
14. VI:H.3345; VI:3461; M 19/68. I have been unable to trace this precise quotation, but Sana'i makes a similar comment in *Hadiqat al-Haqiqa*, in J. Stephenson, ed., *The Enclosed Garden of the Truth* (New York: Samuel Weiser, 1972), Persian text 95.
15. D 735:13; 1062:10; 1198:8; 1551:7; 1955:7; 2764:5; 2779:6; 2846:2; 3045:2; 2872:27/3255:4.
16. D 342:10; 398:7; 591:2; 1389:8; 1458:13; 2056:8; 2333:2; 2531:7; 3183:9; R 1931.
17. D 97:1; 189:1; 578:9; 936:4; 982:1; 1252:5; 2839:13; 2953:2; 3248:11.
18. D 724:10; 1198:8; 2218:3; 2624:2; 2872:27/3255:4.
19. V:3237–39; III:1605–6; D 152:3; 1942:6.
20. In other words, one need not fear sacrificing intellect to the very One from whom all intellect derives, IV:1423–24. Numerous allusions to

the "cutting of the hands" occur in D 46:4; 141:7; 272:6; 332:12; 416:8; 748:3; 1044:1; 1135:15; 1185:6; 1198:7; 1447:4; 1507:2; 1637:2; 1701:2; 1905:5; 1986:3; 2114:3; 2473:9; 2518:7–8/ 3107:7–8; 2654:9; 2685:9; 2741:9; 2820:8; 2922:7; 3474:1.

21. VI:4829; D 60:3; 971:9; 2634:8; 3038:8.

22. VI:3055, 1288, 4829.

23. I:H.3157–70, H.3192–3200; F 195/186; D 1211:5; 1508:8; 1713:14; 2037:11; 2826:6; 2836:9; 3447:9; cf. also more general references to Joseph's beauty in D 16:1; 30:6; 31:6; 187:1; 268:6; 355:9; 441:8; 462:1; 486:7; 530:2; 703:2; 705:12; 707:1; 744:2; 788:10; 797:9; 1100:17; 1104:1; 1105:9; 1228:1; 1339:2; 1497:6; 1551:8; 1570:3; 1942:7; 1950:5; 2046:22; 2088:12; 2220:9; 2230:4; 2440:15; 2484:9; 2602:3; 2614:7; 2782:6; 2807:36; 2840:3; 2843:11; 3045:3; 3340:17; M 41/102.

24. D 504:4; 1923:3; 2593:2; 3126:1; 3172:9.

25. D 1425:5; 1723:11; 3078:11.

26. D 2078:14; 2230:4; 3248:7.

27. I:3162–63; D 1393:19; 1823:7.

28. VI:2015; demonstrating how stories of this sort develop, A. Schimmel writes, "The reed story was taken over from Sana'i (*Hadiqa*, Bk. VII, 485ff.). He spoke of the confidant of a king who became ill because he had been forbidden to tell his ruler's secret to anyone; the physician sent him to a lonely lake, where he gave utterance to his heart's secret, but the reed growing at the shore of the lake was later made into a flute and revealed the secret to the world. This was, originally, the story of 'King Midas with the donkey's ears' . . . A similar story is also told about 'Ali . . . who revealed the divine secrets that the Prophet had entrusted to him" with the caution (according to Rumi's version) that he should tell them only to a well if he must speak at all; MDI 317.

29. II:1276–79; IV:673–74; VI:4570–74; VI:411.

30. D 228:8; 525:9; 599:5; 644:9; 892:9; 911:8; 1002:1–2; 1492:5; 1574:6; 1662.5; 1838:6; 2279:7; 2486:12; 2677:5; 2795:9; 2938:6; 3093:2.

31. D 189:8; 524:8; 2278:6; 3194:2. Many other images of the well appear in D 326:11; 486:8; 500:4; 510:3; 1264:2; 1372:15; 1380:10; 1436:8; 1502:6; 1608:7; 1638:3; 1988:1; 2062:7; 2308:2–3; 2408:3/3502:1; 2437:1; 2498:12; 2603:4; 2611:4; 2821:5; 2854:2/ 3239:2; 2981:7; 3016:7; 3065:1; 3126:1; 3164:4; 3183:9; 3291:17;

3327:4; 3329:5; 3340:21; 3387:3; 3393:9; 3424:11; 3448:5; 3488:5; R 821, 1714. On concluding quote, see III:398, 403; II:3134.

32. VI:H.3400–3415. Further imagery of the prison: D 164:6; 631:3; 1630:10; 1680:4; 2019:7; 2782:6; and of well and prison together: D 179:2; 1292:10; 1433:5; 2339:5; 3297:15; 3441:6; 1651:8.

33. General imagery of shirt and scent: I:125; IV:850, 1846; V:3180, 3256, 3260; D 12:3; 25:27; 217:10; 687:4; 835:6; 997:1; 1153:8; 1250:3; 1395:11; 1734:8; 1743:5; 1796:15; 1826:12; 1893:9; 1990:8/ 2003:10; 1966:16; 2371:5; 2429:15; 2647:12; 2896:17; 3016:3; 3336:24; 3495:4; R 499, 936, 1981.

34. VI:3109; VI:2830; D 2330:8.

Chapter Five: Moses and Company

1. The principal features of Rumi's version appear frequently in the Qur'an, but especially as follows: childhood: 20:36–39; 28:2–13; killing and flight to Midian: 20:40–41; 28:14–28; encounter with God (bush, staff, white hand): 20:9–35; 27:6–15; 28:29–35; mission to Egypt and conflict with Pharaoh: 7:101–32; 10:76–89; 14:5–17; 20:42–78; 23:47–50; 26:9–51; 27:7–14; 28:36–43; 40:24–53; 43:45–56; 44:16–32; 51:38–40; 79:16–25; Exodus and desert trials: 7:133–37; 20:79–84; 26:52–68; Sinai theophany: 7:138–45; 153–56; Samiri and the Calf: 2:48–53; 7:146–53; 20:85–98; cow sacrificed: 2:63–66; Moses with Khizr: 18:59–81. Many of Rumi's details derive from the *Qisas*, as for example details which transform the Moses/Pharaoh relationship into a clear parallel to that of Abraham/Nimrod and details of the plagues and the special properties of the rod (its dragonlike behavior, etc.); and the scene in which Pharaoh's wife warns her husband to heed Moses (reminiscent of the words of the wives of Julius Caesar and Pontius Pilate). QT 147–221; QK 194–225; QKT 208–46.

Ibn 'Arabi holds that Moses in effect became all those lives that were lost in Pharaoh's infanticide—he became the sum of their "psychic predispositions" or "vital spirits." In addition to the Moses/Khizr episode, Ibn 'Arabi concentrates on the ark (in the Nile) as a symbol of Moses' apparent loss, but actual salvation; on Moses' mother's nursing of the child before placing him in the ark so that he would accept no other wet nurse; on Moses' flight after the murder as occurring apparently out of fear but actually out of "love of salvation"; on

Moses' discussion with Pharaoh about the essence of the world; on Moses' then having to demonstrate his answer through miracles; and finally on Pharaoh's drowning-conversion. Aside from a brief mention of the burning bush, no other major elements of the Moses story appear in the *Fusus*, FA 197–213; FB 249–66.

2. MCN III:842 quotes the version found in the Persian *Qisas*.
3. D 3356:19; above summarized from III:H.840–960; cf. also D 512:5ff.; 3356:14ff.
4. II:2969–72; V:701; D 1673:7; 1827:12; 2354:5; 3336:33; M 5/45; FB 255–56.
5. IV:2321–22, 2331–32; D 3081:14; 3109:18; 3423:10.
6. D 2095:7; 2981:17; 3090:4; 3408:7; 3423:11; R 78.
7. III:4367–68; VI:2310; D 176:7; 258:5; 452:19; 676:5; 859:9; 1035:12; 1644:6; 1693:4; 2781:8; 3384:14; 3280:13; suggested also in 896:6.
8. IV:3571; V:338; D 1157:10.
9. D 788:12; 947:4; 2001:8; 2864:12.
10. II:2883; IV:3571; D 3388:8.
11. D 2534:5; 470:7; 1727:13; 1821:11; cf. MM 236–37 on Sufi development of the burning bush motif from Hallaj to Ghazali.
12. Rumi often calls the prophet Kalim II:360; III:1067, 1962, 3368, 3453; IV:1245, 2705, 3012; VI:1091, 1127, 1347, 2486, 3280–81, 3283; D 45:8; 144:2; 217:15; 470:7; 482:9; 1727:13; 1772:6; 1821:11; 1970:2; 2236:1; 2992:4; 3065:4; 3177:7; 3234:7; 3384:14; 3434:8.
13. D 123:9–10; 2213:2; 2687:2.
14. V:3934; cf. also I:1240, III:2788–90 on Moses' former faulty vision of the staff. D 123:8–9; 13ff.; 2095:9.
15. V:234; VI:3058; IV:3314; 252; II:2156.
16. D 96:8; 216:3; 217:3; 841:9; 854:8; 1250:6; 1734:15; 1845:3; 1876:18; 1975:1; 2576:6; 2709:5; 3073:19.
17. D 3384:14; 3390:9; 3392:10.
18. Except where quoted directly or otherwise noted, all of the above is summarized from IV:H.2301–2778.
19. F 184/176; cf. MDI 62ff., MM 269–71 on the origins of the Moses/Pharaoh dialogue in Hallaj's *Tawasin*. Also KPC 23–27 where Izutsu comments on the metaphysical dimension of Ibn 'Arabi's interpretation of the dialogue, and summarizes the pertinent commentaries of both Qashani and Affifi.

20. I:1240; II:1065–66, 2286; IV:1070, 1662, 1673, 2806–10; III:966, 1013, 1054–55, 1168, 1209, 1233, 2788, 3386; V:597. NB, e.g., IV:3523 where rod is "a seven-headed dragon, which the female does not (conceive and) bring to birth from the male"; D 27:9–10; 100:7; 123:14; 255:8; 531:5; 840:2; 909:18; 1414:4; 2236:1; 2723:7; 2784:5–6; 2903:7; 2919:12; 3280:13/3489:4; 3423:9; 3477:8; 3461:6.
21. F80/68; 155/146; III:1010; I:2141–42; V:1539; V:3934; VI:2179; II:2286; III:3453–55: D 159:9; 704:8; 718:18; 836:13/838:16; 871:8; 895:4; 908:8; 909:12; 1250:6; 1531:3,5,6; 1599:4/1603:4; 1673:12–13; 1845:5; 1975:6; 2186:6; 2177:11; 2236:2; 2940:7–8/ 2958:10; 3048:6; 3060:15–16; 3372:1; 3402:12. KPC 119–120 notes that Ibn 'Arabi relates 'asā (staff) to 'asâ (to rebel, disobey), and hayya (snake) to haya (life) an example of the Shaykh's "cabbalistic" bent.
22. F 21/9; IV:1072; V:3807–9; D 192:4; 2903:7; 3060:15; R 78.
23. IV:3521; II:350; III:85, 1167–68, 1177–78.
24. II:146; IV:1065–71; V:1425; III:H.4258–63; D 651:2; 738:4; 1700:6; 2723:8; cf. also for looser association V: 1318–19; D 144:2.
25. D 3375:11; 1889:12; 1061:7.
26. F 21/9; IV:1072; D 895:4; 1206:11; 541:4.
27. IV:3433; cf. also IV:33, 3254, 3527, 3580, 3590; III:3786; V:1233; D 609:7; 644:11; 704 9; 1745–5.
28. IV:2829; I:1188, MCN.
29. Rumi says nothing of the details included in either Qur'an or Qisas regarding Aaron's being chosen as Moses' companion, or about Aaron's role in the calf-worshiping episode. Cf. Q 7:146–53; 20:29–33, 85–97; 28:34–35. QT 152, 157–65, 184–88; QK211–17; QKT 226–32. Ibn 'Arabi, on the other hand, focuses on Aaron's prophethood of mercy as related to being born of the same mother as Moses; he goes on to develop the notion of the divine passion; FA 191–96; FB 241–48.
30. ma'rifa, D 217:15; further Aaron references in D 245:11; 1215:3; 1247:4; 2534:9; 3119:8; 3351 :17.
31. III:2518, 2700, 4263; IV:1070, 3285; V:1328.
32. V:953–5; II:2040; F 65/53; D 836:14/838:4; 1411:6; 1531:2; 1792:9; 2168:23; 2177:10; 2220:11; 2940:6/2958:9–10; 3419:5.
33. I:780; V:953; D 56:11; 1369:5.
34. D 164:9; 2704:8; 2981:15.

35. II:2284–90; D 1172:21/1178:11.
36. D 3496:5; further water/rock imagery: VI:1017–18; D 1282:6; 1329:10; 1585:3; 1817:9; 2176:5; 2502:6.
37. D 94:9; 371:7; 1414:2; 2159:3; 3375:9.
38. D 131:1; 1271:9; 2095:7; 3212:5; 3243:1; 3285:7; 3291:12; 3424:2; R 1758.
39. *arini*, quoting Q 7:144: D 482:9; 1141:5; 2827:4; 2830:14; 2992:4; 3091:6.
40. VI:3065–68; D 401:7; 2901:3. Cf. MM 267–69 on Sufi development and meditation on the scene of Sinai being reduced to cinders, from Hallaj to Ghazali.
41. I:867–68; III:4267; D 414:7; 468:4; 487:6; 934:11; 1012:11; 1215:6; 1594:7; 1845:3; 2051:9; 2524:17; 2599:7; 2656:6; 2817:2; 2953:11; 3234:6; 3257:5; 3452:13.
42. V:1898–1900; I:1135–36; D 12:4; 33:16; 1629:17; 1791:9; 1798:7; 1932:1/R 1728; 2100:11; 2111:13; 2526:4; 2593:6; 2630:25/3142:25; 3065:4; 3350:10; 3386:5.
43. D 562:5; 1080:8; 1787:7–8; 2111:4; 2704:10; 3177:7; R 130/R 340; cf. also other assorted images of Sinai in D 131:3; 187:3; 533:14; 1781:1; 3351:16.
44. D 16:3; 468:4; 2480:9; 2991:4; 2992:4; 3296:1.
45. II:1435–38; III:2523–24, 3897–99; D 892:4; Q 2:63–68.
46. III:2519; MCN gives no source.
47. I:864; II:2367; VI:2168, 2503; D 28:14; 485:13; 1215:7; 1247:5; 1506:8; 1595:6; 1644:6; 1931:16; 2427:3; 2534:9; 2550:7/3119:7; 2709:5; 2784:4; 2828:4; 2948:9; 3351:18; 3381:2; R 1863.
48. Esp. IV:3582–3636 on Moses' receiving instruction on how to proceed with the plagues, etc.
49. I:3843–45; I:277–80; IV: 1670–75; V:2445; VI:4353–54; D 1279:4; 1598:9–10; 1673:12; 2992:5.
50. By *wahy* in II:1750, 1752, H.2156; III:3286; IV:H.2921, 3575; D 1847:16; by *kashf* in V:3914. God reproached Moses for not visiting his Lord (God) in his illness in II:H.2156–64, a text reminiscent of Matt. 25:34ff.
51. I:2969–73; II:436–38; I:236–37; III:1959–70; II:3515–17, 3527–30; D 1772:6; 280:5. MCN I:237 notes, quoting the *Fusus*, Khizr "typifies the esoteric side of prophecy; he possessed a knowledge that was denied to Moses, for 'sometimes God withholds from the apostle knowledge of the divine decree (*sirr al-qadar*), because, if he knew it,

he might fail in his duty, viz. delivery of the Message with which God has entrusted him.' "

52. III:1251–55; D 1247:4; 1599:3/1603:3.

53. Khizr is never mentioned by name in the Qur'an but tradition calls him the companion of Moses in Surat al-Kahf. Ibn 'Arabi and the *Qisas* include Khizr as a prominent actor in their stories of Moses. Though Ibn 'Arabi does not develop the water of life theme, he does portray Khizr as Moses' teacher, superior in knowledge. He relates Khizr's guiltless killing of the youth to Moses' killing of the Copt, associates Khizr's apparent destruction of the boat with the apparent disposal of the child Moses in the Nile, and parallels Khizr's not asking a salary for rebuilding the crumbling wall to Moses' not asking wages for drawing water at Midian. Khizr's sole importance in the Fusus is in relation to Moses, whereas Rumi treats Khizr as more of a personality in his own right. Cf. QT 192–203; QK 230–33; QKT 247–50; and FA 202ff.; FB 256–60.

54. III:1967–69 quoting Q 18:59. VI:1126ff. treated in section on Moses. MCN refers to two interpretations of the "Two Seas," as either the blend of divine with human in Khizr, or Moses as exoteric knowledge as against Khizr as esoteric knowledge—a contrast paralleled in the above text by moon and sun imagery.

55. D 280:6; 1876:18; 2550:8/3119:8; 2944:24; 3133:6.

56. V:714; IV:2756; I:2791.

57. D 836:6; 1255:19; 1422:7; 3074:6.

58. VI:187; D 815:8; 2037:12; 2840:6; 2870:6.

59. VI:4830; D 550:5; 1772:6; 2176:9; 3199:13; 3291:6; 3393:10; R 1222/1261.

60. D 660:5; 180:2; 1109:8.

61. III:4301–17; quotes from vv. 4302 and 4317. Many more images of Khizr and the water of life occur throughout the *Diwan*: 45:2; 50:4; 70:1; 232:6; 294:2; 299:3; 344:2; 504:14; 613:4; 664:4; 729:10; 766:1; 795:10; 836:6; 839:3; 863:18; 874:11; 970:5; 1062:7; 1083:6; 1226:5; 1724:4; 1792:1; 1869:5; 1950:6; 2037:12; 2065:9; 2118:2; 2134:12; 2139:7; 2333:4; 2576:8; 2709:3; 2726:8; 2747:1–2; 2840:6; 2934:2; 3004:12; 3038:12; 3074:6; 3285:9; 3313:12; 3421:5; 3464:6; R 405, 1589, 1779.

62. D 294:2; 929:13; 1792:1.

63. Rumi makes no mention of Ilyas' (Elijah's) resistance to Baal-worship in Q 37:123–32. Wensinck's "Khadir" suggests some reasons for

Rumi's connection of Ilyas with Khizr, particularly the existence of Jewish stories of a journey of Ilyas accompanied by Joshua, during which Ilyas performed actions similar to those of Khizr in Surat al-Kahf (EI2 4:902–5; cf. also his "Ilyas" in EI2 3:1156). That may, incidentally, explain also how Shah Waliallah came to name Joshua as the "young man" accompanying Moses in Q 18, in *Ta'wil al-Ahadith* 50–51. KPC 10–13 notes how the *Fusus* uses a composite Ilyas/Idris as an example of how one must learn to see things symbolically: Ilyas and Idris were in fact two names taken by the same man, representing two different states. In the state of being raised high, the man was called Idris; as an earthly messenger he was Ilyas. In this schizoid condition his knowledge of God could only be imperfect, since only Muhammad was completely successful in uniting the transcendent and the immanent in his knowledge of God. *Fusus* (FA 181–87; FB 228–35) and *Qisas* (QT 223–29; QK 243–50; QKT 263–69) both develop Ilyas far beyond the details that appear in Rumi.

Chapter Six: Jesus and the Other Gospel Figures

1. Rumi adheres closely to the references in Q 3:32–36; 19:1–12; 21:89–90. He adds nothing explicit of the embellishment contained in QT 333–36, 341–42, QK 326ff., and QKT 326–30, except for a very oblique hint at Zacharia's martyrdom. FA 177–80, FB 222–27 does not explicitly mention the prophet by name, apart from naming the whole chapter after him.
2. F 182/173–74; M 117/229 quotes Q 19:6 in which Zacharia asks for a successor of the house of Jacob who would be acceptable to God. FA 175–76, FB 219–20 (on John) also treats this theme.
3. Except for the tale of John's being saved by the mountain, Rumi adheres to details in Q 3:33–36; 19:1–15; 21:89–90. Cf. also QT 336–41. FA 175, FB 218–19 discusses death and resurrection, beginning from an etymology of *Yahya* as derivative of *haya* (life), meaning that John's father "lives on" in John.
4. I:1843–84; III:1018; D 3060:7; 3375:1; R 1899.
5. V:3856, 3982; D 726:4; 1875:9; 2901:4.
6. D 1003:2; 1990:6/2003:8.
7. D 513:2; 1594:9; 2425:2; 2807:14; 2864.8; I:1934.
8. VI:4547; D 24:7; F 80/68; VI:1807; D 1427:12.

9. V:285; VI:1307; on her virginity cf. also D 2807:15; 2854:5/3239:4; R 906.
10. D 1655:13; 1661:4; 2134:18; 2821:6.
11. II:H.3602–15; also F 66/54 on John's description of Jesus in the womb.
12. II:98; F 33/20; D 471:9.
13. V:1189–90; IV:3497; VI:1290; F 33/20; D 122:10; 3424:9; 106:7; 294:13; 1229:5; 2429:16; 2954:7.
14. D 885:4. Further images of the relationship of Jesus to Mary in D 15:6; 619:5; 631:2; 1661:4; 1862:2; 2176:10; 2643:10/3135:10; 2788:8.
15. Materials relevant to Jesus appear in the Qur'an as follows, grouped under the headings used here: Gabriel's visit, birth, speech as infant: 3:37–43; 19:16–34; life and ministry: 5:50–51; 21:91–92; 57:26–27; miracles: 3:43–46; 5:109–15; crucifixion and Ascension: 4:156; 3:47–48; theological issues: 4:169–70; 5:76–79, 116–17; 19:35–36; 43:57–65. Cf. G. Parrinder, *Jesus in the Qur'an* (New York: Oxford University Press, 1977); R.C. Zaehner "The Qur'an and Christ," Appendix to *The Comparison of Religions* (Boston: Beacon Press, 1958), 195–217. The *Qisas* develop especially the themes of life-giver, wandering ascetic, Ascension and second coming, sinlessness; in addition they further embellish the birth and childhood stories and expand the number of Jesus' miracles (QT 342–66; QK 326 ff.; QKT 326–336). *Fusus* begins with the animating power of God's spirit in Jesus, as manifested through Mary and Gabriel. It then discusses the metaphysics of the life-giving breath: Jesus' humility was from Mary, but his resuscitating power was from Gabriel. This meeting of the human and the divine in Jesus has caused, according to the Shaykh, untold misunderstanding. He therefore proceeds to describe the metaphysical intricacies of such an inscrutable mingling. The entire chapter is given to the question of the relationship of the Divine to the creaturely as manifested in Jesus (FA 138–50; FB 172–86). See also James Roy King, "Jesus and Joseph in Rumi's *Mathnawi*," *The Muslim World* 80:2 (April 1990): 81–95.
16. D 1594:9; 2176:10; 2788:8; 3194:5.
17. III:1794; VI:2656; D 2429:16.
18. F 66/54; D 527:15; Q 19:31; further on his speech D 1661:4; 2901:4; 1709:11; 2439:12; I:1733.
19. F 60/48; D 1211:7; 1427:12; 1989:10; 2526:4.

20. F 99/87; IV:1461; D 1534:2; 667:3.
21. D 2550:7/3119:7. See MDI 34–35, 122.
22. F 239/232; IV:H.113–15; M 27/82; 51/122. F 199/190. On hadith about "most difficult thing," AM 322.
23. III:H. 2570–98, H.298–304, 3504; Jesus and monastery D 3285:7; 3375:1.
24. I:865; III:2580; D 1414:5; 1889:13. On the breath referred to in a very general way: D 11:1; 24:7; 425:3; 491:5; 788:11; 894:3; 914:45; 993:4; 1081:11; 1086:6; 1421:2; 1706:15; 1885:6; 1951:9; 2058:2; 2134:18; 2140:3; 2330:8; 2371:15; 2453:9; 2500:2; 2517:11; 2618:11; 2685:18; 2807:13; 2840:3; 2864:8; 2888:5; 3303:5; 3375:1; M 29/84.
25. V:1425, 2814; II:1862, 2110: Stork has breath of Jesus and face of Joseph; crow is a wolf or an ass with a bell.
26. D 96:3; 167:1; 202:4; 371:8; 452:15; 646:10; 736:7; 780:6; 822:6; 1041:3; 1156:12; 1798:7; 2032:4; 2220:12; 2429:14; 2566:3, 2725:1; 3090:4; 3104:15; 3421:5; 3452:3.
27. VI:4115–18; D 155:1; 189:12; 866:2; 1061:8; 1586:3; 2824:5; 2981:15; 2983:10; 3129:5; 3432:12; 3434:9.
28. D 202:4; 214:9; 280:5; 1190:3; 1214:5; 1369:3; 2159:7; 2512:11; 2848:2; 2925:5; 3286:6; 3434:9; kiss: D 1084:9; 1298:5; 1826:4.
29. D 140:6; 169:9/231:2; 1250:4; 1271:10.
30. II:H.140–51, H.457–72. *The Ilahi Nama of 'Attar*, trans. by J. A. Boyle (Manchester: Manchester University Press, 1976), Discourse VII, 108–9.
31. VI:4038–39; V:2503; III:2585–92.
32. II:145–46, 453, 306–7; IV:1068–69; V:1425.
33. IV: 1065–68. Jesus' incantation occurs in numerous verses of the *Diwan* also, spoken both by Jesus and by the authentic lover or teacher: D 191:2; 452:15; 738:4; 1201:9; 1215:4; 1271:10; 1478:7; 1565:9, 1846:7; 2003:3; 2100:4; 2713:5; 2824:5; 3450:8.
34. V:275–76; D 255:9; 772:7; 1271:10; 1279:4; 3477:9.
35. D 45:16; 94:9; 446:6; 631:7; 997:10; 1020:6; 1585:3; 1739:10; 1892:2; 2050:3; 3424:13.
36. I:83–85; V:H.2591. Because a reference to God's turning certain men into "apes and swine," which occurs in Q 5:65, happens to be in the Sura called The Table (of Jesus), Rumi has associated the story with Jesus. Originally the Qur'anic reference was an allusion to the "men of the Sabbath" in Q 2:61 and 7:163–66. According to W.M. Watt's

Companion to the Qur'an (London: Allen and Unwin, 1967), 21–22, the commentators explain those references by means of a David story: "in the days of David the fish at Elath on the Red Sea used to come to shore on the Sabbath to tempt Israelites living there, but kept away on other days; some Israelites broke the Sabbath and caught them or made canals which could be closed so as to trap them; others kept the Sabbath and tried to stop the Sabbath-breakers, but in vain; at length David cursed the latter and they were turned into apes, then after three days swept into the sea by a wind. This story has not been traced in Jewish legend."

37. General reference to ascension III:345, 778; D 16:1; 28:14, 17; 97:9; 144:2; 598:6; 613:8; 631:2; 830:6; 1087:2; 1102:7; 1817:10; 1931:16; 2018:8; 2566:6; 2830:14; 2895:7; 2948:9; 3090:3; 3303:4; 3385:1; 3388:8; 3424:1; 3435:5; specific reference to fourth heaven: I:649, 2787; V:2548; D 114:8; 226:11; 341:6; 446:6; 1754:7; 2307:5. Ibn 'Arabi places Jesus in second heaven.

38. IV:2672; VI:2964, 2971–72; IV:1506; F 117/105; III:3193ff.

39. VI:2973; on the impossibility of the ass's making an ascension, see D 1075:4; 1103:5; 1107:4; 1905:4; 2910:11 .

40. D 24:8; 227:3; 452:15; 1629:7; R 1091; preceding story summarized from I:324ff. intermittently up to I:873; MCN gives a summary and various interpretations of the vizier story at I:H.324ff. According to Muslim lore, the Antichrist (*dajjal* = imposter) will reign for forty days. Then Jesus will overthrow him as a sign of imminent Resurrection—a parallel to the story of the Jinn's usurping the throne of Solomon for forty days. See LWR 104–6 on connection with Ibn 'Arabi.

41. I:359; D 136:5; 342:13; 1229:7; 2200:3.

42. VI:494; V:574ff.; F 98–99/86–87; AM 598.

43. F 33/20–21; same theme in D 513:2; 2643:10/3135:10; 2807:14–15.

44. Of the many images Rumi has fashioned on this theme, some can only be characterized as remarkably crude: D 459:9–10; 613:7; 892:10; 1036:5; 1154:13; 1196:6; 1300:1; 1380:7; 1585:2; 1737:13; 1768:6; 1816:4; 2429:13; 2464:7/3229:7; 2932:5; 2950:11; 3030:16; 3302:2; 3389:2; 3420:13.

45. D 1332:9; 2137:I; 2239:11; 2685:18.

46. I:500–501, VI:1855. In QT and QK Mary apprentices Jesus to a dyer, and Jesus is left to dye some clothes. In QT the dyer returns to find all the garments dyed just the right color, but all from the same vat.

Kisa'i gives the story a slight twist: "You ordered me to dye them, but you did not tell me what colors," Jesus said. Then he asked, "What is your religion?" The man said that he was a Jew. "Say there is no god but God and that I, Jesus, am His messenger, and you will take out each garment in whatever color you want" (QKT 333). Sana'i's *Hadiqat al-Haqiqa* contains the version Rumi seems to prefer: all the robes came out pure white; see *The Enclosed Garden of the Truth*, Major J. Stephenson, trans., 31.

Chapter Seven: The Muhammad of History

1. According to MDI 369, Ahmad Sirhindi explicitly discussed the Prophet's significance under the names of Muhammad and Ahmad, distinguishing between "the two individuations of Muhammad, the bodily human one as contrasted to the spiritually angelic one."

2. Qur'anic references to the Prophet are too numerous to list here; crucial citations are included throughout this chapter. Ibn 'Arabi explains the ternary (or ultimate) perfection of Muhammad by devoting his entire chapter to an ingenious exegesis of the hadith in which Muhammad claimed he loved three things: women, perfume, and prayer. Women were mentioned first because they "represent the passive principle and Universal Nature" which must precede whatever manifests itself. That universal nature, however, is none other than the breath of mercy (i.e., the perfume). Prayer is last, because the Prophet "respected the ascending order of the divine manifestations." The *Fusus* therefore ends with a brief discussion of the significance of prayer; FA 214–26; FB 269–84.

3. Ibn Ishaq says that the child was old enough to walk away, but Rumi does not provide any such information.

4. All from IV:H.915–1040; SN 72–73; Ibn Ishaq does not include the idol breaking or the prayer at the Ka'ba, and says that Warqa found Muhammad in "the upper part of Makka."

5. Summarized from V:H.3535–40; IV:3798; D 2297:12.

6. II:2935; III:2533; VI:2906; D 55:1; 525:7; 879:12; 2131:7.

7. D 16:11; 214:11; 217:6; 324:3; 489:9; 824:3; 1915:15; 2183:8; 2987:12.

8. SN 114–15; MMec 86; MMF 39.

9. I:H.2959–68; III:1941; AM 75.

10. IV:2232; VI:2014. On connection to the reed-flute story of Sana'i see MDI 317.
11. I:H.3500–3670; hadith on Companions in AM 82/87; MCN I:2925; AM 33 on believer's discernment.
12. "Faithful witness to the truth," I:2688; II:922, 2059; D 237:10; 859:7.
13. F 170–72/162–63; D 598:8.
14. F 41/29; Rumi's answer to the taunt and his defense of the piecemeal delivery of the Qur'an will be treated in the second major section of this chapter.
15. VI:1529–31, MCN note on Q 53:19–23; cf. also Ilse Lichtenstaedter, "A Note on the *Gharaniq* and Related Qur'anic Problems," in *Israel Oriental Studies* 5 (1975): 54–61.
16. II:3402; VI:3025; D 491:2–3; 704:14; 766:4; 906:4; 1845:10; 1967:10; 3049:6.
17. III:1663–67; IV:1119–21; VI:2100, 2962.
18. D 1246:10–12, MPR 157. The Companion Bu Hurayra's wallet was a magical food bag which could never be emptied, according to note in MPR 196 and MCN V:H.2786.
19. II:2074–75; D 1205:2; 1274:12.
20. MMec 118–19; MMF 126–27.
21. VI: 1060; preceding summarized from VI:H.887–1110. Abu Bakr's role as agent also in I:575–77.
22. V:224–25; I:1968; VI:1098; D 3234:10.
23. Q 9:40; SN 224: they stayed three days; Q quoted in D 1158:4.
24. D 237:10; 901:10; R 1987; D 1198:4; 2871:3; Spider story in Ibn Hanbal's *Musnad* I, 348.
25. III:1149. In any case, most of these references are to a model love relationship: II:2252, 2845; VI:1077; D 452:9; 718:26; 899:3; 1041:4; 1143:9; 1429:4; 1663:12; 2173:3; 2420:7; 2503:6/2531:8; 2717:5; 3273:22; 3327:4.
26. II:3715–16; summary from II:3712–16; quote from Q 49:10.
27. MCN III:4505–6; Hudaybiya will be considered later in this chapter. Khaybar occurs explicitly in D 645:8, 937:15; cf. also two other well-concealed allusions to Khaybar in MCN I:1989–91, II: 1244.
28. F 189/181. Further miscellaneous references to Jews in D 1216:8; 1732:10; 3439:10.
29. F 14/2; III:H.4473–77, 4520–60.
30. F 189/181; see also 14/2 for related material; Furuzanfar's notes give no further information, nor could I trace down the saying's sources.

31. F 16–17/3–4; Rumi told this story for the benefit of the ruler who had made a great show of being converted, but had been unwilling to put his treasure where his mouth was.
32. This, according to Watt, in response to a dream Muhammad had experienced, relating to Q 48:27, MMed 46ff.
33. VI:166; D 18:1; 28:19; 2227:5; 3452:5.
34. IV:H. 1992–93, H.2030–50, H.2081–85, H.2154–55, H.2159–68; Nicholson comments on Rumi's error in associating Usama with Hudhayl when both Usama and his father Zayd were widely known to be of the Kalb tribe.
35. IV:3374; VI:2117; D 2032:1.
36. D 2503:6/2531:8; 2934:9.
37. D 57:9; 202:10; 235:3; 718:19; 1095:5; 1126:3; 1747:5.
38. D 3496:3; 1859:6; further references in D 1061:7; 1077:3; 1121:11; 1709:2; 3092:4; 3414:3.
39. IV:H.2585–92; MCN cites Muhammad's prayer as an allusion to the words which Muhammad said with his last breath, according to a hadith in Bukhari's *Sahih*, 64, 84, vol. III, 191.
40. VI:754; IV:2273; AM 352; F 24/12; 84/73; D 941:3.
41. III:H. 172–79 in defense of Bilal; IV:H.1992ff. after appointing the young commander; II:2068–82 on Surat 'Abasa.
42. *umma*, D 326:7; M 55/129; *milla*, M 9/54, 112/220, 138/264; F 234/226.
43. V:H.1265; Q 16:124, 60:4.
44. F 75–76/64; VI:H.478–94; AM 598.
45. I:3120, D 3234:13; AM 79; I:3710–16.
46. IV:H.538–41; AM 334; VI:1157; 1595; F 140–41/129; AM 642.
47. VI:501–2; V:2423; IV:3200.
48. E.g., V:1241; D 2407, each line of which ends with the first half of the *Shahada*.
49. F 86/75; cf. also V:454–58 where Rumi puts both fasting and ritual prayer (*namaz*) into a different context: one mote of *'aql* is better, for *'aql* is substance whereas fasting and ritual prayer are accidents.
50. D 370; 1602; 2344.
51. In his ten-volume edition of the *Diwan* (4:140), Furuzanfar cites *Jami' Sagir* 2:49, referring evidently to Jalal ad-Din as-Suyuti's *al-Jami' as-Saghir*. C. Brockelmann, *Geschichte der Arabischen Literatur* (Leiden: Brill, 1943–49), I:172 attributes one of the earliest

collections by the same name to Muhammad ibn Hasan ash-Shaybani (d. 189/904).

52. VI:3572; AM 711; D 1715:4; 3495:7; AM 54.
53. M 32/88, 94/188, 95/189. I have been unable to trace the saying further.
54. I:2223–25; II:380; AM 51.
55. II:895–96; III:4103; AM 130.
56. D 1305 (all); see also 1306:8; 3104:1–3.
57. II:2247; cf. VI:3197f., AM 163.
58. F 124/113; II:2773–74; III:421–29; cf. also three versions of the same story of Muhammad in mosque with Companions in M 1/34; 37/93; 40/101.
59. VI:2338–42; II:2766–67, 70; and especially the story of the man who sighed, II:2773–78.
60. II:3235; III:2401; AM 182; I:381; M 168/247; AM 10. *Du'a'* III:H.1484; III:4782; AM 314.
61. F 192/184; V:H.1084; AM 415.

Chapter Eight: The Ahmad of Faith

1. IV: 1561 ; point illustrated by story of Majnun and the camel, IV:H. 1533–61; F 29/16.
2. F 220/213; I:615–16; references to Q 8:17 in IV:2947; V:H.2243; VI:1523, 2246, 2835, 3197, 4597; I:3789; III:3659–60; II:1306; IV:763; D 948:16; 1954:8. See also TS 163, 263, 283, 309; and WF 117, 124 for further interpretation of Rumi's use of the verse.
3. I:3952–53; IV:2960; D 3387:7; R 79; F 24/12. Note especially Rumi's parody on the fool who presumed to arrogate to himself the hadith referred to in these texts, in F 232/224; AM 100.
4. F 234/227; VI:3256–58; *ahad/ahmad* in I:228, 728; VI:H.888–89; D 144:4; 1578:8; 3228:7; on hadith qudsi, see TS 166, 286.
5. F 28/16; I:3740; IV:H.1641; VI:2008; AM 244. Furuzanfar provides an extended note on the hadith in F 249–50.
6. D 3453:6; hadith in Ibn Hanbal's *Musnad* IV 251, 5.
7. II:3549; III:1226; D 478:20; AM 188. KPC 7 quotes *Fusus*: "Thus whatever vision an Apostle has in his waking hours is of the same nature as what he sees in his sleep. Of course the two states are different from each other, one being sensible and the other occurring in

imagination. But both are the same in that what he sees is a symbol and a form of an aspect of the Reality that lies beyond."

8. IV:H.3300; D 444:5; AM 425.
9. First version in F 18/5; 61–62/50; II:467; D 3475:11; M 82/172; second version in I:2585; VI:3513; AM 116. Cf. *Kashf*, Nicholson, trans., 231, 116.
10. D 1282:9; 1777:4; 2425:3; M 37/93, 49/120, 63/142, 94/188.
11. *alam nashrah* . . . as in III:2356; V:1067–72; D 598:12; 1974:6.
12. SN 71–72; MMec 35–36.
13. III:102 quoting Q 9:61; IV:3534.
14. VI:2617–19; III:1663–67; IV:2083–84; VI:1357–59.
15. IV:H.1834; D 1662:12; 1990:9/2003:11; 3336:25; AM 195.
16. VI:2830; III:161–63; IV:551; 1826–27.
17. V:H.2243; I:1037; II:1918–20; D 2512:16; F 133/123; AM 42. See also TS 263, 344.
18. F 51/39–40; quoting Q 53:3–4; Q 53:4 quoted also in V:H.1430 and 6:4670. Cf. MCN 2:302.
19. F 112/100; III:1300ff.; III:1729 on dream world; VI:H.84 on seeker of knowledge of other world; AM 222, 436; I:322. *'ilm min ladunn*, I:813 quoting Q 18:64; III:179.
20. IV:3082–H.3085; AM 412.
21. Sana'i', *Diwan* 34; D 861:7; 1758:8; 2010:5; 2276:15.
22. Except where noted, all summarized from II:292–300. The association of Muhammad's light with the dawning of a new day appears also in D 1373:8; 1594:4; 1621:2.
23. Cf., e.g., II:293; V:742; I:3659–64; D 2336:1.
24. I:1331; IV:H.1641; V:H.498, 2475–78; VI:2617–19.
25. Q 24:35 in I:1544, 2367; D 64:12; 565:6; 1902:7; 2608:12.
26. F 170–71/162–63; I:2367, 3973, 84; IV:28, 3208.
27. IV:3474–78; image of light as wine also in Adam-text, I:1943–45.
28 Further miscellaneous imagery of the light in relation to Muhammad in D 3:8; 25:2; 190:6; 693:1; 1137:1; 1705:13; 1798:7; 2977:4; 3241:8; 3407:4.
29. VI:685; 2103–6; F 211/203.
30. I.e., Ahmad; II:970–74; hadith alluded to in D 1158:9; 1799:7; 3104:16; AM 546.
31. F 151/142; I:529; D 1989:11.
32. IV:2122; F 51/39; 125/114.

33. IV:2875–76. Further references to the Qur'an appear in D 533:16; 568:10; 729:16; 892:6; 1202:26; 1870:5; 1938:4; 1966:13; 1967:8; 2086:18; 2180:6; 2186:11; 2220:12; 2257:18; 2483:11; 2896:7; 3422:6; R 852.
34. II:921; VI:3445; D 567:14; 2840:2; 2967:5; 3434:10.
35. F 80/68; II:353; VI:3445, 4537.
36. II:353–55; further imagery of this miracle in D 640:7; 683:3; 882:2.
37. I:3949–50; II:1919, 3428; VI:3879.
38. D 1313:13; 572:4; 1117:13; 2417:2; 228:2; 1595:2; 1970:11; 1997:4; 2100:5; 2502:1/2531:3; 2894:9; 2910:11; 3153:6; other imagery of Buraq in D 112:9; 214:11; 258:7; 301:1 quoting Q 94:7; 1212:12; 1283:1; 3234:12. Prophet's mule Duldul in I:3437; II:3794; D 2608:9.
39. II:2226; D 941:8; 2948:6.
40. Rumi is very fond of this play on words and often hints at the Qur'anic text on which it is based II:3752; IV:1309–10, 2640; V:3604; VI:2861; M 47/113, 130/251.
41. Six hundred in D 543:11.
42. IV:H.3755–3808; D 144:2; 724:5; 1793:13; 2220:15; 2364:3; 2989:9.
43. IV:3800–3804; IV:1888–90; I:1064–67.
44. D 845:3; 892:7; 1806:17; 1863:2; 2551:5; 2922:8.
45. III:H.4511–16; F 114/103; AM 298.
46 VI:2861–84. Wine imagery in D 214:11; 980:4; 1776:26; 2433:9; 2630:11/3142:12; 3172:10; further imagery of *Mi'raj* in D 33:2; 133:4; 341:6; 498:6; 525:10; 613:5; 624:13; 638:2; 1172:31/1178:15; 1321:8; 3088:7; 3176:9–10; 3401:10.
47. I:H.2113–20; D 809:12, MPRI 101; 427:6; 1414:6.
48. F 151/142; 155/146; IV:2801.
49. I:1102–6; IV:2800, 2864–74.
50. Q 36:1; II:2203; D 81:3; 1863:1; 1890:8; 2118:4; 2609:6; 2657:7; 3234:10, 15; 3460:6. Cf. M. Epalza, "Los Nombres del Profeta en la Teologia Musulmana," *Miscelanea Comillas* 173 (1975):25.
51. II:922, 2255; IV:495; 3116; V:3539; VI:2495.
52. II:2254, 2483; IV:1420, 2482; VI:1185, 2486.
53. *shahanshah*, III:2196; VI:1159; R 427.
54. *chiragh*, I:3972, 84; IV:28; *siraj*, IV:3208.
55. VI:3445; II:853, 856; IV:990.
56. Cf. already cited texts, I:3952–53; IV:2960; F 24/12.
57. II:3056; III:1128; IV:526; AM 181.

58. D 16:5, quoting *arsalna* from *passim* in the Qur'an.
59. VI:165–66, 171–73; M 56/131; VI:3071.
60. First hadith in M 72/157; Noah in IV: 1458; Umma in IV:H.538–41; D 3495:7; AM 334.
61. F 114/103; III:H.4511f.; AM 298; F 136/125; VI:H.1186–88; AM 632.
62. IV:H.487–95; also on the Prophet's successors, the "four friends" D 972:17; 1140:6.
63. I:2687; IV:991; D 792:8; 1863:10; 2469:4.
64. F 232/224–25; F 212/203; VI:1593.
65. *mawla*, VI:H.4538, the "guard," F 232/224;I:737; D 792:5; IV:2282; VI:333–34.
66. I:3811; IV:H.2577; F 114/103.
67. I:3019; 3824; VI:H.2486–97.
68. I:1328, 1331; 2370; D 1535:2; 2498:13; AM 104.
69. M 33/89; III:1783–88, 1924ff.; IV:H.2933ff.
70. F 231/224, quoting Q 50:2; F 45/34, quoting Q 9:129.
71. F 196/187; 232/225; 231/224.
72. I:1950, 1966; III:1773–74; AM 224; further imagery on the spirit of Muhammad in D 12:3; 19:1; 1974:7; 3447:7; and on companionship with the Prophet in D 25:2; 106:6; 129:13; 462:14; 693:1; 1245:7; 1423:5; 1557:5; 1758:10.
73. D 645:11; 1135:18–19; 1732:10; 1966:11–12; 3391:6.
74. Q 21:107; V:H.64–287; F 145/135; I:717; II:1951; III:4479; D 2:12; 1800:3; 1974:7. AM 449ff.

Afterword

1. Annemarie Schimmel, "Yusuf in Mawlana Rumi's Poetry," in Lewisohn, Leonard, ed. *The Legacy of Medieval Persian Sufism*, (London: Khaniqahi Nimatullahi Publications, 1992), 45–59, esp. 47. See also WF 118–38, and TS 280–89.
2. Thanks to Fatemeh Keshavarz for these suggestions after reading the manuscript of this book.
3. VI:153–54, 3134–40, 3193–99; D 2447:2; R 1590; F 22/10; V:2103ff., 2610.
4. I:1246–47, 1944–5, 2657–63, 3396ff., 3403; II:17–18, 909–10, 1254, 1353–54; III:3198; V:185, 563–64; D 1597:7; 2583:5; 3212:6.
5. MDI 16; see also 419.

6. I:1480–92, 1633–36; II:2507; III:4257; IV:324ff., 363–64, 403–4, 1402, 3413ff.; VI:1216; D 280:7; 1203:2; 1905:3; 2041:10; 2608:10/3121:10; F 39/27; 53/41; 113/101; M 68/150.

7. M 72/157; IV:3357ff.

8. D 729:3. See also Rumi's prayer M 128/243.

9. VI:2652–55; D 879:15.

10. IV:538–41. Additional ark imagery in I:403–4; IV:1414; V:2344; D 148:3; 402:13; 539:10; 541:3; 668:9; 729:3; 876:3; 895:2; 935:6; 1020:2; 1250:5; 1301:5/1302:5; 1343:4; 1369:6; 1674:5; 1840:2; 1889:14; 2017:4; 2090:2; 2391:6; 2646:4; 2684:4; 2747:3; 2830:7; 3090:3; 3351:9; R 159; M 22/74.

11. III: 1450–89, 2306–2569, quoting 2547–48. For literary analysis of the extended tale, see J. R. King, "Narrative Disjunction and Conjunction in Rumi's *Mathnawi*," *Journal of Narrative Technique* 19:3 (1989): 276–85.

12. II:2300; IV:3374; V:2506; VI:1522, 2117, 3313; D 57:9; 202:10; 235:3; 588:8; 718:19; 871:1; 985:6; 1095:5; 1126:3; 1747:5; 1859:6; 1985:7; 2032:1; 2503:6/2531.8; 2934:9; 2965:2; 3496:3; M 138/264.

13. I:1950, 1966; II:3101; III:1773–74.

14. Annemarie Schimmel, "The Prophet Muhammad as a Centre of Muslim Life and Thought, " in *We Believe in One God*, A. Schimmel and A. Falaturi, eds. (New York: Seabury Press, 1979) 35–61, quoting 53.

Selected Bibliography

Affifi, Abu'l-'Ala. *The Mystical Philosophy of Muhyi' Din Ibnul 'Arabi.* Reprint. Lahore: Sh. Muhammad Ashraf, 1964.

Aflaki, Shams ad-Din Ahmad. *Legends of the Sufis: Selections from the Menaqibu' l-'Arifin.* Trans. James W. Redhouse. London: The Theosophical Publishing House Ltd., 1976.

Anawati, G. C., and Gardet, L. *Mystique Musulmane.* Paris: J. Vrin, 1961.

Andrae, Tor. *Die person Muhammads in lehre und glauben seiner gemeinde.* Stockholm, 1918.

———. *Mohammed the Man and His Faith.* Trans. Theophil Menzil. New York: Harper Torchbooks, 1960.

Antes, Peter. *Das Prophetenwunder in der frühen Aš'ariya bis al-Gazali.* Freiburg, 1970.

Arberry, A. J. *Sufism: An Account of the Mystics of Islam.* New York: Harper Torchbooks, 1970.

Baljon, J. M. S., trans. *A Mystical Interpretation of Prophetic Tales by an Indian Muslim: Shah Wali Allah's "Ta'wil al-ahadith."* Leiden: Brill, 1973.

———. "Prophetology of Shah Wali Allah." *Islamic Studies* 9 (1970): 69–80.

Al-Baqillani, Abu Bakr Muhammad. *Miracle and Magic: A Treatise on the Nature of the Apologetic Miracle and Its Differentiation from Charisms, Trickery, Divination, Magic, and Spells.* Ed. with summary and introduction by Richard J. McCarthy, S.J. Beirut: Librairie Orientale, 1958.

Bevan, A. A. "Mohammed's Ascension to Heaven," in *Studien zur semitische Philologie und Religionsgeschichte J. Wellhausen.* 49–61. Giessen: K. Marti, 1914.

Burckhardt, Titus. *An Introduction to Sufi Doctrine.* Trans. D. M. Matheson. Wellingborough: Thorsons Publishers Limited, 1976.

Cahen, Claude. *Pre-Ottoman Turkey.* London: Sidgwick and Jackson, 1968.

Chahine, Osman E. *L'Originalité Créatrice de la Philosophie Musulmane.* Paris: Librairie d'Amerique et d'Orient, 1972.

Chittick, William C. *The Sufi Doctrine of Rumi: An Introduction.* Tehran: Aryamehr University, 1974.

———. *The Sufi Path of Love.* Albany: State University of New York Press, 1983.

Corbin, Henry. *Creative Imagination in the Sufism of Ibn 'Arabi.* Trans. Ralph Mannheim. Princeton: Bollingen, 1969.

Donaldson, Dwight M. *Studies in Muslim Ethics.* London: SPCK, 1953.

Eisenberg, Isaac. *Die Prophetenlegende des Muhammad ben 'Abd-allah al Kisa'i.* Bern, 1898.

Epalza, Mikel. "Los Nombres del Profeta en la Teologia Musulmana." *Miscelanea Comillas* 173 (1975) 2ndo Semestre, No. 63.

Furuzanfar, Badi' az-Zaman. *Ahadith-i Mathnawi.* Tehran: Intisharat-i Danishgah-i Tehran, 1955.

———. *Vie de Jalal ud-Din Rumi.* Tehran, 1954.

Gardet, Louis. *Dieu et la Destinée de l'Homme.* Etudes Musulmanes IX. Paris: Librairie Philosophique J. Vrin, 1967.

Al-Ghazali. *Book XX of al-Ghazali's "Ihya' 'Ulum ad-Din."* Trans. L. Zolondek. Leiden: Brill, 1963.

———. *Al-munqidh min ad-dalal.* Trans. by W.M. Watt in *The Faith and Practice of Al-Ghazali.* London: Allen and Unwin, 1953. Also trans., R. McCarthy as *Freedom and Fulfillment.* Boston: Twayne, 1981.

Hakim, Khalifa 'Abdul. *The Metaphysics of Rumi.* Lahore: Institute of Islamic Culture, 1965.

Haleem, M. A. S. Abdel. "The Story of Joseph in the Qur'an and the Old Testament." *Islam and Christian-Muslim Relations* 1:2 (December 1990): 171–91.

Hartmann, Richard. "Die Himmelreise Muhammads und ihre Bedeutung in der Religion des Islam." *In Vortrage der Bibliothek Warburg.* Hamburg, 1928–29.

Husaini, Saiyid Abdul Qadir. *The Pantheistic Monism of Ibn al-Arabi.* Lahore: Sh. Muhammad Ashraf, 1970.

Ibn 'Arabi, Muhyi ad-Din. *Fusus al-Hikam.* Ed. A. Affifi. Cairo, 1946. Trans. R. W. J. Austin as *The Bezels of Wisdom.* New York: Paulist Press, 1980.

Ibn Ishaq., *The Life of Muhammad*. Trans. A. Guillaume. Lahore: Oxford University Press, 1970.

Ibn Sina. *Fi Ithbat al-Nubuwwat*. Ed. with Introductory notes by Michael Marmura. Beirut: Dar an-Nahar, 1968.

Iqbal, Afzal. *The Life and Work of Muhammad Jalal ad-Din Rumi*. Lahore: Institute of Islamic Culture, (1956) 1974.

Izutsu, Toshihiko. *A Comparative Study of the Key Philosophical Concepts of Sufism and Taosim*. Vol. 1. Tokyo: Keio University, 1966–67.

Khan, Qamarruddin. "Ibn Taymiyah's Views on the Prophetic State." *Islamic Studies* 3 (1964): 521–30.

King, James Roy. "Jesus and Joseph in Rumi's *Mathnawi*." *The Muslim World* 80:2 (April 1990): 81–95.

———. "Narrative Disjunction and Conjunction in Rumi's *Mathnawi*," *Journal of Narrative Technique* 19:3 (1989): 276–85.

Al-Kisa'i, Muhammad ibn 'Abd Allah. *Qisas al-Anbiya'*. Ed. Isaac Eisenberg. 2 parts. Leiden: Brill, 1922–23. Trans. Wheeler M. Tackston as *Tales of the Prophets of al-Kisa'i*. Boston: Twayne, 1978.

Lichtenstaedter, Ilse. "Arabic and Islamic Historiography." *The Muslim World* 35 (1945): 126–32.

———. "A Note on the *gharaniq* and related Qur'anic problems." *Israel Oriental Studies* 5 (1975) 54–61.

Massignon, Louis. *Essai sur les origines du lexique technique de la mystique musulmane*. Paris: J. Vrin, 1928.

McCarthy, Richard J., S.J. "Al-Baqillani's Notion of the Apologetic Miracle." *Studia Biblica et Orientalia* 3 (Analecta Biblica 12) (1959): 247–56.

Meyerovitch, Eva. *Mystique et poesie en Islam, Djalal-ud Din et l'ordre des dervishes tourneurs*. Paris: J. Vrin, 1972.

Mir, Mustansir. "The Qur'anic Story of Joseph: Plot, Themes, and Characters." *The Muslim World* 76:1 (January 1986): 1–15.

Moubarac, Youakim. *Abraham dans le Coran: l'histoire d'Abraham dans le Coran et la naissance de l'Islam*. Paris: J. Vrin, 1958.

———. *Moise dans le Coran*. Paris: J. Vrin, 1954.

Nasr, S.H. *Islamic Studies*. Beirut: Librairie du Liban, 1967.

———. *Sufi Essays*. London: Allen and Unwin, 1972.

Nicholson, R. A. *The Idea of Personality in Sufism*. Cambridge: Cambridge University Press, 1923.

————. *The Mystics of Islam*. London: Routledge and Kegan Paul Ltd., 1914.

————. *Rumi: Poet and Mystic*. London: Allen and Unwin, 1950.

————. *Studies in Islamic Mysticism*. Cambridge: Cambridge University Press, 1921. (See further under Rumi, Jalal ad-Din.)

Nwyia, Paul, S.J. *Exégèse coranique et langage mystique*. Beirut: Dar al-Machreq, 1970.

Önder, Mehmet. *Mevlana bibliografyasi*. 2 Vols. Ankara: Is Bankasi, 1973–75.

Parrinder, Geoffrey. *Jesus in the Qur'an*. New York: Oxford University Press, 1977.

Rahman, Fazlur. *Prophecy in Islam*. London: Allen and Unwin, 1958.

Rasheed, Ghulam Dastagir. "The Development of Na'tia Poetry in Persian Literature," *Islamic Culture* (January 1965): 53–69.

Rosenthal, Erwin I.J. *Studia Semitica, Volume II: Islamic Themes*. Cambridge: Cambridge University Press, 1971.

Rosenthal, Franz. *A History of Muslim Historiography*. Leiden: Brill, 1952.

Rumi, Mawlana Jalal ad-Din. *Mathnawi-i Ma'nawi*. Ed. and trans. R.A. Nicholson, with Commentary. 8 Vols. Gibb Memorial Series. London: Luzac and Co. Ltd., 1925–40.

————. *Fihi Ma Fihi*. Ed. B. Furuzanfar. Tehran, 1338/1959. Trans. by A.J. Arberry as *Discourses of Rumi*. New York: Samuel Weiser, 1972. Note: A new translation of *Fihi Ma Fihi* came to my attention after going to press: *Signs of the Unseen: The Discourses of Jalaluddin Rumi*. Trans. W. M. Thackston, Jr. Putney, VT: Threshold Books, 1994.

————. *Kulliyat-i Diwan-i Shams-i Tabrizi*. Ed. B. Furuzanfar. Tehran, 1351/1970. Selections translated by: R. A. Nicholson in *Selected Poems from the Divani Shami Tabriz*. Cambridge: Cambridge University Press, 1898/1952; and A.J. Arberry in *Mystical Poems of Rumi* and *Mystical Poems of Rumi 2*. Chicago: University of Chicago Press, 1968 and 1973.

————. *Maktubat*. Ed. Yusuf Jamshidpur and Ghulamhusayn Amin. Tehran, 1335/1956.

Schimmel, Annemarie. *And Muhammad Is His Messenger*. Chapel Hill: University of North Carolina Press, 1985.

————. *As Through a Veil*. New York: Columbia University Press, 1982.

————. *I Am Wind, You Are Fire*. Boston and London: Shambhala, 1992.

————. "Maulana Rumi's Story on Prayer." In *Yadname Jan Rypka*. Ed. J. Becka. Prague, 1967.

————. *Mystical Dimensions of Islam*. Chapel Hill: University of North Carolina Press, 1975.

————. "The Place of the Prophet of Islam in Iqbal's Thought." *Islamic Studies* 1:4 (1962): 111–30.

————. "The Symbolical Language of Maulana Jalal al-Din Rumi." *Studies in Islam* 1 (1964): 26–40.

————. *The Triumphal Sun*. London: Fine Books, 1978.

————. "Yusuf in Mawlana Rumi's Poetry." *The Legacy of Medieval Persian Sufism*. Leonard Lewisohn, ed. London: Khaniqahi Nimatullahi Publications, 1992, 45–60.

Sidersky, David. *Les Origines des légendes musulmanes dans le Coran et dans les Vie de Prophètes*. Paris: P. Geuthner, 1933.

Speyer, Heinrich. *Die Biblischen Erzahlungen im Qoran*. Georg Olms Verlag, 1971.

Stern, M. S. "Muhammad and Joseph: A Study of Koranic Narrative." *Journal of Near Eastern Studies* 44:3 (July 1985): 193–204.

Takeshita, Masataka. *Ibn 'Arabi's Theory of the Perfect Man and its Place in the History of Islamic Thought*. Tokyo: Institute for the Study of Languages and Culture of Asia and Africa, 1987.

Tha'labi, al-, Ahmad ibn Muhammad. *'Ara'is al-Majalis: Qisas al-Anbiya'*. Cairo: Dar Ihya 'l-Kutub al-'Arabiya, n.d.

Waldman, Marilyn. "New Approaches to 'Biblical' Materials in the Qur'an." *The Muslim World* 75:1 (January 1985): 1–16.

Wali Allah, Shah. *Tawil al-Ahadith*. Trans. G. N. Jalbani. Lahore: Sh. Muhammad Ashraf, 1973.

Walzer, Richard. *Greek Into Arabic*. Oxford: Bruno Cassirer, 1962.

Watt, W. Montgomery. *Muhammad at Mecca* and *Muhammad at Medina*. Oxford: Clarendon Press, 1953 and 1956.

Widengren, Geo. *The Ascension to Heaven and the Heavenly Book*. Uppsala, 1955.

————. *Muhammad, the Apostle of God, and His Ascension*. Uppsala, 1955.

Wolfson, Harry A. "Hallevi and Maimonides on Prophecy." *Jewish Quarterly Review*, n.s. 32–3 (1942): 345ff, 349ff.

Zaehner, R.C. *The Comparison of Religions*. Chapter 4, "Prophets Outside Israel," and Appendix, "The Qur'an and Christ." Boston: Beacon Press, 1967.

Zakarias, Hanna. *De Moise a Mohammed*. 3 Vols. Chez l'auteur, 1955.

Index of Qur'anic Citations

Index

Aaron: 77, 181n29
'Abbas: 100, 114, 133
abdal: 24
'Abd al-Muttalib: 98–99
Abraham:
  as authentic seeker, 48
  'Attar on, 54
  and repudiation of idols, 48–49, 119–20,
    172n32
  early life of, 42, 47–48
  as exemplar to Muhammad, 55, 119
  failing of, 56
  and hospitality, 50–51, 58, 175n13
  Ibn 'Arabi on, 12, 174n6, 175n11, 175n13
  intercession of, 50, 57–58
  and light, 5, 53–55. *See also* light
  as man of faith, 47–50
  as mosque builder, 46
  and opposition, 21, 51
  and pilgrimage, 48
  and prayer, 56–58
  as prophet, 50–55
  in *Qisas*: 48, 50–51, 52, 54, 55, 174n2, 174n6
  as recipient of revelation, 31
  and sacrificing of son, 49–50, 174n6
  and signs of prophethood, 50–55
Abu Bakr:
  conversion of, 100, 102, 135
  and Muhammad, 107–108
  as truthful witness, 106
Abu Hurayra: 105
Abu Jahl:
  compared to Muhammad, 127, 131
  opposition to Muhammad, 71–72, 105–105,
    139, 143
Abu 'l-Hakam: 105
Abu Lahab: 105, 139
Abu Talib: 100, 103, 148
Abyssinian(s): 111

Adam:
  as first prophet, x
  and knowledge, 28, 36, 153–54
  and light, 5
  and opposition, 21, 72
  and pride, 26
  as a teacher, 8
adversary: *See* opposition
Ahmad: *See* Muhammad
A'isha: 109
'Ali:
  conversion of, 100
  death of, 137
  and *Dhu 'l-Faqar*, 116
  and the Hypocrites, 110
  relationship to Muhammad, 101
almsgiving: 122–23
Anas, Malik ibn: 144
angel(s):
  and Abraham, 175n13
  and the believer, 120
  intercession of, 2, 122
  and light, 45
  and revelation, 81
  superfluity of, 54
  See also Gabriel; Spirit, of God
anger: *See* wrath
annihilation: 15, 71, 83, 134
Ansar, The: *See* Helpers, The
Antichrist: 92, 95, 187n40
antinomianism: 10. *See also* law
'*aql*: *See* intellect; knowledge, prophetic; reason
arrogance: *See* pride
ascension:
  of Idris, 93
  of Jesus, 93
  of Jonah, 141, 147
  See also Muhammad, ascension of
asceticism: 37–38

and signs of prophethood, 43, 70, 82–83
at Sinai, 79–80
sincerity of, 77–79
of the spirit, 83
and true knowledge, 36, 118
mosque: 46, 57, 140, 142
of opposition, 109–111, 156
Muhammad:
as above other prophets, 42, 93, 146
and 'A'isha, 109
ascension of, 31, 99, 107, 139–41, 147
'Attar on, 128
before the call, 97–99
and the believer, 147–49
and breath . . . from Yemen, 65
breaker of idols, 98–99, 105, 115–16,
    119–20, 143, 148
conquers Makka, 115
cosmic mission of, 136–37
death and burial of, 1, 116–18
and divine grace, 105, 127
and example of Abraham, 55, 119
and first converts, 100
and Gabriel, 99
as guide, 156
and the Helpers, 109–10
the Hijra, 108
humility of, 119
Ibn Arabi on, 188n2, 191n7
and intimacy with God, 127–29, 137, 140
and Jacob, 131
and Jesus, 93
and the Jews, 107, 111–12
and jihad, 112–16, 156
and "light" of God, 104, 112, 133–36
and Madinan period, 109–18
names and titles of, 144–46
and Night of Power, 99–100, 133
opposition to, 2, 71–72, 104–107, 110
and prayer, 57, 103, 107, 117, 128–30, 148,
    188n2
preaching of, 1, 2, 6, 119
and predisposition, 131
proof of resurrection, 100
proofs of prophethood, 9, 43, 106, 133–44
in *Qisas*, 3–4
qualities of, 9, 118–19
relationship with 'Ali, 101
religion of, 119–25
and revelation, 28, 99–102, 130–33
and ritual observance, 107, 122–25
Rumi's use of *rasul* for, 23

as Seal of the Prophets, 2, 7, 146–47, 157
and splitting of the moon, 43, 78, 139
story of Bilal, 107
on Sura 68 (The Pen), 104
and Treaty of Hudaybiya, 114–15
as type of Moses, 112
and the *Umma*, 121
and '*umra*, 114
unlettered, 4, 5, 15, 137–38
and his view of Christianity, 113, 121
mu'jiza: *See* miracle(s), evidentiary
Mulla, Sadra (1572–1641): 12
Munafiqun, The: *See* Hypocrites, The
murid: xv, 154–55
Mustafa: *See* Muhammad.
Mu'tazilite(s): 9
al-Muzammil (Sura 73): 100. *See also*
    Revelation; Muhammad, and revelation;
    Quran
mysticism (mystic):
Abraham as, 58
and Ghazali, 10
and inspiration, 11, 52
and Jesus, 96
and knowledge, 8, 37, 55
and Noah, 154
See also Sufism; *ma'rifa*

Nadir (Tribe of): 111
nabi: 23, 24, 36, 81, 94, 156. *See also*
    prophet(s)
nafs:
as enemy, 68, 72, 76–77, 96, 153, 154, 155
as fire, 53, 55
prophets as destroyers of, 18, 33
and revelation, 36
as a wolf, 61
See also jihad, greater
Neoplatonism: xiii. *See also* Perfect Person
Nicholson, R.A.: 25, 28, 30, 48, 111, 136, 144,
    190n34
Night of Power: *See* Muhammad, and Night of
    Power
Night Vigil: 128–29
Nimrod: 21, 42, 47, 50–55, 60
Noah:
birth of, 48
and light, 5
and opposition, 15
and patience, 42
preaching of, 119
shaykh as a, 153–54
nubuwwa: 41, 101